The Female World in Shashi Deshpande's Novels

Tukaram S. Sawant

ATLANTIC
PUBLISHERS & DISTRIBUTORS (P) LTD

Published by
ATLANTIC
PUBLISHERS & DISTRIBUTORS (P) LTD
7/22, Ansari Road, Darya Ganj, New Delhi-110002
Phones : +91-11-40775252, 23273880, 23275880, 23280451
Fax : +91-11-23285873
Web : www.atlanticbooks.com
E-mail : orders@atlanticbooks.com

Branch Office
5, Nallathambi Street, Wallajah Road, Chennai-600002
Phones : +91-44-48531784, 28411383
E-mail : chennai@atlanticbooks.com

Printed in India at Nice Printing Press, A-33/3A, Site-IV,
Industrial Area, Sahibabad, Ghaziabad, U.P.

In the dear memory of my beloved brothers
Late Bhanudas S. Sawant
and
Late Tanaji S. Sawant

Foreword

Ever since the emergence of Indian writing in English, there have been various arguments and controversies regarding the nexus of the identity of Indian cultural heritage and its literature. Nowadays, it has been called a new literature, a part of the Commonwealth Literature, the Third World Literature, or the Post-Colonial Literature. However, to avoid national or political references, it is described as International English Literature in the global context. In India, we have several regional literatures in different languages, as Dr. Ganesh Devy coined the term—Bhasha Literatures; still we cover all of them under the term Indian literature, only because Indian culture and sensibility are shared by all Indian writers in English.

The general assumption is that the national sensibility and creative writings are integrated. There, together, need be the discourse of national consciousnesses in the context of Indian sensibility. To every Indian, nationalism is a God-given religion which is the only way to 'a greater solidarity' in the post-modern era. Even the process of globalization has not been affecting the sense of identity. This religion, the hidden secret of Indian consciousness, has been prevailing in the struggle of preserving the native socio-cultural heritage as an instrument useful for our redemption. This is applicable to both the categories of Indian writers in English, i.e. those who stay in India and those who are expatriates. Indian writing in English has been growing remarkably and Indian English novel has also been growing and flourishing substantially. Indian English novels based on feminism and its different aspects depict the positions of a woman in general. A woman is portrayed as the key figure of Indian families and at the same time she has been projected as the subject of domestic slavery and suppression. The hidden thoughts, suppressed feelings and the self-realization of a woman are found in the female-oriented Indian English novels.

Feminism in India is not as aggressive as feminism in the West. It does not expect the woman to be a complete rebel and revolutionary. It expects her to fight for liberty and equality remaining well within the constraints of her society. It is a movement that fights not only for her rights but also for her status and dignity. Women in India have to suffer in silence on account of male-ego and superiority. Shashi Deshpande's raising her voice against patriarchy is nothing but her feminism reflected in her novels—*The Dark Holds No Terrors, Roots and Shadows, That Long Silence, A Matter of Time* and other novels as well. These novels are good examples of the feministic novels dealing with the native contemporary issues and problems in a men-dominated society. This is the main theme of her novels. She strongly believes that the woman can march towards her empowerment only through making herself strong and confident, and through realizing her talent and potentiality. She wants the woman to emerge as a new woman through self-realization.

This book is a successful attempt to critically analyse the projection of the female world in which the female voice is suppressed in a male-centric Indian society with a special focus on Deshpande's four novels. It contains six chapters: 'Indianness and Indian Sensibility', 'Shashi Deshpande as a Novelist', 'Human Relationships in Deshpande's Novels', 'A Middle Class Indian Woman: A Creature Made by Beliefs and Superstitions', 'A Middle Class Indian Woman: A Victimized Creature', and 'The image of an Emerging New Woman in Deshpande's Novels'. The first chapter defines the concepts of Indianness, Indian sensibility, social units such as individual, family, society and marriage—a social institution. It provides a brief review of a middle-class Indian woman with a special focus on her plight and predicament in Indian patriarchy. The second chapter is devoted to the assessment of Shashi Deshpande, a popular Indian woman novelist in English, who raises a voice of protest against patriarchy. The third chapter is devoted to the study of Deshpande's notion of relatedness and its importance in human life in Indian context. It deals with the theme of human relationships, man-woman relationship, in particular. It underlines the importance of the woman in all relationships. The fourth chapter highlights age-old Indian beliefs, superstitions, customs, conventions and traditions and the role that they play in the life of both, the male and the female. The fifth chapter moves around the depiction of a tradition-bound Indian woman, her plight and predicament, and her never-ending struggle to survive. The sixth chapter projects the image of an emerging 'new' woman who is ready to fight her battle on her own with courage, confidence and determination.

The book seeks to give, as lucidly and simply as possible, a true image of a middle-class Indian woman caught in the trap of Indian patriarchy, citing examples and illustrations from the novels. A tragedy of a middle-class woman has been the main focus of the writer who highlights the basic causes responsible for her tragedy and suggests certain solutions to these problems.

The book, for me, is an attempt to introduce a distinct approach of using the assessment of the fictional discourse for social use and welfare. The writer expresses his agreement with Deshpande that love and trust are the only things which can maintain much-needed balance by strengthening human relationships. By keeping the characters as individualities at the centre and disclosing the underlying forces, the book provides us with the characteristic mentality which makes them behave the way they behave. This comprehensive socio-psychological evaluation of the fiction with a social purpose in mind has really been a very credible contribution to a critical study of Indian English literature. In short, this book with a simple and logical way of studying Indian English fiction from the bottom-to-top approach would really be helpful to the readers of literature.

Dr. P. R. Bhabad

Preface

Indian literature in English reflects Indian life with its various aspects. It mirrors Indianness, an umbrella term which includes everything that is Indian, in one way or the other. A study of Indian literature in English, therefore, is no more than a study of the psyche, consciousness and behavioural patterns of Indians, a study of Indian life, society and culture. The study of any literature, I feel, should have a social purpose. If the study of Indian literature in English is to be profitably undertaken in India, a country with various social issues like caste-system, gender-discrimination, child-marriage, dowry, marital-violence, urge for a male child, patriarchal attitude towards the female members of society, superstitions and many more, its foundation needs to be made solid by making Indians aware of these issues reflected in the writings of Indian writers in English and training them to contribute to the solution of these issues. We should never forget that the solution of any issue or problem lies within us. Though literature, in general, is primarily a means of enjoyment, Indian English literature, Indian English novels in particular, can be used as a means of social change and reform in India.

A true story of Indian English novel began with the writings of 'The Trio of Indian English Fiction'—Raja Rao, R. K. Narayan and Mulk Raj Anand—who used novel as a medium to portray India and Indian life with its strengths and weaknesses, issues and problems, ills and evils. They were basically concerned with the projection of the life of the poor, the deprived, the downtrodden and the exploited. Bhabani Bhattacharya, another big name from the field of English fiction, was sensitive about the issues and problems prevalent in a contemporary Indian society.

However, a true revolutionary change in Indian English fiction came with the publication of Salman Rushdie's novel, *Midnight's Children* which realistically describes a generation of Indians born at midnight on August 15, 1947. Indian English novel witnessed a lot of change owing to the writings of the eminent writers like Arundhati Roy, Jhumpa Lahiri, Shobha De, V. S. Naipaul, Shashi Tharoor, Vikram Seth, Khushwant Singh, Amit Chaudhari, Amitav Ghosh, Vikram Swaroop, Anil Menon, Ruth Prawer Jhabvala, Kiran Desai, Aravind Adiga, Manju Kapur, Rohinton Mistry, Vikram Chandra, Kamala Markandaya, Anita Desai, Nayantara Sahgal, Shashi Deshpande and many others. Indian women novelists in English have been dealing with the issues and problems faced by Indian women in a male-dominated society.

The prime aim of this book is to project, in the simplest possible way, the world of the female, controlled and dominated by the males in Indian patriarchy, with special focus on Shashi Deshpande's four novels, *The Dark Holds No Terrors*, *Roots and Shadows*, *That Long Silence*, and *A Matter of Time*. These novels deal with a common issue of the plight and predicament of a middle-class Indian woman who is subjugated, oppressed, harassed and exploited, in one way or the other, and who ultimately emerges as a 'new' woman ready to move on with her life with courage, confidence and determination. The book intends to take its readers into various layers and nuances of the female life deeply rooted in silence, patience, tolerance and sacrifice. It not only seeks to give an intensive assessment of the female world with its issues and problems in Indian patriarchal set-up, but also suggests solutions to these issues and problems.

A sincere and modest attempt has been made in this book to lay foundation for the proper assessment of the tragedy of a middle-class Indian woman, a victimized creature caught in the trap of Indian patriarchy, and to convey Shashi Deshpande's implied message that the woman herself, to a large extent, is responsible for her tragic lot and that the status and dignity of the woman can be improved only through her self-awareness, self-realization and education. Once the woman realizes that she has been her own enemy and that she needs to help herself in each and every respect, she can emerge as a strong and confident 'new' woman competent enough to move on with her life freely and independently and to have a healthy and constructive competition with her male counterparts in various fields of knowledge and life.

The book, my first endeavour, I humbly believe, is an outcome of the co-operation and encouragement I received from numerous people including my family members, well-wishers, friends, academics, scholars and writers. It is the right moment to record my profound gratefulness to all those who have directly or indirectly helped me to realize my dream, a memorable experience. I take this opportunity to express my gratitude to the writer, Simone de Beauvoir, whose book *The Second Sex* motivated me to write a book on Shashi Deshpande. I would like to express my gratefulness to all the scholars and writers, listed in bibliography, whose ideas and opinions I found useful and relevant to the aim and theme of my book. I sincerely apologise to Shashi Deshpande for having quoted freely from her interviews and novels to serve my purpose.

The book, I believe, will be useful to the students and teachers of English literature, particularly Indian English literature, and researchers in these fields.

Tukaram S. Sawant

Acknowledgements

I am immensely pleased to record my gratitude and reverence to Late Dr. Kumar S. Iyer, who encouraged me by his valuable support and guidance. I would have been very happy if I had published the book during his lifetime. Unfortunately, it was not to happen. I am indebted to a close friend of mine, Prin. Pandurang R. Bhabad for his valuable suggestions at various stages and also for the Foreword that he wrote for the book. I am indebted also to Prin. Dr. Chandrashekhar V. Murumkar and Prin. Dr. Pradip Patil for their help and co-operation. I owe my deep sense of gratitude and special thanks to my friends, Prof. Dr. Suresh C. Salunke, Prof. Keshav S. Dhamal, Prof. Avinash S. Jagtap, Prof. Dr. Ashok E. Kalange, Prof. Dnyaneshwar G. Dhavan and many more for having been the source of encouragement and inspiration for me.

I owe my deep sense of gratitude to my beloved wife, Mrs. Manjusha, who has been with me as my strength and support since the day of our marriage, setting me free for my academic, research and other educational activities, and happily and ungrudgingly shouldering the responsibility of my family. I express my sense of gratitude to Mrs. Swapnali and Mrs. Samriddhi, my lovely daughters, Dr. Rakesh and Mr. Devendra, my sons-in-law, Vihang, my loving, smart and ever-smiling grandson, Akshay, Vivek, and Dr. Kiran, my caring and co-operative nephews, Prof. Mrs. Leena and Mrs. Pooja, my loving daughters-in-law, Smt. Mangal, my sister-in-law, and the last but not least, Smt. Savitra, my mother for their immeasurable support and co-operation.

Tukaram S. Sawant

Contents

CHAPTER 1
Indianness and Indian Sensibility

1.1 Concept of Indianness

The concept of 'Indianness' is really a very complex phenomenon. It has always been a great challenge to define what makes Indianness in the context of India with its astonishingly unique diversity in various fields of life. As India is a multi-lingual, multi-religious and multi-cultural country, it is almost impossible to construct a coherent Indian identity in its true sense. However, defining Indianness has become very important today. Indianness seems to imply common Indian features and characteristics, irrespective of caste, creed, religion, region, language, status and the like. It implies India's spiritual and cultural heritage, dreams and aspirations, values and principles, customs and conventions, mythology and philosophy, beliefs and superstitions, virtues such as tolerance, sacrifice and non-violence, and most importantly, unity in diversity. Though Indians are divided by region, caste, religion, language, these divisions certainly vanish when they are faced with a national crisis. The five *Pandavas* and one hundred *Kauravas*, bitter enemies of each other, used to be one hundred and five together, one and united, while facing a common enemy. During the British rule over India, a vast majority of Indians were united in one purpose, irrespective of their caste, religion, region and language. This is what we call Indianness.

Indianness is an innate, abstract and inherent force that binds and unites all Indians together. It is something where all differences naturally melt and vanish. It is an umbrella term that comprises everything deeply rooted in Indian context. It is a concept which projects India through its languages, customs, conventions, traditions, norms, values, beliefs, superstitions, dreams, aspirations, mythology, culture, philosophy, and sensibility—everything that makes an Indian the Indian. It can be defined in terms of what and how Indians are and what makes them what they are. Prof. David McCutchion defines it as life-attitudes and modes of perception. According to Prof. V. K. Gokak, it is a composite awareness in the matter of race, milieu, language and religion. It is an inherent and integral part of Indian life. In short, caste, religion, race, class, zonal surroundings, religious, ethical, philosophical, moral, political ideologies, social stratum, traditions, heritage, religious and cultural diversities, and, above all, unity in diversity are the distinctive features of Indianness.

1.2 Indian Sensibility

Sensibility is nothing but an individual's emotional, intellectual, spiritual, mental and moral responsiveness to and awareness of the internal as well as the external world. Any normal individual possesses an alert cognitive faculty which makes him aware of himself and the world around him and his place and position in it. His sensitivity makes him naturally respond to that world. It comprises various powers such as observation, perception, appreciation, insight-formation, responsiveness on the part of the individual. Indianness and Indian sensibility are the two sides of the same coin. Indian sensibility implies Indian ways of looking at life that exists around. It has a very strong and solid foundation which is deeply rooted in Indian traditions, philosophy and culture. As it is difficult to define Indianness, it is difficult to define Indian sensibility. H. H. Shri Swami Vishveshwarnandaji, the Guest of Honour at the inaugural function of the 53rd All India English Teachers' Conference on Indian Sensibility in Indian English Literature organized at Gurukul Kangri University, Haridwar, on 18th December, 2008, said: "I confess that when the subject came to me, I was searching left and right for a good answer, via computer and so on, but I was not satisfied. I consulted writers and highly learned people to get their opinion regarding this Indian sensibility in Indian English Literature. Though a lot of different, quite interesting answers I got, I was still not convinced to catch the right point" (Vishveshwarnandaji 2008).

Indian sensibility, according to Shri Swami Vishveshwarnandaji, is "a treasure in the heart of the Indian people, to be more precise, it is God's gift". It is something which can lead men towards great ideals. It is a product of enormous purity, spiritual advancement, great thinking, a well-disciplined living and a divine vision. It is rooted in Indian Vedic culture which is second to none in the world. Shri Swami Vishveshwarnandaji, in his speech, further, appeals: "Dear friends, we have to preserve this great culture, and we should improve this wonderful sensibility more and more in favour of others, in favour of the entire mankind and, of course, in favour of ourselves". It is something that motivates us to be a good and responsible human being, to think like a genius, work like a giant and to live like a saint.

We Indians are Indians only because we are not like others who are not Indians. To be an Indian makes us count the features of Indianness, our typical Indian responsiveness, awareness, insight, intuition, taste, appreciation, delicacy, sensitivity, discernment, perceptiveness, etc. All these features are measured in terms of the observations of Indians' internal and external behaviour in different contexts in order to provide an authenticity to Indians who are distinct from the rest of the multitudes of the world. Our patterns of behaviour, customs and traditions, culture and philosophy, values and norms, heritage, beliefs and superstitions, strengths or weaknesses, ways of appreciating or criticizing others, reacting to the happenings around, defining the qualities and distinctness of our abilities and faculties of perceiving the pros and cons of all the elements of the reality, etc. are the prominent facets and components of Indian sensibility. We can learn a lot about Indian sensibilities through feelings, thoughts, emotions, situational reactions, and moral and ethical values of Indians. Indian sensibility may establish and maintain Indianness and Indian identities leading towards defining ourselves anthropologically as Indians.

Indians possess and exhibit a distinct sense of social, religious, and cultural behaviour in the course of life. A sense of reverence for others, especially for the elders, Gandhian principles of truth and non-violence, divine virtues such as tolerance and sacrifice, a sense of neighbourhood, a sense of compassion have been the main driving force to Indians. Accordingly, the determination of the concept of personality, the orientation of personality development, the individual or social expectations and efforts for the achievement of the targeted personality traits have been attained by Indians. Individualities are the components of social stratum who move and work for the sake of identities; the social surroundings and motivations become the elements of the manifestations of humanities in the given regions and regional ties.

Today, the world is too much with us. We have been blinded by money and power. We have sold our spirit to the god of materialism. Our materialistic attitude is leading us towards our spiritual decay and destruction. Films, radio, television, mobile, internet, etc. have intellectually and spiritually corrupted our life to a large extent. The very course of modern human life has been adversely affected. A lot of damage has been done to human life. The much needed purity in the human heart has been destroyed. Human beings have been demoralized and dehumanized. They have been pushed into the deep dark world. Our realization of the very significance of Indian culture and Indian sensibility and our belief in the very strength of Indian culture and philosophy can save us from decay and destruction. Indian culture, the very source of Indian sensibility, is a treasure house of divine virtues such as love, affection, co-operation, respect, hospitality, truth, non-violence, loyalty, integrity, unity, tolerance, sacrifice, peace, sympathy, compassion, nobility, generosity, values, ideals, philosophical thoughts, and moral and spiritual life.

1.3 Concept of the Family

Family is a small social unit in which its members, in spite of differences among them, live together under one roof, resemble one another in some degree, in body and in mind, co-operate with one another. It is a group of persons of opposite sexes, related by blood, marriage or adoption, playing various roles depending upon their age, sex and relationship, living together in a single household. Basic human needs, sex drive, reproductive urge, and emotional, social and economic needs are the basic conditions which compel human beings to come together and form an organization in the form of a family. Universality, emotional basis, formative influence, limited size, nuclear position in the social structure; duties and responsibilities of the members and social reputation are some of the distinctive features of a family. Ideally, a complete family is the place where one feels good, comfortable, and secure. It is the place where nobody will put you down, where nobody will make you feel small, where nobody will laugh at your follies, shortcomings and weaknesses, and where nobody will be judgemental. It is the only place where you will always get love and respect, support and co-operation. It is as good as a paradise on the earth. It is, no doubt, a picture of an ideal family. However, families today are far away from being ideal and complete.

Though Indian family is in a crisis today, it is an integral part of the wider system of kinship relationship. It plays a major role in establishing, maintaining and strengthening the conjugal, filial and fraternal bonds in our society. The social relationships between members of families are based on duties, responsibilities, obligations, emotional support, co-operation, love, trust, sincerity, loyalty, integrity and unity. Living together peacefully, helping and co-operating with one another, maintaining strong bonds with family members, neighbours and relatives, being hospitable to everyone who comes to your home, treating the guest as God, worshiping God, practising Yoga and meditation, respecting the elder members of a family are some of the values of Indian family.

There is a two-way and complementary relationship between an individual and a family. Each member of a family seeks something and gives something. He plays a give-and-take role within a family. Family is a way of living together and meeting emotional needs of its members through communication, interaction and co-operation. Interaction in a family is a collaborative activity where all the participants are equally important. Silence and misunderstanding in a family kill the very spirit human relationship. The individual contributes to the change, transformation, growth and development of a family whereas the family provides the individual with opportunities for self-discovery, development of individuality and personality and also for understanding the importance of inter-personal relationship within and outside a family. The significance of Indian family lies in the fact that people with different tastes, traits, dreams, aspirations, attitudes and aptitudes live together under one roof.

1.4 Concept of the Society

Society is a group, an organization which shapes, moulds, guides and controls the behaviour of its members. This organization not only liberates but also checks, restricts and controls the actions and activities of men and women, sets up standards for them to be followed, practised and maintained. The individual, a member of a society, is a social animal that is dependent on society for protection, comfort, nurture, education, equipments, opportunities, almost for everything. The relationship between the individual and society is organic and complementary. The individual does not enter into relations with other men by juxtaposition, but organically in as much as he belongs to organic societies which range from the simplest to the most complex.

There has always been a two-way relationship between man and society. One cannot live life without society. Wherever there is human life, there is society. Human life and society are inseparable. Man is dependent upon family and society to which he belongs and looks for protection, comfort, nurture, education, resources and opportunities remaining well within the restrictions of family and society. He is dependent upon his society for the development of his individuality and personality, for the realization of his dreams and aspirations. Both are essential for the development of each other. The individual is a creature as well as a creator of his society. Every individual is a creation of a social relationship. A social human relationship evokes and directs our personality by moulding our attitudes, beliefs, ideals and morals.

Patriarchal attitude to the woman, gender-discrimination, preference for a male child, differences of language, status, religion, caste-system, racial, ethical and cultural diversity, and most importantly, unity in diversity mark the special features of Indian society. Males are preferred to females; they are given more importance than women. Men are considered independent, self-reliant, liberal, demanding and domineering while women silent, meek, submissive, obedient, selfless, conservative, dependent and tolerant in Indian society. Indian women are made to depend on their male-counterparts throughout their life. They are assigned a conventional and traditional duty of looking after their homes and their husbands, caring for their children and so on.

Every society has its own culture. Culture is nothing but a special heritage of a particular people. It implies a kind of force that influences, controls, conditions and moderates the growth and development of a human being. Compared to other beings, man is considered a cultured and civilized human being. Culture and civilization make him a good human being. MacIver and Page write: "By civilization, then, we mean the whole mechanism and organization which man has devised in his endeavour to control the conditions of his life. It would include not only our systems of social organization but also our techniques and our material instruments". (MacIver and Page 498). It can be treated as an invisible force directed to moulding and regulating the behaviour of human beings.

Indian culture is rich, diverse and unique in its own way. Our habits, manners, etiquettes, attitudes, ideas, beliefs, values, morals, the way we communicate with one another, the way we behave, the way we live in the company of one another, are some of the components of Indian culture. Love and respect for the elders as well as for the guests, respect for one another, hospitability, helpful and cooperative nature, beliefs, superstitions, customs, conventions, traditions, feminine sensibility, male-oriented focus, are a few striking features of Indian culture. Gandhian philosophy rooted in truth and non-violence, tolerance and sacrifice, and unity in diversity are the essential foundations of Indian culture and civilization. In addition to these, multilingualism, secularism, sense of fraternity, dance forms, attires, rites and rituals, festivals, family structure, even the caste-system are inseparable parts of Indian culture. To worship gods and goddesses, to observe fasts on different occasions such as the *Hartalika*, the *Karva Chauth* has been very common in Indian culture. Our *Vedas* and Scriptures, Epics and Mythology, Yoga, Meditation and Ayurveda reflect Indian culture. Indians, irrespective of their class, caste, and religion are brought together to celebrate festivals like Diwali, Christmas, Id as a result of culture. Ganesh festival, in the State of Maharashtra, is celebrated with great excitement and enthusiasm by all, irrespective of their class and status, caste and creed. Folk music and folk dances are the very heritage of India. The *Bharatnatyam*, the *Kuchupidi*, the *Kathakali*, the *Ghumar* dance of Rajasthan, the *Lavani* of Maharashtra, the *Gharba* dance, the Manipuri dance, the Oddissi dance and many others are the Indian dance forms which are rooted in Indian culture.

Indian tradition is deeply rooted in beliefs and values that transcend space and time. Indians give up their superstitions, change and modify their false beliefs, norms and values depending on the needs and requirements of society. Indians are highly and surprisingly tolerant and flexible in the sense that they accept changes dictated by Western influence and yet clearly and strongly stick to their belief in their culture. It is one of the wonders of Indian culture that a girl gets married into a new family and adjusts herself to the routine and rituals of that family and becomes an inseparable part of that family culture. India is a secular nation which allows complete freedom of worship according to beliefs and faith of the people from different religions. Indian religions have some common festivals, rituals and practices. They spend their time in the pursuit of religion and god in their own way. They get involved in religious practices like prayers, rituals, pilgrimages, fasts, discourses, sermons and the like. They are known for their customs, conventions, traditions, culture, civilization, heritage and philosophy.

Indian society, on the whole, is traditional. Though traditional, it is not static. It undergoes slow, gradual and continuous change. It is undergoing changes at different levels—economic, political, familial, social and cultural. It is changing into a modern society. Modernization aims at achieving a descent standard of living for the people. It also aims at making a modern man in the true sense of the term. But the question remains: Who is a modern man? "A modern man," Ram Ahuja says, "is one who gives up the traditional ways of thinking and feeling, who has an open mind to accept new ideas, who is rational and secular and who believes in equality, freedom and justice". (Ahuja 430). The factors such as urbanization, industrialization, modernization and Western education have brought about social changes in Indian society.

Indian society is facing many problems today. There has been a clash between tradition and modernity. The youth is on the path of revolt as his society fails in meeting many of his needs, requirements and expectations. There has been an inter-generational gap between the old and the young. There has been a serious problem of gender-discrimination on account of which women suffer a lot even today. The system of child-marriage still exists in some Indian communities. Widow re-marriage is looked down upon in our society. The system of dowry, in one form or the other, still, exists in both the urban as well as the rural India. Women have been demanding and fighting for their rights. They have been trying to be economically self-dependent and self-sufficient. Today, quite a large number of women are holding high positions in the public as well as private sectors. They are not prepared to be the slaves of men and to be merely the source of their pleasure. Several women organizations are now engaged in protecting rights and privileges of women. They have been fighting for women empowerment.

1.5 An Indian Woman

The Hindu moral code, known as 'The Laws of Manu', denies the woman a separate and independent existence apart from that of her husband and family. The age-old respect for these laws dictates the place and position of the woman within a family. The woman cannot be independent and is meant to submit her life to the authority of a man: father, husband, brother or son. It is said that she derives her status from her husband and power from her son. Her father is the first guardian-cum-master of the woman. In the absence of her father, his role is performed by his son or his male relatives; and with her marriage, her possession is transferred to her husband. In marriage, she is separated from the family in which she was born and brought up, and is automatically connected to her husband's family.

Man always wants the woman to be the object and means of enjoyment. She does not have her own choice. She is an integral part of the universe which is controlled and governed by males and in which she has a secondary and subordinate role to play. She is not allowed to have desire of her own. She is not allowed to open the door of her heart; it is the man who speaks for her. Simone de Beauvoir writes: "History has shown us that men have always kept in their hands all concrete powers; since the earlier days of the patriarchate they have thought best to keep woman in a state of dependence; their codes of law have been set up against her; and thus she has been definitely established as the Other". (Beauvoir 171). Man always endeavours to have hold and control upon her; he endeavours to mould her to his desire. She too submits passively to his will and desire. She sees herself and makes her choices not in accordance with her nature, but as man defines her.

The Indian woman is an index of Indian customs, conventions, traditions, culture and civilization. She is known for feminine virtues such as silence, patience, tolerance and sacrifice. Her very presence in the kitchen teaches her the importance of compromise and adjustment, tolerance and sacrifice, patience and passivity. She is taught to obey the fire and the water, to wait for the sugar to melt, for the wash to dry, for the fruits to ripen and for many other things silently, patiently and ungrudgingly. She is taught to adjust herself to time, place and circumstances. Resignation has been one of her distinguishing traits. Simone de Beauvoir opines: "This resignation inspires the patience often admired in women. They can bear physical pain much better than men; they are capable of stoical courage when circumstances demand it; lacking the male's aggressive audacity, many women distinguish themselves by their calm tenacity in passive resistance. They face crisis, poverty, misfortune more energetically than their husbands . . . In a generous woman, resignation takes the form of forbearance: she puts up with everything, she condemns no one, because she holds that neither people nor things can be other than what they are . . . women are always trying to conserve, to adapt, to arrange, rather than to destroy and build a new; they prefer compromise and adjustment to revolution". (Beauvoir 613). The woman with these traits is considered a complete and perfect human being. She is the soul of her home, family and society.

A patriarchal society to which she belongs is, to a large extent, responsible to hamper the development of her 'self' and 'individuality'. She has been facing exploitation, subjugation, tyranny and injustice forcefully inflicted on her in a male-centric Indian society. It has been a general belief that the role of the woman is restricted and confined to the four walls of the home and she has been expected to be involved in household activities. Her life is passed in cooking, washing pots and pans, managing her house, pleasing her husband, rearing children and looking after her husband, children and family. She forgets herself, her dreams and aspirations, self and individuality, in favour of her husband, children and home. She is not free and independent in her world which is ruled over by males. She has been assigned a subordinate role of a parasite in the masculine world. Shut up and confined in her home, she feels nervous and helpless before the male members of society who set goals and establish norms and values. Her life is not directed towards any ends because she does not have her own ends. Though Indian culture has given the woman a status of 'Mother' or '*Devi*', worthy of great reverence and worship, she has been facing subjugation and exploitation in one form or the other. She is treated as a commodity, a property, and a possession. The woman, who is exploited and dehumanized by the institutionalized mechanism of prescriptive behaviour in the form of patriarchy, finds herself in an inevitable state of affairs.

The Indian woman is a victim of gender-discrimination in Indian patriarchy where sons are preferred to daughters. Sarabjit Sandhu observes: "The mother is very much attached to her son. Her attitude is a typical one; after all, he is a male child and therefore one who will propagate the family lineage. In another sense also, the male child is considered more important than a girl, because he is qualified to give '*agni*' to his dead parents. The soul of the dead person would otherwise wander restlessly". (Sandhu 1991). It is surprising that it is the mother who wants to get rid of her daughter's responsibility by giving her away in a marriage as early as possible. Veena Das says: "Daughters are comparable to something kept in trust for another (*Anamat*) . . . Once a daughter is properly married and goes on to her own house, it is like a debt that has been paid". (Das 93). Mothers, instead of protecting the interests of their daughters, become responsible and instrumental in torturing and harassing them. The patriarchal set-up plots against girls right from their birth. The birth of a male child in a family, strangely and surprisingly, changes mothers' attitude to their daughters. It almost proves the end of all their dreams and aspirations. Before they could assert themselves, they are burdened with the responsibility of taking care of their baby brothers. Tired of injustice done to them, they dream to use marriage as an escape route to set themselves free from the trap of their ancestral homes. They consider marriage a gateway through which they can move towards liberation from the established norms and conventions of a patriarchal family.

Marriage, as an institution, plays a vital role in the life of men and women in India. It is supposed to provide for their need for love, security and children. It is a solid base of Indian families. To be true, ideally, it is a beautiful thing. It is a special kind of friendship, a special kind of partnership between two people from the opposite sex. Success of this friendship depends on mutual trust, love, and understanding. It is very essential for the well-being of a human society. However, a happy marriage is not everyone's cup of tea. The demand of the lifetime commitment it makes is not possible for everyone. Most marriages are not happy on account of various factors such as sexual promiscuity, male-ego, male-domination, women's growing economic independence and awareness, the patriarchal attitude to women, men's treating women as the objects of sex, inequality between men and women and so on. Though a victim of male-ego and male-domination, though caught in the trap of marriage, the woman makes adjustments and compromises and continues to live with her husband, tolerating her destiny in the form of marital sex and violence.

Marriage is a turning point, an ordeal especially for the woman as she is expected to adjust herself to a new environment of her husband's home. She marries to fulfil her simple need to be free and independent, but unfortunately, in her attempt to set herself free from her parental trap, she is caught in a new trap, i.e. marriage. Her tragedy lies in the fact that she sets herself free from one cage only to be caught in another cage. Marriage, ironically, becomes an obstacle in her way of being a free and independent individual. Simone de Beauvoir opines: "Marriage is the destiny traditionally offered to women by society. It is still true that most women are married, or have been, or plan to be, or suffer from not being. The celibate woman is to be explained and defined with reference to marriage, whether she is frustrated, rebellious, or even indifferent in regard to that institution . . . It has always been a very different thing for man and for woman. The two sexes are necessary to each other, but this necessity has never brought about a condition of reciprocity between them . . . A man is socially an independent and complete individual . . . the girl seems absolutely passive; she is married, given in marriage by her parents . . . In marrying . . . she takes his name; she belongs to his religion, his class; she joins his family, she becomes his 'half' . . . She gives him her person, virginity and a rigorous fidelity being required . . . No doubt marriage can afford certain material and sexual conveniences: it frees the individual from loneliness, it establishes him security in space and time by giving him a home and children; it is a definite fulfillment of his existence". (Beauvoir 445-51).

The functions assigned to the woman after her marriage are: to satisfy her husband's sexual needs, to provide children to his family, and to take care of her husband, children and household. Marriage is the beginning of greater sacrifices for her, sacrifices in the form of her name, person, self, identity, freedom, virginity, her dreams and aspirations. Simone de Beauvoir writes: "The tragedy of marriage is not that it fails to assure woman the promised happiness—there is no such thing as assurance in regard to happiness—but that it mutilates her; it dooms her to repetition and routine". (Beauvoir 496). Repetition and routine kills the very emotional aspect of her life. Though she suffers a lot in her marital life, she considers herself incomplete without her husband; she prefers wifehood to both girlhood and widowhood.

According to Sudhir Kakkar, "Indian woman has to adhere to the image of a good and ideal woman—'*pativrata*', subordinating her life to her husband's happiness. The '*pativrata*' conduct is not a mere matter of sexual fidelity, but an issue of great importance in all patriarchal societies". (Kakkar 66). Indian society allows the husband to have all the freedom to enjoy his conjugal rights as and when he desires, but the wife does not have that freedom. Indian husband has liberty to have another woman if he is not satisfied with his wife. Lord Rama-like '*ek-patni*' conduct is not expected from the husband. Full freedom is given to him to satify his physical hunger the way he likes. However, the woman is not allowed to get involved in extra-marital relationship. It is treated as a crime of adultery. She is expected to be true and faithful to her husband in each and every respect.

India, the largest democracy of the world, has almost an equal number of men and women. Owing to westernization, wide-spread education, and deliberate efforts of social reformers like Mahatma Phule, Rajarshi Shahu Maharaj, Maharshi Karve, Mahatma Gandhi, Karmaveer Bhaurao Patil, and others, Indian women, both from the urban and rural areas, are getting educated today. As a result of growing industrialization, urbanization, growing awareness and spread of education, they have started coming out of their homes and have secured decent jobs and positions in different fields of life. They have started getting involved in the higher type of professional activities. They have started questioning and opposing the conventional and traditional practices. They have been fighting to acquire a place, position and status as an important and equal member of her family. They have been endeavouring to recapture their dignity, individuality and status. They are marching side by side with men in various fields of life. They are contributing significantly towards the building of modern India. They are now participating in various activities such as education, sports, politics, media, art, culture, service sectors, science and technology.

Shashi Deshpande as a Novelist

CHAPTER 2

2.1 Deshpande: A Popular Indian Woman Novelist in English

Deshpande, an award-winning Indian woman novelist, started her literary career as a short-story writer with the publication of her first short story in 1970. Her collection of short stories was published in 1978 whereas her first novel, *The Dark Holds No Terrors*, that brought her a lot of praise and admiration, came out in 1980. Her novel, *That Long Silence*, published in the UK in 1988, and India in 1989, won her the Sahitya Academy Award and Nanjangad Thirumlamaba Award. She was also awarded Padma Shri in 2009 for her contribution to the field of Indian English novel. Her other novels are: *If I Die Today*, *Come Up and Be Dead*, *Roots and Shadows*, *The Binding Vine*, *Small Remedies*, *A Matter of Time*, *Moving On* and *In the Country of Deceit*. In addition to her novels, she has written four children's books and essays available in a volume, *Writing from the Margin and Other Stories*.

As a popular woman novelist, she is basically concerned with the theme of intricate human relationships in which the woman is at the centre, the place and position, the plight and predicament of the woman in Indian patriarchal society, the role of customs, conventions, traditions, beliefs, superstitions, mythology, culture and philosophy in her life, her dreams and aspirations, her natural urge to prove herself as an independent human being and her struggle for self-assertion and self-realization in this callous and malignant environment in India. She is concerned about the disparity between the male and female members of society and about the secondary and inferior position given to the woman. Her sensitive and emotional middle-class heroines, Saru in *The Dark Holds No Terrors*, Indu in *Roots and Shadows*, Jaya in *That Long Silence* and Sumi in *A Matter of Time* are fully conscious of the fact that they are the victims of gender-discrimination and marital-violence prevalent in Indian patriarchy. Caught between traditional values and the fast approaching new life, they are carrying the burden of home and workplace, child-bearing and nurturing, age-old norms, conventions, and traditions, orthodox beliefs and superstitions, duties and responsibilities. They have been struggling for freedom, justice, individuality, identity and survival. They are fighting their own battle, with an urge to find their own way through self-dependence, self-confidence, self-respect and self-assertion. They try to emerge as new women remaining well within the limits of marriage and family.

2.2 Deshpande's Novels: A Brief Review

Her first novel, *The Dark Holds No Terrors*, moves around Sarita, the protagonist, who suffers a lot throughout her life in the name of gender-discrimination and marital violence. It explores the inner psyche and consciousness of the Indian woman, a victim of Indian patriarchy. It deals with various issues related to girlhood, womanhood and motherhood which constantly torture and haunt the female mind. It projects the dilemma of a modern woman who relentlessy fights for her rights, identity, individuality, justice and liberty. It is a story of her conflict as a daughter and also as a wife. In her pre-marital life, she suffers a lot in the name of gender-discrimination. She marries Manohar with a hope to set herself free from the tyranny of her life as a daughter. However, her hope is shattered to pieces and she is compelled to live her life as a trapped creature bearing her husband's sexual assaults. After having tolerated sexual exploitation for seventeen years, on hearing about her mother's death, she returns to her parental home, fully determinied not to return to her husband. Her stay in her father's house gives her an opportunity to review the strength of feminine traits in her and also the nature of her relationship with others. She gathers courage and confidence and decides to return to her marital home to live, control and guide her life the way she likes, remaining well within the restrictions of marriage. She represents a typical Indian woman who struggles to set herself free from the shackles of customs, conventions and traditions, and who strives for the development of her individuality and for the realization of her feminine strength through courage, confidence, determination and education. She bravely fights to survive as an independent being in the world which is filled with darkness, blackness, emptiness and nothingness.

If I Die Today is a perfect detective novel or a fictional story. Initially, it was published as a short story, but later, developed into a novel. Though a defective novel, it deals with issues related to the woman's education and economic independence, and to the nature of womanhood and motherhood. It also highlights issues such as gender-discrimination and urge for a male child deeply rooted in Indian patriarchy. It moves around Manju, the woman protagonist, a young college lecturer, who gets married to a doctor. She lives on the campus of a big medical college and hospital with her husband. She is a sincere, honest, straightforward, broad-minded, kind-hearted and intelligent woman whose marital life with a doctor is not happy. Her life is filled with loneliness, frustration, silence and various barriers. Though she tries her level best, she fails in her attempt to bring happiness and harmony in her marital life. Mriga, a 14 years old girl, one of the memorable characters in the novel, is a typical Indian girl who is a victim of gender-distinction. Dr. Kulkarni, her father, appears to be modern, but he is haunted by the desire for a son and never forgives Mriga for not being a son. Mriga's mother, being a weak person, never lives according to her own wish. She is a sad and suppressed creature, too weak to give Mriga the support and love she wants very badly.

Come Up and Be Dead is a psychological mystery thriller. It deals with the theme of suicide of a schoolgirl in a school. Miss. Kshama Rao, the Head Mistress of the school, though competent, fails to deal with the situation. Two more deaths follow, making the school a place of fear and suspicion. Devi, Kshama's cousin, is successfully looking after Kshama's house and her brother, Pratap. She thinks that Pratap is directly or indirectly involved in the girl's murder. But before she can know the truth, Pratap dies. Devi feels that he too has been killed. She hears different facts from different characters such as Sapna, a school-teacher, Sona, the dead girl's friend and Girish, a doctor. Devi also unwittingly offers herself to 'come up and be dead'.

Roots and Shadows is a novel which highlights Indu's plight and predicament, dreams and aspirations, failures and frustrations, pain and agony. Indu, the woman protagonist, struggles to overcome her pain and suppression and to discover her real 'self', and 'identity', but unfortunately every time she gets deceived and ultimately fails on account of the undue expectations of a male-dominated society. She enjoys no freedom before as well as after her marriage. Before marriage, she was taught to be silent, meek, submissive and obedient. Caught between customs, conventions, traditions and patriarchy, on one side, and modernity and her urge for self-discovery, on the other, she revolts against patriarchy and marries Jayant against the wish of her ancestral family, especially, Akka. However, since the day of her marriage, she has been frustrated as Jayant attempts to develop her identity and personality according to his own ideas and norms. She sacrifices everything—her aspirations, dreams and desires in order to avoid conflict in her marital life. By becoming a traditional wife, she forgets her 'self', her 'identity'. She tries to gather courage to seek freedom within the ambit of obligations and responsibilities of a marriage. Always ready to please her husband, she submits to his wills and desires, totally surrenders her body and soul to him. She sheds her 'I' into her husband and does everything to reflect his image. She believes that she is the architect of her own destiny. However, she ultimately decides to go back to her husband and to live her life as per her desires.

That Long Silence is an attempt to explore Jaya's relations as a wife, a mother, and most importantly, as a human being with others in a male-centric Indian society. The novel highlights Jaya's marital relationship with Mohan which is deeply rooted in silence. It explores the female psyche and mysteries of the female life affected by conventions and traditions prevalent in Indian society. Jaya, the woman protagonist, who is from a conservative family, possesses the potential and inner strength of character which is suppressed by conventional beliefs and ideas. She has been trained to be silent right from her childhood. Like other female protagonists, she, too, has a strong feeling of dislike for and aversion to social taboos. Mohan's mother is a silent sufferer throughout her life. She faces and tolerates all insults heaped upon her and injustice done to her by her husband. For her, silence is the only weapon that she uses to move on with her life, totally depending on her husband. Jaya follows the same path by suppressing her own wishes and aspirations, and lives according to the desire of her husband. She accepts her husband as a sheltering tree and forgets her own 'self' and 'identity'. She accepts a traditional role of an ideal wife by following her husband blindly and mechanically. She, in a sense, is a modern Gandhari. She makes adjustments and compromises wherever and whenever required. However, in the end, she hopefully and confidently decides to find means to live her life afresh on her own.

The Binding Vine explores the innermost recesses of the woman's heart through the perspectives of Urmila, the woman protagonist, who is a clever and educated woman working as a lecturer in a degree college. She, in a moment of crisis, makes an inward journey which enables her to analyse the place and role of a woman in a family. She is portrayed as an independent woman who is psychologically and emotionally very strong. She rebels against the patriarchal tyranny and expresses her anger against injustice and oppression enforced on her by a cruel and callous male-dominated society. She has a strong desire to bring about radical changes in the place and position of a woman and to improve her status and dignity. In order to have her own way in her life, she marries Kishore against the wish of her parents. Unfortunately, the peace and happiness of her marital life is destroyed because of the unexpected death of her female child, Anu. After Anu's death, she begins to brood over social evils that destroy the very identity of the woman. In spite of her sorrows and sufferings, she never sheds tears and tries to deal with her grief on her own. Her comments on gender-discrimination, the tragedy of a girl child in a family, marriage, marital-violence constitute the very core of the novel. Deshpande highlights the need and urgency of the abolition of marital violence in the form of sex imposed on the young and innocent girls like Kalpana. She wants her women to fight for freedom, freedom from male-violence, gender-distinction and sexual harassment.

A Matter of Time is a multi-generational tale which exposes the human predicament of four women—Manorama, Kalyani, Sumitra and Arundhati, representing four generations of the same family. It deals with issues related to womanhood, motherhood, human relationships and a joint-family system in India. It is about physical and mental exploitation of women, sex and sexuality and many other issues related to feminine sensibility in a male-dominated society. It moves around a Hindu married woman with her sorrows, sufferings, suppression and oppression. It narrates a story of a middle-class family of Gopal and Sumi with their three daughters, Arundhati, Charulata and Seema. Gopal's walking away from his marital life makes all the members of the family including Sumi face mental pain and suffering. Sumi, a victim of Gopal's desertion, lapses into a state of complete and utter silence. As a representative of a typical Indian wife, Sumi feels: "What is the woman without her husband? . . . Is it enough to have a husband, and never mind the fact that he has not looked at your face for years, never mind the fact that he has not spoken to you for decades? . . . Does this wifehood make up for everything, for the deprivation of a man's love, for the feel of his body against yours, the warmth of his breath on your face, the touch of his lips on yours, his hands on your breast . . . but her *kumkum* is intact and she can move in the company of women with the pride of a wife". (Deshpande 167).

Small Remedies is a novel which artistically and realistically presents and portrays changes and transitions that occur in Indian society with changing time. Trapped between tradition and modernity, Madhu, a sensitive woman, is fully conscious of the fact that she is a victim of gender-discrimination prevalent in a conservative male-dominated society. Being a representative of a 'new' woman, she is concerned with the revelation of women's conduct, behaviour and existence in a male-dominated society. Savitribai and Leela represent 'new' Indian women who have courage, confidence, urge and ambition to rebel against and violate the established norms, beliefs, customs, and conventions. The protagonist is characterized by the spirit of rebelliousness which is expressed through the woman's rejection of her assigned role in her family and society, her refusal to follow the traditional ways of life, her aversion to the practice of favouring the male child and her disregard for the conventional social taboos.

Moving On is an exploration of a typical middle-class Indian woman's journey from meekness, submissiveness, patience, silence, obedience and passive resistance to her self-discovery, self-reliance, self-realization, development of individuality and to the making of a 'new' woman who is strong and confident enough to have her own way in life without any co-operation from and dependence on the male. It, like *A Matter of Time*, is a multi-generational story that moves around four generations with special focus on human relationships. The protagonist rebels against the oppressive patriarchal society, and the spirit of revolt provides her the right impetus, inspiration and motivation to move on with courage, confidence and determination. It is a story of Vasu, Badrinath's wife, who is characterized by silence, shyness, obedience, sincerity and honesty which are the very ornaments of feminine sensibility. She has a strong desire to be liberal and independent. She expresses her anger at and avarice to a patriarchal society through the stories she writes. Her stories are an expression of her 'self', her genius and personality. Writing becomes an important means for her to fight against her society that imposes many norms and restraints on the female. In a sense, she uses her writing as a means of social change and reform. Manjari, Vasu's daughter, too, opposes and reacts against the things which she doesn't like. She, like her mother, struggles for liberation and freedom. After her husband, Shyam's death, she boldly and confidently tries her level best to be self-dependent and self-sufficient. Being an Indian mother, she desires to look after her children, but the desires of her body begin to distract her attention. Sexual desire in her is so dominant that she gets involved in physical relationships with other men. She considers herself an optimist who believes in the potentiality of life, and realizes that life, at any cost, has to move on and on.

In the Country of Deceit is a novel that deals with the theme of extra-marital love and affairs. It is about Devyani, an unmarried lady who falls in love with a married man who is much older than her. The first part of the novel describes how Devyani is living a free and independent life in her new house after the death of her mother. All her relatives including her married sister, Savita are trying to find her a suitable companion but she doesn't want to destroy her peace and independence by getting caught in the trap of a marriage. She feels that marriage will deprive her of freedom and independence. She meets Ashok and enters into a physical relationship with him. Her relationship with Ashok is an oasis in her dreary life. The element of deceit and betrayal in Rani's love story constitutes the very theme of the novel. The novel projects different lifestyles, presenting in the end an idea of condemnation of a universal crime beyond redemption; and the reader is left wondering: Is it the crime of Love or that of Deceit?

2.3 Deshpande's Novels: Woman-oriented

Deshpande's novels are a product of her observations and experiences of the life of middle-class Indian women caught in the trap of Indian patriarchy. She writes sincerely of what she sees around her. She seems to be engaged in portraying the realistic pictures of educated middle-class Indian women with their feminine traits, their strengths and weaknesses. Her novels, deeply rooted in Indian context, usually, have women as protagonists. The projection of feminine virtues such as silence, patience, sacrifice, tolerance is the very essence of her novels. They deal with themes such as loss, loneliness, pain, agony, anguish, frustration, subjugation, exploitation of Indian women, and also with their dreams and aspirations, their desire to be free and complete women in the true sense of the term. As a popular woman novelist, she has been basically concerned with the plight and predicament, sorrows and sufferings of the female members of a contemporary Indian patriarchal society. Her major concern is with the pathetic condition of Indian women. She raises her feminine voice of protest against their subjugation, suppression, oppression and exploitation.

She is worried about the issue of gender-discrimination and the male-female imbalance deeply rooted in Indian society. She has shown her serious concern about the woman who is restless on account of established conventions and traditions which are in favour of the males. The Hindu moral code, known as the Laws of Manu, denies the woman an existence apart from that of her husband. The woman cannot be free and independent and is forced to submit her life to the authority of the male in Indian patriarchy. It is unfortunately believed that she derives her status from her husband and power from her son. Deshpande raises her voice against the Laws of Manu, according to which, a girl should be under her father's control in her childhood, under her husband's control in her youth, and when her husband is dead, she should be under her son's control, but she should never have independence at any stage in her life. An Indian woman, unfortunately, has been looked down upon with contempt, reduced to the status of a plaything, a machine, a lifeless object used to fulfil men's sexual desire, treated as a commodity to be used, and controlled and disposed of by men the way they like in Indian society.

Deshpande believes that the woman occupies an important position as a daughter, a sister, a wife, a mother, and most importantly, as a human being in all human relationships. However, in a man-woman relationship, the woman is made to play a secondary role. She is dominated and surrounded by the male universe. She differs from her male-counterpart in the sense that she pursues a dream of mute and passive submission and subordination while a man a dream of control, authority, domination and independent identification. It is unfortunate that men and women are not treated equally. Men are, after all, men while women merely women. They do not share the world in equality as the world belongs to the males. They have always been mute and silent sufferers totally dependent on their male counterparts for everything. Nature has really played a trick on women by making them tolerate everything in the name of gender-distinction and marriage. It has also played a trick on them by making them dream of seeking happiness only through a man. It is but natural for them to aspire for natural companionship, physical, mental and emotional satisfaction, social status, dignity, respect and also material comforts, but they are far away from the realization of their dreams and aspirations. Women themselves, to a large extent, are the architects of their own destiny.

Simone de Beauvoir writes: "Thus humanity is male and man defines woman not in herself but as relative to him; she is not regarded as an autonomous being". (Beauvoir 16). They are simply what men see, define and decree. They are just what men want them to be. They, to a large extent, appear to the male as sexual beings. They are destined to passively submit to the sexual desire of their husbands. Beauvoir opines: "Man can think of himself without woman. She cannot think of herself without man . . . she appears essentially to the male as a sexual being". (Beauvoir 25). This has been their inevitable and unavoidable tragedy. Everything in their life has been ultimately directed to the one and only purpose of pleasing the male. Beauvoir rightly raises certain fundamental questions related to the female world which need to be answered. They are: "How can a human being in woman's situation attain fulfillment? What roads are open to her? Which are blocked? How can independence be recovered in a state of dependency? What circumstances limit woman's liberty and how can they be overcome?" (Beauvoir 29). Are these questions not thought-provoking?

We need to realize that women know the female world more intensively and intimately than men do because they have their roots in it. They are familiar with the root causes of their problems. We need to approach their problems with a mind free from bias and prejudice. The solution to their problems lies neither in fighting for equal position nor denying it, neither in retreat into the home nor escape from it. They should neither allow themselves to be swept off their feet by superficial trends and movements nor to be chained to the orthodox conventions. They should ensure the continuity which strengthens roots and simultaneously engineer change and growth to keep society dynamic, abreast of knowledge, sensitive to changes and fast-moving events. They need to fight against age-old norms, beliefs, conventions and traditions rooted in Indian patriarchy. Women, Deshpande feels, must not be reduced to the level of a mere breeding machine. She told in an interview: "I have a very strong feeling that until very recently women in our society have been looked down upon as breeding animals. They have no other role in life. I have a strong objection to treating any human being in that manner". (Gangadharan).

In view of different approaches to established norms, beliefs, values, customs, conventions and traditions prevalent in Indian society, there are three types of women portrayed in Indian English Fiction. These are: the mother figure, i.e. the protagonist's mother, the woman who is rebellious and the woman who is a compromise between the two. The mother figure is a traditional type of woman who believes that she has to be true and faithful to her husband, meek, silent, obedient, submissive and tolerant under any circumstances. She feels that she has no identity, no existence apart from her husband and family. She allows herself to be a victim of a patriarchal society. The second type of the woman, on the contray, is bold, confident, courageous, self-dependent and rebellious. The first and the second types are the two poles apart. The third type of the woman is a compromise between the woman who is totally submissive and traditional on one side, and the woman who strongly rebels against the patriarchal society on the other. Deshpande's female protagonists are of this type. They are neither traditional nor modern. They might protest against patriarchy, but gradually realize that their revolt cannot be the only solution of their problem. They also realize that they need to fight their battle on their own. Sarala Palkar comments: "It is only through self-analysis and self-understanding, through vigilance and courage; they can begin to change their lives. They will have to fight their own battle; nobody is going to do it for them". (Palkar 134).

Deshpande doesn't consider women inferior and subordinate members of a society. She wants them to be aware of their inner strength and potentiality leading them towards self-realization. She makes them emerge as new women strong enough to live their lives with courage, confidence and determination. She does not want them to be a mere shadow of their husbands, but wants them to assert themselves by taking their own decisions all by themselves. She treats them as individuals equal to men, as competent as men with exceptional and unique capabilities and potentials. She wants them to be economically, ideologically mentally, intellectually and emotionally free and strong. She wants them not to remain passive and submissive but to emerge as strong, confident and assertive individuals, attempting to and succeeding in striking a fine balance between traditional beliefs and individual needs and requirements, dreams and aspirations. She wants them to be complete and independent human individuals, to be 'new' and 'modern', equal to their male-counterparts.

Who is a new and modern woman? A modern woman is one who is rebellious and revolutionary, who has an open mind to accept new ideas and who believes in the principles of individuality, equality and freedom. She is one who strongly reacts against orthodox norms and beliefs, traditional ways of living and feeling. She is one who thoughtfully takes her decisions on her own. She is as strong as her male-counterpart in many respects. Simone de Beauvoir writes: "Society, being codified by man, decrees that woman is inferior: she can do away with this inferiority only by destroying the male's superiority. She sets about mutilating, dominating man, she contradicts him, she denies his truth and his values . . . The emancipated woman wants to be active, a taker, and refuses the passivity man means to impose on her. The 'modern' woman accepts masculine values: she prides herself on thinking, taking action, working, creating, on the same terms as men; instead of seeking to disparage them, she declares herself their equal". (Beauvoir 726-27).

Deshpande makes her woman protagonist move towards self-awareness and self-realization and finally to an assertion for autonomy and freedom. She makes her emerge as a self-reliant, intelligent, confident, assertive and happy individual. She makes her exhibit great strength, courage, confidence and determination to reject her traditional role models and dare to go through a process of introspection and emerge as a 'new' woman. Her woman protagonist gradually learns to fight her own battle through self-effacing dependence, aggressive self-assertion, and iconoclastic rage. She becomes a 'new' woman who is conscious of herself as a free and independent individual, who is free from her traditional, social and moral constraints, and who is able to live with a heightened sense of dignity, status and individuality. She casts aside her passivity, silence and invisibility and destroys the image of a meek, obedient, submissive, silent and tolerant human being.

2.4 Deshpande's Feminism

The origin of feminism can be traced in the struggle for Women's Rights during the last decade of the 18th century in the West. It is a movement that seeks to liberate women from male-ego and male-domination. Its intention is to banish patriarchy and provide an opportunity to women to have free and fresh air, and to behave and live as per their dreams, aspirations, beliefs and ideas. It raises a voice of protest against male-domination, male-centric society, male-created beliefs and ideologies. It intends to carry women chained in customs, conventions and traditions towards liberation and self-realization. It is a movement which embraces numerous phases of women's freedom and emancipation. One of the major concerns of feminism is to see and treat women as beings who are capable of finding their own way in life.

Indian feminism, which started in India late in the 1970s, has been influenced by Western feminism. However, it is not a blind, mechanical and slavish imitation of Western thoughts, ideologies and movements. It is nothing but an expression of resentment at the unjust treatment given to and injustice done to Indian women in the name of gender-discrimination. Social reformers like Raja Ram Mohan Roy, Mahatma Phule, Pandit Ramabai and others fought for the cause of women. It was Mahatma Gandhiji who gave a new direction and dimension to the feminist movement in India. He wanted to free women from exploitation, oppression and suppression in a male-centric society. Owing to the rise of feminism in India, Indian women writers have started using novel as a tool to express their bitter revolt against the masculine world in which the woman is a victimized creature. They have been dealing with the plight and predicament of Indian women, their problems, and their physical, mental, financial and emotional suppression and exploitation in various fields of life. Many female writers such as Anita Desai, Bharati Mukherjee, Shobha De, Nayantara Sehgal, Shashi Deshpande and others with a few male writers like R.K. Narayan, Raj Rao and Mulk Raj Anand are concerned with the projection of the female psyche, female consciousness and the inner conflict going on in the minds of women. Indian writers' attempt to free Indian women from Indian patriarchy is, in a sense, Indian feminism.

Deshpande has been dealing with the female psyche and consciousness, the female dilemma and the tempest raging within women in her writings. Herself being a woman, she sympathizes with women and says in an interview: "If others see something feminist in my writings, I must say that it is not consciously done. It is because the world of women is like that and I am mirroring the world". She wants to be known, assessed and evaluated simply as a writer, not as a woman writer. She, in her essay, Why I am a feminist, says: "It took me years to say even to myself, I am a feminist. It was the culmination of the voyage that began within myself, and went on to be the ocean of women's place in the world. Today when I call myself a feminist I believe that the female as the species has the same right to be born and survive, to fulfil herself and shape her life according to her needs and the potential that lies within her, as the male has. I believe that women are neither inferior not subordinate human beings . . . I believe that Nature, when conferring its gifts on humans, did not differentiate between males and females; except for the single purpose of procreation". (Deshpande 83). She insisted in an interview: "I am not a feminist, I am a human being and I write about other human beings who happen to be women . . . My work has helped to break the silence on a number of issues which were once a taboo to talk about".

Her feminism is typically Indian in the sense that it is rooted in Indian soil and context. It refers to her intense awareness of her identity as a woman, her concerns for the feminine issues and problems. It is not a blind imitation of Western feminism. It implies her intense awareness of her identity as a woman, her concern for the feminine issues and problems. It is neither aggressive nor cynical. She believes that feminism is very much an individual working out her problem. Her intention is only to make the Indian woman realize her 'self', her strength and potentiality. She is a true promoter of feminine sensibility in the context of Indian patriarchy. She has been expressing the pain, anguish, agony, sorrows and sufferings of a modern middle-class Indian woman who is caught between tradition and modernity. She depicts the woman's struggle for self-realization, self-assertion, self-expression and development of her individuality and personality. Her approach to the female world is natural, positive, optimistic and humanistic. She does not consider herself a feminist writer. She says that she is a feminist, but she doesn't write to propagate an 'ism'. She feels that while she is a feminist, her novels are novels, works of art which are deeply and firmly rooted in Indian context.

Human Relationships in Deshpande's Novels

CHAPTER 3

3.1 Deshpande's Notion of Relatedness

Deshpande is keenly interested in the projection of human beings in their relationship with one another. She strongly desires to reach a stage where she could write about human beings and not about men and women. The underlying themes in her novels are human relationships, especially the ones that exist between husband and wife, mother and daughter, and father and daughter. The woman, according to her, is at the centre in all these relationships. Human beings do possess a strong desire to be related and attached to one another. This very urge for relatedness to one another within and outside family emerges as a discovery on behalf of the individual, the male as well as the female, in her novels. Since man is a social creature, his need and urge to be related is natural and universal. It is difficult, rather impossible for a human being to live, grow and develop without relating to others in one way or the other.

The Dark Holds No Terrors portrays the woman's fight to survive in the callous and malignant patriarchal world that offers no easy outs to her. Sarita, the woman protagonist, gradually realizes that there is more in the life of the female than just depending on her husband and parents, on institutions such as family, society and marriage. Marriage, as we know, plays a very crucial role in the life of an individual, both the male and the female. Both Saru, in *The Dark Holds No Terrors*, and Indu, in *Roots and Shadows*, marry with a simple and natural hope to set themselves free from their caged existence at their ancestral homes. However, in their quest for freedom, ironically, they are caught in another trap in the form of marriage. Though caught in a marital trap, it is the hope in them that enables them to keep going in their lives. Old Uncle, in *Roots and Shadows*, rightly says: "That's the hope that keeps us going. That makes us willing to let go finally". (Deshpande 108).

Jaya, too, in *That Long Silence,* stresses the need of facing the future course of her life hopefully or optimistically. She strongly believes: "People don't change . . . It's true. We don't change overnight. It's possible that we may not change even over long periods of time. But we can always hope. Without that, life would be impossible. And if there is anything I know now it is this: life has always to be made possible". (Deshpande 193). Life is not possible without hope, without emotional attachment, and without bond of love. When Mohan leaves Jaya, she hopes: "Yes, Mohan would be back. Not only that, he would be repentant, showing his repentance in myriad devious ways . . . In the dark he would hold me close . . . He would make love to me . . . We would go on as before". (Deshpande 127). It is the hope that makes her life possible and bearable after Mohan leaves her. *A Matter of Time* is an attempt to unfold the history of the family in its struggle to survive with dignity and strength, with courage and confidence, rather than submitting passively or cravenly. Gopal, with the hope to escape, finally leaves, never to return, with the thought: "If it is indeed true that we are bound to our destinies, that there is no point struggling against them, even this remains—that we do not submit passively or cravenly, but with dignity and strength". (Deshpande 246).

3.1.1 Sarita's Hopeful Fight to Survive in the World of Males

The Dark Holds No Terrors is a powerful projection of Sarita's fight to successfully survive in the world which, since time immemorial, belongs to men. It highlights the inner struggle of an Indian woman represented by Sarita with reference to her relationship with her husband, her mother, and her father. In reality, Saru is a child with a lot of curiosity which is reflected in her playfulness, her visiting her friends, and her outdoor games. She enjoys roaming about the mango groove, enjoying the rain and many other things from the world of nature. However, she, a typical middle-class Indian girl, suffers a lot on account of a social evil in the form of gender-discrimination. Being a girl child, a variety of restraints are imposed on her by her mother. She wants to liberate herself from the shackles of Indian customs, conventions and traditions. Her initial experiences in her life as a child and as a young girl influence her so strongly that she wants to be a powerful and dominant person in her life, and she knows that she can do it only through education.

As a daughter, she is disappointed as her relationship with her mother is strained as a result of her mother's preferring her son to her daughter, and her caring more for her son than for her daughter. Deprived of motherly care and affection, she realizes that she is an unwanted and unloved daughter. She feels ignored, rejected and neglected in her family. She develops a sense of hatred for her mother. She gets enraged and rebels against her parents by marrying Manu who is from a lower caste, with a hope to attain freedom and autonomy of her 'self' and to assert and affirm her feminine sensibility and individuality. But unfortunately, she is deceived by her marriage. During the course of her journey, she slowly realizes that there is something more to life than mere depending on her husband and parents. To prove herself, she works hard as a student. She shows interest in nothing except her studies. When her friend, Smita wants her to attend the inauguration of Literary Society, she tells her bluntly: "I'm not coming. You know I'm not interested in these things". (Deshpande 50). To succeed at any cost becomes the one and only purpose of her life. She believes: "I had to work hard, to be a success . . . I had to make myself secure so that no one would ever say to me again . . . Why are you alive?" (Deshpande 50).

During her college days she was almost in the heaven in the company of Manohar, a secretary of Literary Association. She was attracted towards him, was excited by his gay personality, his effortless control over the others, his anger at their mistakes, and his smiles that came and went in a flash. She was delighted when he said: "When we're together, it's heaven, wherever we are". (Deshpande 38). She felt shy and trapped when he spoke of marriage. She felt humble when she found him caring for her, or rather loving her. She felt: "It was impossible that I could mean so much to any human being. It was impossible that such things could happen to me. They happen only to girls in movies and books, not to girls like me. And yet, I could not doubt his love. He cared for my feelings as no one had ever done . . . Yes, he loved me . . . True, we had been so far, considering our opportunities, almost impossibly innocent in our relationship, never going beyond holding hands . . . we stayed physically apart . . . It's my painful middle-class inhibitions . . . making marriage the open sesame of all enjoyment for me". (Deshpande 39-40).

Very soon Sarita married him against the wish of her parents, especially, her mother; and experienced what it meant to be wanted, needed, cared and loved. She was almost in the heaven in the early days of her marital life. However, she was made to taste the bitter fruits of marriage in the form of marital violence imposed on her by her so-called caring and loving husband, and she lost her faith in love and marriage. Scornfully, she said: "Love . . . there was no such thing between man and woman. There was only a need which both fought against, futilely, the very futility turning into the thing they called 'love'. It's only a word . . . Take away the word, the idea, and the concept will wither away". (Deshpande 72). Deprived of care, respect and love at her marital home, on hearing of her mother's death, she returned to her parental home once again with a hope to receive help and co-operation, care and love, comfort and consolation from her father; and with a desire to share her pain, agony, loneliness and failure with her father.

A human being's need to have somebody to care for him, love him stands at the core of *The Dark Holds No Terrors*. The urge to confide in someone, to talk to someone, and to share with someone grows in Sarita. She gets terrified at the very thought of loneliness. She finds herself eagerly and hopefully staring at the people around her. Many a time, waking up at night with a start, confusion and fear, she thinks: ". . . I am alone". (Deshpande 43). She feels lonely because she received no love, with a few exceptions, all through her life, before as well as after her marriage. She feels totally deserted in her life. She even seeks to have the support and blessings of God by getting involved in *pujas*, fasts, rituals and prayers, but in vain. She just experiences a feeling of being a fraud, an actress performing the role she does not believe in. She has a strong desire to say: "Baba, I'm unhappy. Help me, Baba, I'm in trouble. Tell me what to do". (Deshpande 44), but she doesn't. She keeps her suppressed loneliness, suppressed unhappiness only to herself. She is tempted to confide to Madhav, to tell him everything and to ask for his advice. But she has no courage to do so. However, during her stay at her parental home, she understands the nature of her relationship with others, especially with her mother and her husband. She learnt a lot from Madhav, who confidently said that he would not spoil his life because of his brother, and that it was his life, after all. Saru is motivated by Madhav and his words and decides not to spoil her life for her husband but to return to her husband with a new ray of hope and determination to live her life afresh.

3.1.2 Indu's Urge for Self-assertion through her Relatedness with Others

Indu's inner self and her desire for the assertion of her individuality and liberty with reference to her relationship, her attachment and interaction not only with her husband, Jayant, but also with the people from her ancestral family find exploration in the novel, *Roots and Shadows*. Indu, the woman protagonist, grows and develops as an individual and attains completeness in her life only through her bond with the members of her marital family and those of her ancestral family. As a female member of a large joint family, in her childhood, she was taught to be a typical Indian girl, to be meek, obedient, docile, submissive and unquestioning. However, being rebellious, she wants to have her own way in her life. Suppressed in Indian patriarchy, she rebels against age-old and orthodox conventions, by marrying Jayant, who is not from her caste, at the age of eighteen, with the intention of making herself a complete individual. After her marriage, she surrenders and submits herself completely and whole-heartedly to her husband in the name of love. But very soon she realizes that like any other Indian husband, Jayant, too, wants her to live according to his views and ideas, his dreams and aspirations. She, too, forgets her 'self' and 'identity' and sheds her 'I' into her husband. Her dream to be a free and complete individual remains only a dream. She feels deceived and disillusioned in her marital life. In her professional life of a journalist, she has to surrender to the dictates of the editor. She is deprived of liberty in her marital life as well as in her professional life. She wants to escape from the burden of wifehood and considers 'marriage' a trap. She strongly feels: "Behind the facade of romanticism, sentiment and tradition, what was marriage, after all, but two people brought together after cold-blooded bargaining to meet, mate and reproduce so that the generations might continue". (Deshpande 3). She begins to believe that love has no role to play in her marital life.

She loses her belief in conjugal love. She feels: "And anyway, love, that's a word I don't really understand. It seems to me an overworked word, overburdened by the weight we put upon it. I love a book, a word, a sari, a curry, a dog, a child, a man. God, how hopelessly inefficient to use the same word for such different emotions, such varied reactions . . . What I feel for Jayant . . . can I compress all of it within this word?" (Deshpande 88-89). She considers herself a woman who loves her husband too much, too passionately, but is ashamed of it. She is disillusioned by her husband's hard-to-understand and uncaring nature. She is not happy in her marital life as she does not get what she desires to get. On her return to her ancestral home after ten years, she gets emotionally attached to her ancestral family, and becomes a part and parcel of that family. She gets involved with Naren who has his own theory of love. Love, according to him, is another word for a human physical contact. He says: "I have a theory about contact, Indu. I mean literal contact, people touching each other. We always need it. Babies crave to be touched by the mother, a parent. Then we move away from the family to generalized contact. Have you seen boys and girls going about, their arms around each other? Later craving gets a vocal point. You want to be touched by, to touch, one person of the other sex. It gets magnified and exaggerated beyond proportion". (Deshpande 160). Physical contact, another name for love, enables the people to keep their relationships normal, healthy and intact.

After she becomes Akka's successor, a *Mahabharata* begins in the family, with its members fighting for their share of the ancestral money and property. She thinks to herself: "I had always imagined that as soon as a person died, the relatives came panting to find out what had happened to the money. Now Akka was dead, and they had, all of them, always been parasites on her; and yet no one, not even her husband's nephew Shridhar, who had come to perform the ceremonies, had shown the least curiosity about the money". (Deshpande 41-42). After Akka's death, the family members are in a hurry to sell the house. Kaki, who has been in the house since the day of her marriage, is on the side of the sale of the house. She hopes to live comfortably in a new house with Hemant, her son. Her dream is to live in a small house with a small kitchen, a gas to cook on, clean and shining pots and pans lined on shelves. Sunanda-atya, like Kaka, is against the sale of the house. Her feelings for the house are different from those of Kaki. She says: "Vahini wasn't born in this house. She doesn't have the same feeling for it that we . . . Anant and I do. If I had a wish, I would say . . . let me die here where I was born. Our father died here, and mother, and Akka. It's all right for Vahini . . . she has sons and can stay with them without feeling an intruder. Where can I go? My brothers, thank God, have been so good for me. I've never been unwanted here. And I belong here, nowhere else". (Deshpande 121). It is the sense of belonging that matters most to her. Anant-kaka who is worried about Mini's marriage, hopes to convince Indu to spend for her marriage. He, who was against Mini's marrying Naren, now, hopefully believes: "And Naren . . . why not? He's a good boy. I told you I always liked him. A little irresponsible, may be. But once he's married and has a wife and kids, he'll settle down. I know he will. After all, he's a clever boy. Well qualified too". (Deshpande 131). He hopes that once he marries, has a wife and children, he will settle in his life.

Indu is inspired by Old Uncle and his philosophy. In spite of his losing his wife in his youth, his only son in his middle age, and his only grandson, Naren, his only link with life, in his old age, to her surprise, he considers himself singularly fortunate. She learns a lot from him for whom success has nothing to do with money. Earning and spending is not the only thing that matters in human life. 'What do I want?' is a question not easy to be answered. It is impossible, unimaginable, or rather unbearable for Indu not to succeed, not to have the best in her life. She is in a sad state of affairs. Away from her husband, she seems to be happy and comfortable in her ancestral home. However, the truth is otherwise. She thinks: "I turned about and made myself comfortable here now. But that's only for a time. This is an interlude. I don't belong here anymore. And yet I don't fit into the world I have left behind me, either. Where then do I belong?" (Deshpande 102). This sense of not belonging either to her marital home or to her ancestral home, a sense of nothingness destroys not only the peace of her mind but also her confidence. She finds herself on the verge of a complete bankruptcy. She does not know what she wants to have in her life.

Old Uncle is worried about Naren, a fatherless and motherless young man, who is treated as an outsider in the family. His care for his grandson is a kind of pain, a kind of punishment for him in his old age. Attachment, for him, is the law of human life. Nobody can escape it. One cannot protect oneself against love. Love is the only thing that matters in life. Hope is something that keeps human life in motion; it is something that keeps life move on. He is right when he says: "In spite of the hurt, the suffering, the humiliations, you go on getting involved. That's the human predicament". (Deshpande 109). Indu, too, accepts her predicament. Though, she tries her level best, she fails to keep the family, a large group of people with diverse pulls, conflicting interests and conflicting feelings, united and intact, spends for Mini's marriage, chooses Vithal as one of the first to be benefitted from Akka's trust, sells the house to Shankarappa, and completes the circle by returning to her marital home, with confidence and determination, to achieve complete happiness. The paradox of the situation lies in the fact that though, not happy with Jayant, she cannot live without him. She is hopeful to be happy with him. She hopes: "Jayant and I . . . I wish I could say we have achieved complete happiness . . . I want to be loved, I want to be happy. The cries are now stilled. Not because I am satisfied, or yet hopeless, but because such demands now seem to me to be an exercise in futility. Neither love nor happiness comes to us for the asking . . . The other day, I came away from my writing, tired, disheveled, almost in tears. 'I'll publish it for you', Jayant said, putting his arms comfortingly around me . . . Happiness . . . I never knew it was made up of such simple things". (Deshpande 13).

What does the Indian woman expect from her husband? She expects care, support, co-operation, and affection from him. Affection in a family should be a living presence. Indu finds a kind of ease in her relationship with her husband. She begins to believe that freedom lies in giving oneself to others and one can find freedom when one fulfils one's obligations and discharges one's responsibilities within a limited circle. She realizes: "I know this now. But twice in my life I had thought that I was free, once, when I left home as a young girl, and the second time, when, once again I left the family after Naren's death and returned to Jayant. Both times I found out how wrong I was. New bonds replace the old. That is all". (Deshpande 14). Life, both in the world of man as well as in the world of nature, continues endless, limitless and full of grace. Continuity is the law of life. It is the only thing that matters in life. Indu is surprised when Old Uncle said: "But when you get to my age, you'll understand. It's the only thing that matters. It means continuity. It means I'll never die . . . That's the hope that keeps us going. That makes us willing to let go finally. Not all of me shall die. There shall be something of me left". (Deshpande 108). The hope that life continues plays a great role in human life. One era ends so that the other might begin. Akka's era has been replaced by Indu's. Shankarappa is planning to build a hotel in place of the house. Even the *champak* tree, with evergreen leaves, the golden flowers, which is right in the middle of the house, in the back courtyard will go down. It will cease to exist. However, Indu rejects the idea of non-existence. She feels: "Non-existence? No, there is no such thing. To accept it will be to deny the miracle of life itself. If not this stump, there is another. If not this tree, there will be others. Other trees will grow, other flowers will bloom, and other fragrances will pervade other airs". (Deshpande 184). Indu understands a great secret of life, the secret that life never ceases to exist.

3.1.3 Jaya's Hope of Erasing her Long Silence

Jaya, the protagonist of the novel, *That Long Silence*, is a sensitive, educated middle-class woman who lives with her insensitive husband and children. She is a typical Indian woman who is caught between her aspirations and restrictions imposed on her in Indian patriarchy. After her marriage, Mohan, her husband, remains a stranger to her for a few days. She is hopeful and optimistic to achieve much-required closeness and intimacy with her husband gradually. She thinks: "We were married; we were husband and wife, so everything, according to him, was permissible. He had taken it for granted that I thought the same way. And so perhaps it was only I who had been surprised when intimacy had come, all of a sudden; with the physical link . . . whatever my feelings had been then, I had never spoken of them to him . . . In fact, we had never spoken of sex at all . . . First there is love, then there's sex . . . What else could I call it but love when I thought of how I had longed for his physical presence, when I remembered how readily, almost greedily, I had responded to his touch? . . . The strength of my feelings for him had both shamed and terrified me . . . I had rationalized: we're all frightened of the dark, frightened of being alone. And so we cling to one another, saying . . . I love you, I want you, I need you". (Deshpande

94-97). Human need to love and to be loved, to want and to be wanted, to care and to be cared is the foundation stone of human life.

She steps into her role as a dutiful wife and a loving and caring mother. However, as time progresses, her married life becomes a dull routine. She believes that she can stay away from her husband without any pain, fear or grief. She can sleep with him without any desire, interest and intimacy now. She describes her marriage as "a pair of bullocks yoked together . . . a clever phrase, but can it substitute to reality? A man and a woman married for seventeen years, a couple with two children, and a family somewhat like the one caught and preserved for posterity by the advertising visuals I so loved. But the reality was only this. We were two persons, a man, and a woman". (Deshpande 8). After Mohan has been caught in the scandal, Mohan and Jaya begin to face an uneasy silence. It is very difficult for Jaya to face blankness, emptiness and nothingness. She does not see herself as free and independent Jaya, but as Mohan's wife, and Rahul and Riti's mother. She becomes a symbol of a silent, tolerant, obedient, and submissive housewife. The home, she feels, should be a place where one can be safe, secure, assured and confident. But in reality, it is a small and dark world where the woman is not only guarded, protected, shaped, and directed, but also restrained, narrowed, and weakened. It is the place which decides and determines the destiny of the female. For Simone de Beauvoir, "the home is not merely an 'interior' within which the couple is shut away; it is also the expression of that couple's standard of life, its financial status, its taste". (Beauvoir 542).

Jaya has her own philosophy of physical contact and touch. She feels: "Physical touching is for me a momentous thing. It was only Appa who hugged me as a child, and after him there was Mohan. We were husband and wife and he could hold me, touch me, and caress me. But it was never a casual or light-hearted thing for either of us". (Deshpande 15). She can differentiate between Appa's hugging her as a child and Mohan's holding her as a wife. But she understands the meaning of 'male touch' for the first time when Kamat, her neighbour touches her. It is true that women are gifted with an innate and inborn competence that enables them to read the physical touch and eyes of the males. What Indu said to Sunanda-atya, in *Roots and Shadows*, speaks a lot about this latent competence of the female. She says: "I know, my knowledge dates from the time I was fifteen . . . I was learning to ride the bicycle. And he, your husband, my uncle, had offered to help me. I had accepted the help gladly, until I had felt his 'helping hands' giving me the age-old messages of male to female. At fifteen, you're woman enough to have an instinctive knowledge of male hunger, and child enough to panic at being the object of it. I have avoided him ever since". (Deshpande 136).

A sense of belonging plays a vital role in human life. The individual always wants to be in the company, in the contact of someone. A game of friendship is played enthusiastically by men and women. Jaya remembers her so-called friendship with Rupa. She recollects: "We met as families once a week, Rupa and I rang each other up twice a week, we went shopping together, we saw movies together, we were the members of the same women's club . . . And yet the truth was that Rupa and I were strangers. We never talked to each other, not like Seema and I had done in school. Seema and I had told each other everything, whereas, Rupa and I skated, hastily and fearfully, over the thin ice of our daily routine life. We didn't probe deeper; we didn't even want to . . . Nevertheless, we kept up this fiction of our friendship with great enthusiasm". (Deshpande 47-48). It is not a true friendly relationship. It is a kind of 'let's pretend' game of friendship. It is a piece of family fiction. But even such type of relationship, a kind of change, makes our daily dull and mechanical routine bearable.

3.1.4 Role of the Hope in the Life of Women in 'A Matter of Time'

A Matter of Time highlights the importance of relatedness in human life and the intricate relationship within an extended family, covering four generations of men and women. Aru, the eighteen-year-old girl, hopefully struggles to understand a strange and strained relationship between her father and mother, and between her grandfather and grandmother. We need to realize that we have to build our lives on the solid foundation of hope, love and trust. Human relationship does not last long in the absence of this foundation. Gopal, Aru's father thinks to himself: "We bury our fears deep, we stamp hard on the earth, we build our lives on this solid, hard foundation, but suddenly the fears come to life, and the earth shakes with their struggle to surface. It was Sudha, the sight of her when she came to us after her illness that brought my fear back, so close that the sound of its flapping wings filled my years to the exclusion of everything else". (Deshpande 51).

Sudha, Gopal's step-sister, a vigorous, healthy, confident and cheerful girl, looks empty, peevish, self-centred, invalid and constantly complaining of her loss, pain and agony, as if it is all over for her after P. K.'s sudden death and after the surgery for her tumour. Gopal feels that it is something more than P. K.'s death and her sickness that has made her the way she is. Gopal realizes: "She had retreated from us; none of us . . . could reach her. And she was frightened of this world of loneliness she suddenly found herself in". (Deshpande 51). If this happens to Sudha, the most generous and loving woman, who has invested all of herself in relationships, what hope is there for others not to be empty and dejected? Gopal, finally, realizes: "Emptiness is always waiting for us . . . And so it's a lie, it means nothing, it's just deceiving ourselves when we say we are not alone. It is the desperation of a drowning person that makes him cling to other humans. All human ties are only a masquerade". (Deshpande 52).

After his marriage, Gopal believes that he needs his wife, her warmth, her humanness, and her womanness. During the early days of his marital life, he realizes: "It is through our bodies that we find our first connections to this world. I knew it when I saw Aru as a baby, her tiny mouth open, ceaselessly searching for the nipple, the milky fountain, for the softness and warmth of her mother's breast. Yes, for me it was right to live with Sumi. And there were my children . . . I wanted it all. And I did everything—caring for my babies, tending them, caressing them—with joy and passion. Those hours in the night when I was alone with them, holding the small warm bundles in my arms, I was filled with an emotion I had never known until then". (Deshpande 68). This sense of belonging to one another plays a vital role in strengthening human relationships.

Human need to be related to one another, human will and desire keeping all things in motion in human life matter most in the drama of mankind. It is the hope, the hope of something better to happen in human life, makes us move on with our lives. Manorama and Vithalrao, for example, are much worried about their daughter, Kalyani and her coming back home as a deserted wife. Vithalrao, a man of science, to everybody's surprise, turns to astrology with a hope that some astrologer will tell him about his daughter's return to her marital home. He is searching for someone who will tell him: "Your daughter will soon be united with her husband, they will live happily together". (Deshpande 152). When all the doors are closed for a man, it is the hope that opens a new door for him.

After Gopal's desertion, his wife, Sumi's routine, to the fear and astonishment of her daughters, Aru, Charu and Seema is as usual. Aru, in particular, experiences the panic and disorientation of being lost, and feels deprived of the need of love and affection she and her sisters expect to get from their father. They are confused, but they naturally follow their mother by going through their normal routine. Sumi's calmness and normality make it possible for them to hope that their father will come back. After over a month since Gopal left home, Sumi thinks that they need to vacate the rented house immediately. Aru, who disagrees with her mother, believes that to give up the house is to kill that hope. Even when they are brought to the Big House, every time the gate creaks, they hope it could be their father, every time the phone rings; there is the hope that they could hear Gopal's voice. Even Sumi, despite her apparent indifference and stoicism, is not immune from this hope. They try to keep the ray of hope burning in them. During Premi's visit to her after Gopal's desertion, Premi remembers Sumi's hopeful and confident response to Gopal's resigning: "He'll get a job—he told me someone has already approached him . . . Oh, I'm not worried!" (Deshpande 16). Sumi remembers her argument on the word *Sa-hriday* with Gopal. She remembers him saying: "There's no word in English that can fit the concept. English is a practical language; it has no words for the impossible. *Sa-hriday* in the sense of oneness is an impossible concept". (Deshpande 24).

Sumi, according to whom, love, attachment and companionship are necessary in human life, is worried about Aru's marriage, her indifference to Rohit, her ignoring Rohit's feelings about her. In a response to her father who says that she need not worry about her daughters' marriage, she thinks to herself: "But I do worry, I have begun to worry about their marriage . . . Will Aru learn that love, however brief, however unsatisfactory, however tragic, is necessary? Will she realize that without that kind of a companionship some part of us withers and dies?" (Deshpande 169). It is true that Sumi's failure in her marital life, in spite of the fact that Gopal and Sumi love each other, makes her think of love, a noble feeling, as momentary, unsatisfactory and tragic. Though, it is so, she wants Aru not to reject Rohit's friendship. She wants to say to her: "I'm not thinking of your marrying him; you're far too young for that . . . Just don't reject his friendship, don't reject it because he's a man". (Deshpande 170). Healthy friendships and relationships within and outside a family, though rare, are necessary to have normalcy in human life.

Aru and Charu are greatly affected by their father's walking away on their family. Charu cannot concentrate on her studies. She tells her mother, "You know, Ma, just before I fell asleep, I couldn't read. I couldn't see any words on the pages; I just kept seeing us, as we were before . . . But I want us to be like that again, the way we were. I keep thinking—surely Papa will want to be back with us, he'll come home and we'll be like before". (Deshpande 193-94). She, hopefully, wants her father to come back; she wants the entire family live together as they used to before.

Surekha, the lawyer, comes to see Aru's father. She wants to see the man who could walk out on such a daughter. During their meeting, Gopal expresses his belief in the words from the *Upnishadas*: "For the desire for sons is the desire for wealth and the desire for the wealth is the desire for the worlds". (Deshpande 214). He has always thought that the love for daughters is less tainted but more disinterested. He feels that his daughters don't need him anymore. Surekha strongly reacts to Gopal and says: "They don't need you? You're fooling yourself. Is there any moment when our need for one another ceases?" (Deshpande 214). She strongly believes that human need for one another, an inseparable part of human life, makes life possible. But for Aru, after having learnt about her mother's decision to accept the job in a residential school, her family life seems to over. She says: "It's over . . . Our family life . . . When Papa went I thought, I hoped, we would get it back some day, it was still possible, I could dream of it, but, now—I don't know . . .". (Deshpande 230).

3.2 Human Relationships: Soul of Deshpande's Novels

Deshpande deals with the theme of human relationships, in general, and husband-wife relationship, in particular, in her novels. Her greatness as a novelist lies in her potentiality to probe deep into the inner psyche and consciousness especially of the female human beings in their relations with others in Indian setting and context. She is interested in the projection of the very ambiguities, intricacies and complexities of human relationships within and outside a family. She believes that a woman is at the centre of any relationship in a family. Human beings are naturally required to live within relationships which contribute to the growth and development of their individuality, to the shaping and moulding of their lives. Society, with all its beliefs and superstitions, norms and values, conventions and traditions, rites and rituals, culture and civilization, equipments and institutions, provides form and order, shape and direction to human life.

3.2.1 Marital Relationship in 'The Dark Holds No Terrors'

The Dark Holds No Terrors is an intense piece of work that moves around the relationship between Manohar and Sarita, husband and wife, and Saru's relations with her father and mother as well. Deshpande gives a muted and essentially sympathetic treatment to the issues and problems related to marital relationships in it. The opening of the novel, holding the breath of the reader, underlines the nature of the relationship between Manohar and Sarita, the relationship rooted in marital violence in the form of sex. Sarita frightfully remembers: "The beginning was abrupt; there had been no preparation for it . . . At first it was a nightmare of hands. Questing hands that left a trail of pain . . . and then, the nightmare was compounded of lips and teeth as well. Hands and teeth? No, hammers and pincers. I could taste blood on my lips . . . I struggled to utter the usual words of protest, to say . . . No, not now, stop it. But the words strangled in my throat. The face above mine was the face of a stranger . . . Panic and terror mounted in me as the hands, deliberately, with a kind of casual cruelty, gradually tightened round my throat. Oh God, I was going to die . . . The dream, the nightmare, whatever it was, continued. Changing now, like some protean monster, into the horror of rape. This was not to be death by strangulation; it was a monstrous invasion of my body. I tried to move . . . it was impossible . . . Now the horror of what was happening to me was lost in a fierce desire to end it. I could not, would not bear it . . .". (Deshpande 11-12). The first two pages of the novel, vividly, describe the wife's rape by her husband, thus, arousing curiosity of the reader about the nature of husband-wife relationship which has nothing to do with emotions and feelings. In an interview with Vanamala Vishwanatha, Deshpande, herself, has admitted: "*The Dark Holds No Terrors* came to me when I saw a couple. The wife had a better job and there was an obvious tension between them. He was aggressive and surely, that set it off". (Vishwanatha 3). However, it is true that she did not write the novel only with the notion of rape, marital violence or sexual domination in her mind.

Sarita was reminded of her gender as a girl child by her mother, a typical orthodox and traditional Indian woman. She had been a victim of gender-discrimination. The distinction that her mother made between her and her younger brother, Dhruva made Sarita hate her mother like anything. Her biased and loveless relationship with her parents, especially with her mother, gave rise to a sense of insecurity in her. Her hatred for her mother and her ambition to be a doctor with the support of her father brought her to Mumbai to seek medicine as a career. She fell in love with Manohar, who was not a Brahmin but from a lower caste poor family, and married him just out of her hatred for her mother. She was almost in the heaven during the early days of her married life. She remembers: "After the first moment of apprehension . . . a purely physical response or lack of it, rather . . . there was never any withholding in me. I became in an instant a physically aroused woman, with an infinite capacity for loving and giving, with a passionate desire to be absorbed by the man I loved. All the clichés were, I discovered, were true, kisses were soft and unbearably sweet, embraces hard and passionate, hands caressing and tender, and loving, as well as being loved, was an intense joy . . . I was insatiable, not for sex, but for love. Each act of sex was a triumphant assertion of our love, of my being loved, and of my being wanted. If I had any doubts, I had only to turn to him and ask him to prove his love for me. And he would . . . again and again and again". (Deshpande 40). She was extremely happy with her husband even in a small room in a chawl with a common toilet and with the corridors smelling of urine, amongst women with inquisitive, unfriendly eyes; and amongst men with lascivious stares. However, the life of happy moments in her life was very short, unreal and illusionary.

Manohar's attitude to his wife began to change as soon as her status as a doctor gave her special dignity and importance in the neighbourhood. Being a young doctor, she was excited and thrilled while examining, advising and prescribing the real patients. She could not hide her enthusiasm even from her life partner. She noticed: ". . . when we walked out of the room, there were nods and smiles, murmured greetings and namastes. But they were all for me, only for me. There was nothing for him. He was almost totally neglected". (Deshpande 42). Manohar's ego, pride and superiority complex, an outcome of Indian patriarchy, did not allow him to tolerate her success and popularity. She noticed affected indifference in Manohar's behaviour. He became sick of the place where he was ignored, the place where his wife was very busy with her profession. The celebration of love through marriage came to an end with Saru's gaining recognition as a doctor. Her marriage began to crush under the weight of her successful career as a doctor.

Manohar failed to share his wife's excitement and enjoyment, her success and popularity, her status and prestige. Hurt and humiliated, he became sexually violent and aggressive. He began to attack his wife like a wild animal. She was scared and found it difficult to face her sexually aggressive and violent husband. She came to the realization that she had to suffer a lot due to her husband's sexual attacks on her. Her fortune was not in her favour as after her marriage she was made a victim of male-brutality, male-superiority and male-domination. During sex, she felt that she was being raped, and that her husband was not himself but a stranger. She was totally shattered and emotionally disturbed by these nightmares. She could do nothing against his maniac strength. She was incapable of resisting her panic, pain and agony. She wanted to cry: "I can't, I won't endure it any more. I would rather die. I can't go on". (Deshpande 99). It was the beginning of a mute and unending struggle between them.

It is a fatal truth that in a man-woman relationship, it is the man who treats the woman as inferior, passive and submissive, it is the man who wants to be dominating, it is the man who wants to be the ultimate winner, it is the man who expresses the desire and the woman, who is sexually subjective, is the object of his desire, and it is the man who takes the female and it is the female who is taken. Manohar's sexual desire and attack, which were violent and brutal, made her just an injured and victimized creature. He deliberately wanted to make his wife feel humiliated and possessed. He made the act of love a battle in which his wife was hurt and defeated. He wanted and needed her company only to enjoy sex regularly against her desire. He committed rape in the name of marriage itself. His wife, a helpless sexual object, received no pleasure out of her sexual relations with him. Her husband's brutality and his sudden, abrupt and violent sexual attack caused trauma and aroused hatred and disgust in her. Brien writes: "Men often use violence against their wives when they lack in other means of control such as economic or educational superiority over women". (Brien 136). Manu proves Brien right by the way he treats his wife.

The husband in Manohar forgot that marriage is a holy union, and any sexual pleasure taken in it forcefully has to be restrained and controlled. She believed: "But now I know that it was there it began . . . this terrible thing that has destroyed our marriage. I know this too . . . that the human personality has an infinite capacity for growth. And so the esteem with which I was surrounded made me inches taller. But perhaps, the same thing that made me inches taller, made him inches shorter. He had been the young man and I his bride. Now I was the lady doctor and he was my husband". (Deshpande 42). Care and love had no place in their marriage. She scorned the word 'love' itself. She thought: "There was no such thing between man and woman. There was only a need which both fought against, futilely, the very futility turning into the thing they called 'love'. It's only a word . . . take away the word, the idea, and the concept will wither away". (Deshpande 72). She now began to hate the word 'love' itself and refused to believe that such a thing exists between man and woman. She realized: "And I? Now, I knew it was not just the consequences I feared and hated, but the thing itself. What had I imagined? Love? Romance? Both, I knew too well, were illusions, and not relevant to my life anyway. And the code word of our age is neither love nor romance, but sex. Fulfillment and happiness came, not through love alone, but sex. And for me sex was now a dirty word". (Deshpande 133).

Sarita was tired of her relentless routine, her hospital, her teaching, her visits, her home, her children; and above all, the nightmares. She was terribly frightened at the very thought of sex, a marital-violence. She failed to strike a balance between her role as a doctor, and that of a wife. She, therefore, decided to stop working as a doctor with a simple intention to give justice to her role as a wife and a mother. She just wanted to stay at home, cook and clean, and to look after her children.

Manohar was shocked at her decision. He asked her: "And how will we live? On my salary? Come on, Saru, don't be silly. You know how much I earn. You think we can live this way on that?. . . Can you bear to send the children to a third-rate school? To buy them the cheapest clothes, the cheapest of everything?. . . No, Saru, there can be no going back. We have to go on". (Deshpande 81). He wanted her not to stop working. He wanted her to earn not only butter but bread as well. She had a strong desire to: "Tell him what he does. Tell him you can't stand it any longer. Tell him you're prepared to sacrifice everything as long as he leaves you alone. To sleep alone in a room, to be by myself on a bed, to be untouched, unhandled . . . only then I can be clean again". (Deshpande 80). However, being a typical Indian woman, she remained mute and silent. Her silence kept her sorrows, her pain and agony to herself. She felt: "I should have spoken about it the very first day. But I didn't. And each time it happens and I don't speak, I put another brick on the wall of silence between us. May be one day I will be walled alive within it and die a slow, painful death. Perhaps the process has already begun and what I am is a creature only half alive. And it seems I can do nothing to save myself". (Deshpande 96). She was caught between Manu's two selves, between two surprisingly different men, Manu a fearful stranger of the night, and a pathetic Manu during the day. She was terribly frightened by this dichotomy, his sexual attack at night, and his cheerfulness the next morning, his air of being as usual, a complete, total normality.

Her marriage had made her a terrified animal, sitting in the same room with her husband, watching the same familiar gaze coming over his eyes, the mask-like rigidity coming over his face, and at night waiting for the terror to strike. Marriage became a burden, a catastrophe for her. She considered her marriage an unfortunate failure. Her marriage ceased to be a commitment to share, to adjust, to understand, to help, to co-operate, and to love. She lost her interest in marriage which denied her freedom and liberty in her professional life; and also a true sexual pleasure in her marital life. All her inner sentiments, her sensitivities, her dreams of a happy and successful life had been trampled and crushed by marriage, where wife, in one way or the other, was raped by her husband. In loneliness she experienced a strange fear of disintegration, a terrified feeling of not existing. She considered herself a lifeless puppet. Her life was full of uneasiness, nothingness and emptiness. Once she, in the hospital, found herself cutting a piece of paper, telling herself: ". . . these are bits of my mind falling on the ground". (Deshpande 22). She feared that she was losing, rather, had lost something, almost everything. Feeling lonely, she had an urge to confide in someone, to talk to someone. There was no one who could comfort her, console her. She, therefore, on knowing about her mother's death, decided to rush to her parental home, not to comfort her afflicted father, but to comfort herself by sharing her painful failure with her father. Actually, her coming back to her parental home was a kind of escape from her sadist husband and her loveless marriage. To her, it was an escape route, something that led her out of her loveless trap.

Once, in a dream, she found herself at home, in her own room, then walking out of the house, out of the gate, and on to the road . . . She, hopefully, thought that the road in the dream had brought her back to her parental home where she was staying without her children, her husband, her home, her practice, and her patients. It was difficult for her to go on without them either. It would have been possible for her to go on, she thought, if "she had belonged to another time, where a woman had no choice but to go on. Human nature may not change, but isn't there such a thing as a frame of mind, a way of thinking, which is shaped by the age you live in? It was so much easier for women in those days to accept, not to struggle . . . And they called that Fate". (Deshpande 70). She knew that a man and his state of mind, his nature, temperament and his personality are shaped and moulded by the age he lives in, the place to which he belongs, and the milieu in which he is brought up and grows.

Saru thought of her grandmother who had been deserted by her husband only a few years after marriage, leaving her as a young woman with two little daughters, one of whom had been her mother. Her grandmother's father looked after them and got the girls married. Her grandmother always carried the burden of being unwanted, a dependent and a parasite, but she never complained. She accepted her lot believing that she was a puppet in the hands of her destiny. She said: "It's my luck, my fate. It was written on my forehead". (Deshpande 70). Saru was frightened by the very thought of fate believed to have been written on her forehead. She did not believe that she was fated to accept and endure passively and patiently. She knew that her passivity, her silence, her tolerance had turned her into a puppet manipulated by others, especially by her husband. She herself was responsible for her own tragedy. However, hope in her made her tolerate her tragic lot. She hoped: "Yet in the daytime, when the terrors which came with the dark disappeared, there was always the hope that there would be someone. One could never be so totally deserted, after all. And yet, she had the dismal feeling that it was she who had frozen herself into an isolated, lonely suffering she could never break out of". (Deshpande 43-44).

At her parental home, away from her husband and his sexual assault, she got a chance to recollect her relationship with her parents. It was from Madhav she came to know that her mother was lying sick in her room nearly for one year. Her mother's agony was so intense and acute that she thought only of her pain, and not of her dead son, her unwanted daughter, and her weak and feeble husband. After her death, her husband, Saru's father never went to her room. Saru, on her return, went into the same room and opened the almirah. She found a packet full of photographs in it. One of the photographs was of her parents, obviously taken in a studio soon after their marriage. She, in it, saw her mother "sitting stiff, unsmiling in a chair, he on the arm of it equally stiff, the two of them a pair of puppets, posing there because they had been told to . . . a pair of strangers". (Deshpande 57). She knew that her parents, husband and wife, had been strangers throughout their married life. The photograph reminded her of a very strange relationship between her father and mother.

The relationship between Madhav's mother and father throws some more light on a conventional husband-wife relationship in Indian context. Madhav's mother, a typical Indian woman, happily accepts a secondary role in her marital life. She considers it a punishment to be deprived of a chance to serve her husband who does not eat anything she cooks. Saru is reminded of the woman from the Sanskrit story, the story from her textbook. She remembers the woman "who would not disturb her husband's sleep even to save her child from the fire". (Deshpande 207). Saru believes that the story must have been written by a man who has been telling all the women for all the time: "Your duty to ME comes first. And women, poor fools, believed him". (Deshpande 207). With their full trust in the woman from the story, middle-class Indian women blindly believe that their duty to their husbands is of prime importance, and to serve and to please their husbands is the only purpose of their lives.

3.2.2 Strained Husband-Wife Relationship in 'Roots and Shadows'

Indu, the protagonist of the novel, *Roots and Shadows*, like Sarita, is rebellious by nature. She rebels against Akka, the head of the matriarchal family, and marries Jayant, a man of a different caste, but of her own choice, with the hope to get escape from her caged existence in her conventional and orthodox ancestral family with its rigid values and beliefs, customs and conventions. She sees marriage as an alternative to the restrictions imposed on her in the name of gender-distinction in her ancestral family. In marrying Jayant, she enters into an independent and free world of her dreams. She feels: "I had thought I had found my alter ego in Jayant. I had felt that in marrying him, I had become complete. I had felt incomplete, not as a woman, but as a person. And in Jayant, I had thought I had found the other part of my whole self, not only that, but total understanding, perfect communication. And then, I had realized this was an illusion. I had felt cheated". (Deshpande 114-15). But she feels deceived by the very institution of marriage itself. It is the irony of her life that she, in her attempt to set herself free from Akka's domination, gets trapped in another cage in the form of marriage. But very soon, in the absence of perfect understanding between them, she begins to taste the bitter fruits of her decision of getting married to Jayant.

She is physically and emotionally dissatisfied with her husband who has only a practical approach to life. Her feminine dreams are suppressed as her husband takes her for granted and expects her to submit in one way or the other. Her marriage with Jayant fails to give her true freedom and complete happiness. The chains of her marriage are really heavy, and she is expected to adjust and modify herself to the situation from which it is difficult for her to escape. She wants to be loved, and happy, but her wish remains unfulfilled. She is not satisfied because she gets neither love nor support. Her answer to Atya's question, 'Are you happy with him, Indu?' is: "Happy? Who can say that? But I know I can't be without him". (Deshpande 67). She herself does not know whether she is happy or not. Atya is reminded of Akka's words: "Such marriages never work. Different castes, different languages . . . it's all right for a while. Then they realize . . .". (Deshpande 68). Akka, who wanted everyone in the family to be happy, did not have a good opinion about inter-caste marriages.

Indu seeks fulfillment in education and career, works as a journalist for a woman's magazine, but soon gets disgusted with her work as a journalist, gets tired of women with their issues and problems, and begins to work for other magazines. Her husband is a barrier in the way of her feminine urge of self-expression through her writing. According to him, one person like Indu can do nothing against the whole system by using her pen. Being practical, Jayant says: "That's life! What can one person do against the whole system? No point making a spectacle of yourself with futile gestures. We need the money, don't we? Don't forget, we have a long way to go". (Deshpande 17). He wants his wife to continue with her work as a journalist, and not to spend her time in creative writing. He thus suppresses her desire to be a creative writer. She loses her temper when her husband wants her to make compromises and not to leave her job.

Indu, now a meek and yielding creature, goes back silently to her work, hating it and hating herself, feeling trapped, seeing herself endlessly chained to the long dusty road that lay ahead of her. She realizes: "I no longer have any desire to mould people, to change them, to reform society. There is only one thing I know I can do . . . I can write . . . Whether any publisher will accept it, whether it will win acclaim, appreciation, accolades . . . I school myself not to dream of such things . . . But can I withstand other pressures? The desire to be known, to succeed for Jayant's sake . . . will they not impel me to compromise, to write the kind of things that are acceptable, popular and easily sold?" (Deshpande 15). Though, she cannot enjoy liberty as a writer, she continues to write because her husband wants her to write only to earn money. It is painful for her to hear Naren who, on her writings, says: "Tell me what the hell you've been doing?. . . The kind of writing you've been doing. I've had my eye on you, young woman. I've read most of the things you've written. And now . . . interviewing society dames and showering them with adjectives. What do you do that for?" (Deshpande 24). Though, Indu does not want to respond to him, her spontaneous response, "Money, what else? It's my job" (Deshpande 24), pinpoints the real purpose of her writing.

Though, she is not happy with Jayant, she always tries to please her husband. She considers herself incomplete without her husband. Away from her husband at her ancestral home, she thinks: "This is my real sorrow that I can never be complete in myself. Until I had met Jayant I had not known it . . . that there was, somewhere outside me, a part of me without which I remained incomplete. Then I met Jayant, and lost the ability to be alone". (Deshpande 31). In her attempt to please her husband, she loses her identity. She totally surrenders herself to her husband in each and every respect. Before her marriage, she was trained to be obedient, unquestioning, meek and submissive only because she was a girl. After her marriage, her husband, Jayant, too, expects her to submit and surrender. She remembers: "Then I had met Jayant. And I had found out that he too expected me to submit. No, not expected. He took it for granted that I would. And I did it, because, I told myself, I loved him. As if that justified everything . . . And remembering how I had surrendered to him, step by step, I realize now, that it was not for love, as I had been telling myself, but because I did not want conflict . . . that I had clung tenaciously to Jayant, to my marriage, not for love alone, but because I was afraid of failure . . . And so I went on lying, even to myself, compromising, shedding bits of myself along the way, which meant that I, who had despised Devdas for being a coward, was the same thing myself. I had killed myself as surely as he had done". (Deshpande 158-59). She compares herself with Devdas, and in despising Devdas, she despises herself.

Indu and her life moves only around her husband. She has killed her feelings, emotions, dreams and aspirations. She changes, shapes and moulds herself as per her husband's desires and needs. Jayant, a practical, authoritative, and dominating male not only suppresses Indu's voice, but makes her life dull and mechanical. The woman in Indu can neither express herself nor choose for herself on her own. She can neither love nor hate but pretend to be happy with the gift of silence. Her marriage has also strengthened her capacity for pretence and deceptions. She knows she can shatter her husband with withdrawal and rejection. But she hides her reactions and pretends to act out a pleasant willingness to respond. Though, she prefers involvement to detachment, she never gets what she wants. She has successfully put on the mask of a meek and submissive 'wife'. She knows: "But my marriage had taught me this too. I had found in myself an immense capacity for deception. I had learnt to reveal to Jayant nothing but what he wanted to see, to say to him nothing but what he wanted to hear. I hid my responses and emotions as if they were bits of garbage". (Deshpande 38). She understands that she is different from her husband and they are on different planes. Her husband chooses his level while she tries to choose the one he would like her to be on.

She is so frank and bold that she tells everything about her relationship with her husband to Naren. She says: "And so I pretend. I'm passive, and unresponsive. I'm still and dead . . . So that's all I am, Naren. Not a pure woman, not a faithful woman, but an anachronism, a woman who loves her husband too much, too passionately, and is ashamed of it". (Deshpande 83). She is shocked to find herself a woman with no choice, no wants, no dreams, no aspirations, no identity and no individuality. Always ready to please her husband, she submits to his wills and desires and does everything for him. She even forgets to dress herself the way she wants, the way she likes. She admits: "When I look in the mirror, I think of Jayant. When I dress, I think of Jayant. When I undress, I think of him, always what he wants, what he would like, what would please him. And I can't blame him. It's not he who has pressurized me into this. It's the way I want it to be. And the day I had thought . . . isn't there anything I want at all? Have I become fluid, with no shape, no form of my own? . . . Am I on my way to becoming an ideal woman, a woman who sheds her 'I', who loses her identity in her husband's?" (Deshpande 49). She becomes a typical Indian woman living her life as per the expectations of her husband.

She realizes that her love for her husband is quite disturbing and her complete surrender to him is painful and frightening. She feels disgusted and frustrated by her silence and passivity. She even thinks of leaving her husband hoping to be free and 'whole' self again, but she has no courage to do so. She feels guilty to have cheated Jayant by entering into a physical relationship with Naren twice. She questions herself: "What, then, had I achieved by giving him my body, apart from wronging Jayant? Wronging Jayant? . . . But had I not wronged Jayant even before this? By pretending, by giving him a spurious coin instead of the genuine kind? I had cheated him of my true self". (Deshpande 171). She decides to continue with her marital life even though she knows that her marriage is a failure. She surrenders to Jayant in order to prove her family that hers is a happy and successful marriage. She has dreamt of a happy marital life, but unfortunately her calculations go wrong after her marriage with Jayant.

Akka, a matriarchal head of the family, was one of the victims of a child marriage. She underwent an inhuman treatment and sexual harassment in her marital home. Though, marriage plays a very important role in the life of both, man and woman, it is something that suffocates the woman in the name of conventions and traditions, it is something that suppresses her dreams and aspirations, it is something that treats her as a prey and a plaything, it is something that deprives her of her liberty, it is something that hampers the growth of her individuality, and it is something that makes her forget her self and identity. For the woman, marriage is living with a man, totally depending on him for everything, tolerating his habits and his way of life, enduring his smell and touch, his likes and dislikes, his whims and absurdities, sleeping with him, bearing him children, looking after him, his children and home, and surprisingly everything. Indu defines 'marriage' in her own way. Indu says: "But Mini . . . marriage is . . . It means living with a man. You have to listen to him, endure his habits, his smell, his touch, his likes, his dislikes. You have to sleep with him, bear him children". (Deshpande 124).

3.2.3 Intricacies and Complexities in Man-Woman Relationship in 'That Long Silence'

That Long Silence gives a realistic projection of and a sympathetic treatment to the issues and problems, intricacies and complexities related to marital relationship, relationship between Mohan and Jaya. After their marriage, Jaya's husband, in order to prove his male authority and domination, changes her name. Jaya, now, becomes Suhasini, the name that Mohan gave her after their marriage. Jaya joins his family; she becomes his 'half'; she gives him her person, her virginity, almost everything. She gives him a home and children. She accepts Mohan as a sheltering tree. She becomes "Sita following her husband into exile, Savitri dogging Death to reclaim her husband, Draupadi stoically sharing her husband's travails . . .". (Deshpande 11). She follows her husband blindly and obediently. She strongly feels: "If Gandhari, who bandaged her eyes to become blind like her husband, could be called an ideal wife, I was an ideal wife too. I bandaged my eyes tightly. I didn't want to know anything". (Deshpande 61). She, on her own, shapes herself resolutely to his life, dreams, desires and aspirations. She lives for her husband and children, and not for herself.

She accepts her husband's authority willingly. She says: "No, I have to be honest with myself. It was not he who had relinquished his authority; it was I who no longer conceded any authority to him. But I have to be fair to myself as well. That was no sudden, cruel volte—face on my part; no, it was part of the same subtle resistance I had offered, the guerrilla warfare I had waged for so many years. We all do it; it is part of family life". (Deshpande 9). However, she seems to have a sense of pride in her husband, who, according to her, does not believe in battles within families. He is concerned about his family, his wife and children. Jaya believes: "Mohan has always had very clear ideas about himself. He was a dutiful son; he is a dutiful father, husband, brother. It had never mattered much to me until he said: "It was for you and the children that I did this. I wanted you to have a good life. I wanted the children to have all those things I never had". (Deshpande 9).

Their marital relationship gets affected and disturbed due to the probability of Mohan's joblessness, the prosecution and disgrace brought to him by the charge of corruption and the scandal he is involved in. There is a sudden change in his behaviour, in his attitude to others, especially, to his wife. He begins to experience an inner conflict. He tries to console himself and his wife. He pretends that he is not afraid of any disaster. He says: "No, nothing will happen; nothing can happen. So many men are in this situation. Can anyone live on just a salary? I've panicked for no reason. I'm sure it has blown over". (Deshpande 30). In a confused state of mind, he seeks his wife's support. Suhasini wants to ask him to confess his sins, to kneel down, to kiss the earth and ask for forgiveness, but, she doesn't. She says nothing. She just thinks to herself: "But . . . he might well retort then—Kneel down youself. Have you forgotten it is for you I did this? For you and the children . . . The children can plead ignorance and get off, but I will have to take on the burden of being a partner in the crime, an ally, an accessory before the fact". (Deshpande 31). Mohan and Suhasini are on the verge of losing the props of their lives. After having lost his job, Mohan seems to be no one at all; certainly not that man, Jaya's husband, around whose needs and desires her own life revolves. She cries in despair: "There was nothing he needed, so there was nothing for me to do, nothing I had to do. My own career as a wife was in jeopardy. The woman who had shopped and cooked, cleaned, organized and cared for her home and her family with such passion . . . where had she gone?" (Deshpande 24-25).

She experiences a conflict between her two selves, individual self and creative self. She faces a crucial need of giving justice to both. In her attempt to relate her individual self with her creative one, she is compelled into 'self-exploration' which makes her aware of her contribution to and responsibility in her husband's crime of corruption and of her own betrayal of Mohan. She strives to maintain a balance between Mohan's making marriage a trap for her and her own willingness to fit in the archetypal role model of a happy wife and a successful mother. Veena Sheshadri judges the character of Jaya as a betrayer of Mohan. She comments: "One ends up by wondering whether Jaya has imposed that long silence on herself . . . in order to camouflage the streaks of ugliness in her". (Sheshadri 95). She is right in saying so as Jaya deliberately keeps her husband in the dark about her writing and her relationship with Kamat.

Jaya is compelled to reject her creative self because of its incompatibility with her role of a wife. She prefers the role of a wife and a mother to that of a writer. She feels convinced that Mohan is hurt by her prize-winning story. Mohan thinks that the story is about their personal and private life. She remembers what he said: "Jaya, how could you, how could you have done it? They will all know, all those people who read this and know us, they will know that these two persons are us, they will think I am this kind of a man, they will think I am this man . . . how could you write such ugly things? How will you face people after this? How can you reveal us? How can you reveal our lives to the world in this way?" (Deshpande 143-44). Jaya fails to convince him that the story has nothing to do with their life; it is not a self-revelation, and that it is a story about a couple, a man who could reach out to his wife only through her body. She thinks that she has done wrong to her husband and she decides to stop writing. However, she continues to write stories which have been rejected and hidden in her house. She carries a sense of failure as a writer owing to her inability and incapability to coordinate between her role as a creative writer and that of Mohan's wife with two children, Rahul and Rati.

She herself accepts the duty of looking after her home, husband, and children. She believes: Stay at home, look after your babies, keep out of the rest of the world, and you are safe. She forgets her own identity as an individual. She says: "Even a worm has a hole it can crawl into. I had mine—as Mohan's wife, as Rahul's and Riti's mother . . . And so I had crawled back into my hole. I had felt safe there, comfortable, unassailable. And so I had stopped writing". (Deshpande 148). She follows her husband and goes along with him, who, she thinks, has a clear idea of each and everything, of what he wants, of the kind of life he wants to live and of the kind of home he wants to live in. She, therefore, goes with him to the Dadar flat away from their carefully furnished home at Churchgate, where, as members of a happy family, they all smiled and laughed, where Jaya, the mother, served her husband and children with love and care, where Mohan, the head of the family, smiled indulgently, and where the children were happy and exited, lively and playful. Jaya, like any other middle-class Indian woman, has an illusion of a comfortable, smiling, happy and complete family. She truly loves a happy home and a family in the fairy tales in which people always live happily, far away from the thorns of life. Her marital life with her husband on the top position, with two children, one boy and the other girl, appears to be happy. But appearances are always deceptive, as, in reality, she silently pines for happiness in her marital life.

Her marital life, to a large extent, has been moulded by Vanitamami's advice. She always remembers her words: "Remember, Jaya, a husband is like a sheltering tree . . . Without the tree, you're dangerously unprotected and vulnerable . . . This followed logically. And so you have to keep the tree alive and flourishing, even if you have to water it with deceit and lies". (Deshpande 32). This advice given to a future wife becomes a foundation of Jaya's marital life rooted in long and unbearable silence. She struggles to nurture and to keep that tree ever-green and alive. She slowly gives up her sense of being an individual with personal dreams and aspirations; and moulds herself to the needs and requirements, beliefs and principles of her husband. By doing so, she deceives, not only others, but herself as well.

Jaya wonders how can the relation of a man to a woman, the relation of a husband to his wife be natural if they hurt each other, if they deceive each other, and if they do wrong to each other. How can be a man naturally related to a woman if their relationship is rooted in deceptions, lies and evasions. Jaya cleverly and cunningly keeps Mohan in the dark about her relationship with Kamat. As human memory is selective, she remembers her great act of treachery against Mohan, the treachery of aborting the child without his knowledge. She uses 'treachery' as a tool to keep her marital relationship intact. She keeps her husband in the dark as she believes in Ramukaka and Vanitamami, according to whom, happiness of her husband and family depends on her. She accepts silence, endurance, tolerance and patience as her destiny. She has been a silent and patient sufferer right from her infancy. She feels that women are born only to wait and to suffer in silence, and that the waiting game in the life of a woman continues throughout her life. She never gets tired of that game. She feels: "But for women the waiting game starts early in childhood. Wait until you get married. Wait until your husband comes. Wait until you go to your in-law's home. Wait until you have kids. Yes, ever since I got married, I had done nothing but wait, waiting for Mohan to come home, waiting for the children to be born, for them to start school, and waiting for them to come home . . .". (Deshpande 30).

During the early years of their marital life, though they were strangers to each other, though, they were ignorant of intimacy through physical link, through sex, they enjoyed sex. She gradually understands the truth about love and romance which are inseparable from sex, a physical need of a man and a woman. She begins to believe that it is the sex that binds the man and the woman together. The act of sex, Jaya feels, affirms and confirms our loneliness. When Mohan turns away from Jaya, or rather, when Mohan turns on her, Jaya thinks: "Each relationship evolves its own vocabulary. Ours had been that of the workaday world. The vocabulary of love, which I had thought would come to us naturally and inevitably, had passed us by; so too had the vocabulary of anger. No, it was I who had left that alone after the day when my first disastrous foray into verbalizing emotions had almost ripped our marriage apart. Since then, we'd never gone beyond those first basic 'mudras'. Now suddenly, unfairly, he'd overtaken me. His fingers flickered, creating images, not of beauty, but of darkness and deceit". (Deshpande 116).

However, in the course of time, she admits that her family life has been unendurable. She is disillusioned with her marital life. She is frustrated by the boredom of unchanging pattern, the unending monotony of her life. Mohan's constant presence has become a burden to her. Mohan's actions before, after and during sex, the same positions, the same movements, the same time, have been so typical and predictable that Jaya can predict them each and every time and that she can almost stand back and watch the whole thing from a distance. She remembers the night on which she was very eager for sex, the night on which she responded passionately to her husband, she recollects: ". . . and then it was over. He had turned away from me—it had been as usual, there had been nothing unusual about any of his actions, or mine either, nothing that marked that night out from the rest of our times together . . . The contact, the coming together, had been not only momentary, but wholly illusionary as well. We had never come together, only our bodies had done that". (Deshpande 98). She is terrified to realize the strength of her bitter feelings for her husband. She begins to feel that her emotions and feelings for her husband are a kind of disease or a disability. She feels: "We're all frightened of the dark, frightened of being alone. And so we cling to one another, saying . . . I love you, I want you, I need you. Often I had told myself: love is a myth, without which sex with the same person for a lifetime would be unendurable". (Deshpande 97). She now begins to consider her marital life a kind of a catastrophe, a disaster.

3.2.4 Marital Relationship Rooted in Oppressive Silence in 'A Matter of Time'

Human relationship gets affected by the conventions and traditions, norms and beliefs, values and ideologies prevalent in a society. It is shaped by the age human beings live in. It is moulded by everything that exists around them and by circumstances. *A Matter of Time* is an exploration of the strained marital relationship between Shripati and Kalyani deeply rooted in a strangely oppressive silence and the failed mysterious marital relationship between Gopal and Sumi as well. In addition to these marital relationships, it projects a few more marital relationships, those between Vithalrao and Manorama, Anil and Premi, Satyanarayan and Goda, Vasudev Murthy and Devaki, Ramesh and Chitra, and between P. K. and Sudha. All these relationships, in one way or the other, get affected by Indian patriarchal set-up.

The novel opens with a description of the ancestral house, which is called The Big House or *Vishwas* to which Sumi is brought with her three daughters after her husband's deserting his family for the reasons nobody knows. Gopal stays a few miles away from his wife and daughters in the house of Shankar, one of his old students. He, too, does not know the exact reason of his abandoning his wife and children. However, he is preparing himself for the answer to the question, 'Why did you do such a thing? He thinks to himself: "I had prepared myself for this question, I had rehearsed my answers before I spoke to Sumi, I had been ready to counter her arguments . . . What do I say? What were the lines I had prepared? . . . I heard a voice . . . No, I can't say that . . . It's a kind of illness, a virus, perhaps, which makes me incapable of functioning as a full human being, as a husband and father . . . Sumi is one person who may understand this, she will know what I mean. But this is not enough; I have to be more honest to her, more explicit . . . What then? What do I say? . . . I stopped believing in life I was leading, suddenly it seemed unreal to me and I knew I could not go on . . . is this the truth? Is this why I left my home, my wife and children? Could I have said this to Sumi? . . . I have not been fair to Sumi . . . I should have spoken to her earlier, given her some hint of what was happening to me". (Deshpande 40-41). He seems to be totally confused. If his probable counter arguments fail to please him, how can they please others? To state the truth, he is running away from his duties and responsibilities towards his wife and daughters.

Sumi's coming back to The Big House, as a deserted wife, is a great shock to her mother, Kalyani, who cries out in agony: "No, my god, not again". (Deshpande 12). She, who is much worried about Sumi, goes to see Gopal and bursts out: "What have you done to my daughter, Gopala, don't do this, don't let it happen to my daughter, what happened to me? . . . When Sumi married you, she was too young; but I was not anxious for her, you were older, you were sensible and you cared for her . . . how can you change so much, Gopala?" (Deshpande 46). Gopal is amazed to see her speaking not with anger and hostility, but with affection and tenderness. She earnestly requests him not to punish her. Out of her concern for her daughter, she goes on saying: "I know she didn't bother too much about her home. But Gopala . . . how could she have known what being a good wife means when she never saw her mother being one? I taught her nothing, it's all, my fault, Gopala, forgive me and don't punish her for it . . . Is it money, Gopala? If it is, you know that Sumi and you will have everything of mine. Premi is comfortable; I am not worried about her. Even my jewellery—most of it is for Sumi . . . What about your daughters? Have you thought of them?" (Deshpande 47-48). Gopal tries to tell her that he has nothing against Sumi, she has done nothing wrong. He tries to convince her that he never expected her to create for him the world he wanted, that he did not make her responsible for giving him all that he wanted in life. She is, however, not convinced and she leaves him with a sense of regret and failure. Like Kalyani, Aru, too, tries to know the reason of her father's desertion, and when she fails, she, with a sense of bitterness, calls her father a callous husband, an unloving father and an unfeeling man, Premi and other family members also attempt to find out the reason behind Gopal's strange and mysterious decision but in vain.

During the early years of his marital life, Gopal was very happy with his wife. He was filled with emotions and excitement. Almost in the heaven, he thought to himself: "So I married Sumi. And I knew I was right, it was my body that told me the truth. I never had any doubts about my feelings for her . . . I knew I needed her, her warmth, her humanness, her womanness . . . It was my body that told me the truth once again, my body that could lie beside Sumi night after night, quiescent, feeling nothing. After the earlier humiliation of my inability to sustain my excitement, of being unable to go on, this was peaceful. But I could not avoid the truth; I knew it was over . . . But how could I have said this to Aru: Marriage is not for everyone. The demand it makes—a lifetime of commitment—is not possible for all of us". (Deshpande 68-69). He feels humiliated by his inability to sustain his excitement laying beside his wife night after night, his inability to go on with his physical relationship with his wife. He begins to believe that the life of the body has to end. The demand of lifetime commitment that marriage makes, he feels, is not possible. This, perhaps, may be the reason of his walking away from his wife and daughters.

Sumi sees Gopal for the first time, since the day he left the home, since the night he told her about his desire to go away. There is an unbearable burden of unsaid things between them. They need to talk to each other as silence between them is more dangerous, more treacherous. To begin with, they speak of Shankar and his family, of the children playing outside, of Gopal's work in the press. There is a tension between them, the tension of which they are aware. Sumi now realizes that they can never be together again, he has gone on living, his life has moved on, and that it will go on without her. She also knows that her life too goes on without him. She accepts: "Our lives have diverged; they now move separately, two different streams". (Deshpande 85). Both Gopal and Sumi fail to say what really they want to say. They, like strangers, just stare at each other in silence. It is the silence that constructs a wall between them. Like Saru in, *The Dark Holds No Terrors*, Sumi wants to be alone, to be by herself, to be free and to sleep alone. She wants to enjoy the pleasure and liberty of being alone, and not to be disturbed on her bed at night by her husband. She is tired of sharing her bed with her husband every night.

Since her return to her parental family, things have changed. It is Sumi and Gopal's marriage which is now at the centre of everybody's talk in the family. Listening to them, "Sumi sometimes has a picture of her marriage moving slowly through this dark tunnel of whispers to the yawning silent darkness into which Kalyani's own marriage has disappeared". (Deshpande 102). Devaki, who is hit by Sumi's failed marriage, arranges a family get-together to which both Sumi and Gopal are invited. It is Devaki's unsuccessful attempt at reconciliation between them. Gopal sees Sumi who is sitting erect in a tall chair, her profile delicate and sharp against the glitter and colour of a Tanjore painting on the wall behind her. He can see her who has made herself up, something she does only for the parties. He remembers the way she got ready for such occasions. He can see her now, "sitting before the mirror, looking earnestly at herself, drawing the lipstick carefully across her lips pursuing them together, a thoughtful look on her face as if she is tasting the lipstick. And then, standing up to wear the sari, her left hand deftly making the pleats, drawing her breath in so that she can tuck them in, patting them flat, and smoothing them down". (Deshpande 106). He can also see the same two bangles she has been wearing since the day of her marriage. He is fascinated by her looks even today. He sees her smiling at him without any embarrassment. He is amazed and awed by the way she talks to the strangers.

Sumi is clever enough to know what Devaki is hoping for. She asks: "Did you expect Gopal and me to fall into each other's arms in your living room? . . . You silly girl, why are you crying? . . . I've never been able to cry easily, you know that. And what do I say, Devi? That my husband has left me and I don't know why and maybe he doesn't really know, either? And that I'm angry and humiliated and confused". (Deshpande 107). Sumi knows that the tears in Devaki's eyes are for both Sumi and Gopal, and their failed marriage. She also knows: "To both Premi and Devaki, Gopal and she were 'the lovers', the touchstone for all lovers henceforth". (Deshpande 107). Now, these 'lovers' have become the two poles apart, the streams flowing in opposite directions.

Sumi wonders whether the love and the desire for possession are enough to keep the marriage intact. She remembers: "For a brief while, Gopal and I were part of this eternal story too. We fell in love. I fell in love with his physical being first. I have to admit that . . . but this passes. We don't need to be saints to turn away from physical pleasures. We don't have to go such a long way, either, as Yayati did, to realize that a time comes when the pleasures of the body pall. They taste flat, insipid, perhaps, even bitter. We want love to last, we think when we begin that it will, but it never does; it transforms itself into a desire for possession, a struggle for power. What lasts then? The loss of the familiar rustling by my side at night is what I mourn, not our lovemaking. I feel cold without the presence of Gopal in my life; sex has nothing to do with it, no, nothing at all". (Deshpande 168).

She regrets that love does not last long and it transforms into a mere desire for possession, which on its own fails to keep the marriage intact. Though, she feels cold in the absence of Gopal in her life after his desertion, she accepts the reality of her being an abandoned wife and tries to cope with it with grace and courage. She recollects Nagi's philosophy summed up in a sentence: "Some people are like that". (Deshpande 179). She realizes that it is universally accepted that everything is excused and everything is understood. She feels: "For Nagi, perhaps, with an irresponsible husband, one son dead, the other uncaring, and a dependent daughter, this *mantra* is the only thing that makes life possible. What other way of survival is there?" (Deshpande 180). She seems to have decided to follow Nagi's *mantra* in her life with a view to make her life possible.

It is difficult even for Gopal to forget his wife and her beauty. During his meeting with Surekha, for whom Sumi is beautiful, Gopal does not hesitate to praise Sumi and her beauty. He gets excited and says: "You should have seen her as a girl . . . I think she was at her best after Aru's birth. But there's more to Sumi than her looks. And she has no vanity at all about her appearance. She's proud of her quickness and her memory". (Deshpande 212). To Surekha's surprise, though, he speaks like a doting husband, he has left her. She is surprised to hear him say that our journeys are always separate and that his wife and daughters do not need him anymore. He says: "They don't need me anymore. There was a time when I used to wake up in a cold sweat thinking of dying, of leaving my children fatherless. I thought I had an obligation to stay alive because of them. But that's over". (Deshpande 215). He feels that his wife and daughters can live, can survive without him. This strange feeling of Gopal is, perhaps, responsible to make him walk out on them.

During her final visit to Gopal, Sumi is too intent on her own purpose to realize that they are conversing like a couple, a husband and a wife, talking about their daughter. They are talking to each other normally and comfortably as if nothing has happened between them. But for Gopal, the talk between them, at the moment, is different from the talk they used to have when they were together. He thinks: "This is not how it was when we were together; this is how it would have been after a few years. It's as if we've lost a whole section of our lives, we've jumped over time and reached a much later stage of our life together". (Deshpande 221). Sumi's concern and distress for Aru is only a part of what has brought her to her husband one year after his desertion. Her real intention is to remind him of what he said to her the night they decided to get married. She says: "You said that at any time if either of us wanted to be free, the other would let go. We are not going to be tied together . . . and I agreed . . . Then you began to move away from me . . . When you left, I knew I would not question you; I would just let you go. None of them, not even our daughters . . . could understand me . . . And I had to go back home with my daughters, I had to live with my parents. I had to see what had happened to my mother. I was frightened.

It seemed like something being repeated—my mother then, me now . . . But now I know my life is not like my mother's. Our life, yours and mine, was complete". (Deshpande 221-22). She thinks that her life is different from that of her mother, who has not spoken to her husband for more than thirty-five years, in the sense that she is free to talk to her husband at her will. She considers herself more fortunate than her mother who is compelled to live in oppressive silence.

Gopal can realize his dream of being totally free only because his wife sets him free of his duties and responsibilities towards his wife and daughters. All of a sudden, the girl he had married comes to his mind. He remembers Sumi, sleeping in the bus with her head on his shoulder, unaware of the crowd around them. He is in his thoughts of their travel together as husband and wife in the bus. He recollects every minute details of the time they spent together: "When we reached our destination, I woke you up and you got off obediently and staggered after me like a sleepy child. We got to the guest house where we were to spend our honeymoon . . . And there was no food for us . . . So we ate what we had with us and then I bathed but you went off to sleep almost immediately. It was a deep and easy sleep . . . When I woke up in the morning you were not in bed . . . I got out of the room, went down the steps and there was the river. You were in it as I had expected, floating, as if you were weightless . . . I joined you in the river. You were wearing your nightdress and it was clinging to you above your waist, but below, in the water, it billowed and ballooned about your body so that I could touch your bare flesh. I could feel it respond to my touch. I touched your face with my hands, with my lips and it was like touching a flower wet with dew . . . We came out of the water then, we went to our room and it was there, with the sound of the river in ours still that we came together for the first time. And I knew then that it was for this, this losing yourself in another human being, that men give up their dreams of freedom". (Deshpande 222-23). Gopal is excited at the thought of coming together to lose oneself completely in another human being, at the thought of their physically coming together. He comes out of his thoughts and realizes that his body, after almost a year, is awake with a desire to be physically united with Sumi. He is angry with himself and his thoughts. Sumi knows that she can do nothing for him. She gets up and is prepared to leave never to meet him again.

For Manorama, Kalyani's mother, who is denied a son, Kalyani becomes a visible symbol of their failure to have a son. When Manorama realizes that she can no more give birth to a child now, she fears that her husband, Vithalrao may adopt a son or marry again. She feels insecure at the thought of Kalyani's getting married and becoming a part of another family. Kalyani, though clever and aspiring to be an engineer, is not allowed to complete her education, and instead, is married off to her mother's brother, Shripati. After this marriage, Manorama feels secure now at the certainty that the family property will remain in the family. Since her marriage, 'The Big House' becomes a living presence for Kalyani. The accident that takes place in the form of her son, Madhav's loss, changes the very course of her marital life. While coming home to Bangalore for the holidays, she loses her four-year old mentally retarded child. Kalyani and her daughters are left on the platform surrounded by the curious strangers. Kalyani is brought back from Bombay by her father. They do not see Shripati nearly for two months. He goes about the city like a madman, searching the streets, railway platforms, beaches, even hospitals and mortuaries, but never finding his lost son, the only heir to his property. He has not spoken to his wife since the day it happened.

Aru and Charu undertake a futile exercise to know the reason for Kalyani's silence and her shouldering the burden of injustice done to her by her husband. They argue about the oppressive silence between their grand parents. They try to reach a conclusion without knowing the history of the relationship between them. They know nothing about the reason of their marriage, of Shripati's unwillingness to marry her, of Manorama's selfish appeal to Shripati's sense of gratitude, and of the cruelty that makes Kalyani accept a feared uncle as her husband. They have no idea of the hopelessness that lay within the relationship between Kalyani and Shripati. Aru is always confused and irritated to see her grandmother's mysterious silence. It is the silence that becomes her strength. She uses her 'silence' as a weapon, a mode of resistance that does not allow anyone to have a glimpse of her inner feelings.

Kalyani, Sumi's mother is a typical Indian woman who is a victim of mental violence and torture. Hers is a story of a strange oppressive silence imposed on her by her husband. Surprisingly, she has not spoken to her husband for more than thirty-five years. Shripati cannot tolerate even the shadow of his wife. His keeping himself away from her speaks a lot about a strained relationship between them. He has almost shut himself in the room upstairs. Kalyani is deliberately kept away from that room. She, too, is silent and frozen at the sight of her husband and is unable to shake off the paralysis of fear. Sumi remembers, once, after having seen her father in his room upstairs, she closes the door gently behind her. And as she stands there, thinking of her father, a strange thing happens. It is like a visitation, an apparition that she sees, developing before her like a sketch, and finally becoming a recognizable figure. To her surprise, the figure is no other than her mother herself. She sees her standing before the closed door, banging on it with her open palms, shrieking out something, slumping at last on the floor. She remembers everything, sees herself as a child standing there terrified, watching her mother lie in a huddle. After all these years, on her return to the Big House, She knows: "It did happen. I saw it, I saw my mother lying there". (Deshpande 74). The image of that blood-edged human shape is still with her. She remembers Kalyani banging wildly, vainly on the closed door of her husband's room.

The question is: why does Kalyani tolerate injustice and savagery? Is it because she is a wife and not a widow? Is it because she wants to enjoy the right to all the privileges of the wife of a living husband? Is it because she thinks herself to be fortunate to have a living husband, no matter he has not looked at her face for years, no matter he has not spoken to her for years? She must have been ready with answers to all these questions, but, being a typical Indian woman, she keeps her answers to herself. She lives happily because her *Kumkum* is intact, because she can move freely in the company of other women with the pride of a wife. Sumi wonders: "Is this what has helped Kalyani to endure everything, the fact that she is a wife and not a widow?" (Deshpande 167).

She is worried about her father who, she remembers, said to her: "Let your girls learn to stand on their feet. Don't worry too much about getting them married". (Deshpande 169). She fails to understand the reason of his turning to isolation, of keeping himself aloof from the rest of the family, including his daughters. She thinks to herself: "My father gave up everything and turned to solitude . . . he turned his back on his wife because he was frightened of himself of what he could do in his anger. I have sensed it in him, a kind of suppressed savagery. Or maybe that was only an excuse which helped him to get out of a marriage he had never wanted. Who knows the truth? I only know that, sometimes, he seems to me as much a victim as Kalyani . . . When Aru speaks of the 'sins of patriarchy', I am uneasy . . . For things are never so simple. We can never know all the incalculables hidden in the human heart. Why did my father come back? Was it his sense of responsibility towards his wife and daughters? To return to a wife he had spurned, to give up the ambitions and career which had become his whole life—no, that is something I can never understand". (Deshpande 168-69). She realizes her inability to understand what he has done to his wife, to his daughters, and also to himself. Though she tries, she fails to know the nature of the relationship between her parents.

Sumi and Shripati get killed in an accident. On receiving the news of their death, Kalyani, immediately turning to Goda, cries out in a terrible voice: "Look at me, Goda, look at me". (Deshpande 233), and falls down on the floor in a slow motion. Late at night, she is found sitting up and crying out the name by which she had called the man who was later to become her husband, crying at last for him. It is difficult for Aru to forget two pictures: "a woman, her two daughters by her side, frozen into an image of endurance and desperation, and a man, moving all over a city, tirelessly searching for his lost son". (Deshpande 244). After his accidental death, Shripati has left the house, not to Kalyani, his wife, but to Kalyani, the daughter of Vithalrao and Manorama. As the will is being read by Anil, Goda anxiously looks at Kalyani, but for Kalyani, "There was no sting in the words that took away her marital status. On the contrary, it is as if the words have given her something she had lost; they seem, in fact, to have strengthened her". (Deshpande 245). The words seem to have given her something more than the house; the words seem to have restored the strength of her mind.

Premi, Sumi's sister, a successful professional, a mother of Nikhil, a seven-year-old son, is a wife of a successful and prosperous lawyer, Anil. After their marriage, Anil does not believe his wife telling him that her father did not speak to her until she was ten. Premi, who comes from a family where its members do not talk to one another freely and comfortably, is surprised to find her marital family free and happy. Her marital family is just like a family in a movie. She feels: "At first it had been like watching a movie—it was pleasing, interesting, pretty, but it could not possibly be true. People did not really talk to each other so easily, they did not hug and touch and use words of endearment so casually. No, it was a false picture; the truth was a father who stayed in his room, who never came out, never spoke to you, and a mother who put her hand on your mouth so that you did not cry out . . .". (Deshpande 18). It is difficult for Premi to believe that such type of a family, a family like Anil's, exists. Compared to her mother and her sister, she is happy in her marital life.

She remembers: "He had scarcely looked at me before we got engaged; I was only the awkward girl, the daughter of a family friend who spent occasional weekends in their home. And then we got engaged and he played his role of fiancé to the hilt. But to me there was something false in the picture, there was some irritant in it that hurt me, like a piece of grit in the eye. He said the word 'love' often, as if it was a magic word that could convert all the things he did—the phone calls, the gifts, the going out together, the endearments—into something real . . . It was only then that Anil became real to me; he was the father of my child". (Deshpande 135). Premi believes that the woman needs a husband and her life is incomplete without him. Her spontaneous response to Aru, the response that Nikhil is the outcome of their marriage, highlights her happiness and excitement at the birth of Nikhil, a son. Hers, in a sense, is a happy family far away from cares and worries, issues and problems. However, the story narrated by Premi, the story of one of her patients, the pregnant wife of an AIDS patient, who, aware of his disease and critical condition, married the girl so that he would have someone to look after him, brings out new dimensions of betrayal and cruelty in the man-woman relationship.

Kalyani's mother, Manorama, a daughter of a poor man from a village, a wife of Vithalrao, has never been happy in her marital life, not on account of her husband, but on account of her unfulfilled desire to have a son. Kalyani praises the beauty of her mother. She proudly says: "You should have seen my mother's saris. She never wore anything but silks. Such silks! And her diamonds—you could see them flashing a long distance away. My father used to say you needn't need a lantern at night if she was with you". (Deshpande 117). Goda supports her when she says: "I've never seen anyone as beautiful as Mami. She was as fair as milk. And so tall—she was like a queen". (Deshpande 117). Aru expresses her disbelief both in Kalyani and Goda for whom Manorama is a beautiful woman. In the picture in the hall, she looks stern with a rounded face almost blank in its inscrutability. Aru thinks: "Perhaps, that was the way people presented themselves for a picture in those days, for Vithalrao in the companion picture is just as serious and grave as his wife . . . Manorama seems to be all of a piece: the pose is the woman". (Deshpande 117). She has always wanted a son but there is Kalyani, the root cause of her disappointment and displeasure. She is disappointed at Kalyani's coming back home as a deserted wife with her two daughters. Her cruel treatment given to her daughter, her anger towards her daughter leads to a breach between Vithalrao and Manorama, the first time since their marriage. The rift between them never gets healed. He is mentally disturbed; he has a stroke, and after a few days, he dies. Manorama holds Kalyani responsible for his death. Kalyani never forgets her words: "You are my enemy; you were born to make my life miserable". (Deshpande 153). She, too, dies soon after Shripati's coming home.

There has been a sister-like bond and attachment between Kalyani and Goda, a bond that stands even the stress of Kalyani's mother, Manorama. During Goda's weekly visits to the Big House, her marital life with Satyanarayan is at the centre of her conversation with Sumi. Though, her marital life is comfortable, she, a typical Indian woman, is always complaining about her husband. The conversation between Goda and Kalyani follows a regular pattern beginning with her complaints about her husband. Her luck seems to be in her favour in her childhood as well as in her marital life. Her husband is an easy-tempered man, a good provider and a loving and cheerful companion always ready to please his wife. He is devoted to his wife even after forty years of their marriage. However, Goda makes complaints against her husband, complaints about trivial things such as his deceiving her on his diet, about his insistence on their grandson, Hrishi's driving their old fiat and his extravagance in buying all the magazines in English and Kannada available on the stands. Compared to Kalyani and her marital life, her life is happy and comfortable. Though, Kalyani has been deserted by her husband, she never complains against him and accepts her lot silently and uncomplainingly.

Devaki, who was a skinny, awkward girl in glasses, wearing a short and straight dress, conscious of her unpleasing image, blossoms into a chic young woman after her marriage. Conscious of her limitations and shortcomings, she has deliberately shaped herself and successfully overcome the awkward corners of her self and personality. After her marriage with Vasudev Murthy, a successful architect from a renowned family, she develops confidence and successfully fits and adjusts herself to a kind of life her husband wants. It is with his help and support that she becomes an independent and successful woman entrepreneur. Like Devaki, Ramesh's wife, Chitra, too, proves herself a devoted wife and a loving mother of twins, Jai and Deep. Sumi, who has never been fair to Chitra, never done her justice, has thought her cold and indifferent to everyone but her own sons, caring for no one, not even Ramesh, changes her attitude to her when she finds her helpful and cooperative to her during Aru's hospitalization. She finds Ramesh and Chitra true companions. Overcome by remorse, she talks to Ramesh about Chitra, about her devotion to Jai and Deep, about how she has transformed herself from being an ambitious athlete to a devoted wife and mother, how wonderfully she is shaping the twins, doing so much for them, going jogging in the morning, tennis practice in the evening and many more such things for her children. Hers is truly a complete, happy and ideal family living with one another and living for one another. Devaki and Vasudev Murthy, Ramesh and Chitra prove that success of marital life depends on both, husband and wife living in co-ordination with each other, knowing each other and co-operating with each other. In this sense, Devaki and Vasudev Murthy, Chitra and Ramesh are successful husbands and wives. Gopal and Sumi, Shripati and Kalyani, on the other hand, are the pairs away from a happy and successful marital life.

3.3 Relationships within a Family

Deshpande mainly writes about Indian families in which we breathe, grow and live. She expresses her worry and concern about the spaces that Indian women inhibit and the silences that reside within them as the members of a family. Jasbir Jain writes: "Deshpande's novels show a concern with families and space. There are families, nuclear families with memories of living in joint family structures, families with arms extended in every direction, those who hold together and those who won't". (Jain 34). Familial relationships are at the centre of Deshpande's novels. She believes that it is necessary not only for women but also for men to live in co-ordination within relationships. Her novels, which are about families with their strengths and weaknesses, beliefs and superstitions, customs and conventions, bindings and confinements of relationships within them, highlight the nature of relationships within a family. They also deal with various issues and problems related to all these relationships. Members of a family with different interests and attitudes live together in co-ordination and co-operation with one another. Indu, in *Roots and Shadows*, says: "I had seen the concept of the family taking shape, living in front of eyes. It had struck me how suddenly, if only momentarily, we had become an entity, a family, united by a strong bond, a common loyalty. It was 'we' now, not 'they' or 'us'". (Deshpande 4).

3.3.1 Familial Relationships in 'The Dark Holds No Terrors'

The Dark Holds No Terrors is a realistic projection of two families, Saru's parental family and her marital family. It moves around Saru and her place in these two families where she is destined to suffer. Her parental family, including herself, consisted of four members, her parents, her mother, her younger brother, Dhruva. Hers was a typical traditional Indian family following rites and rituals, and celebrating religious ceremonies and festivals. It was a matriarchal family in the sense that her mother was a dominating figure in her family. Saru had a very bad childhood due to her mother who always tortured her in the name of gender-discrimination and who preferred her son to her daughter. Saru, in her very childhood, was made to realize that, being a girl, she was inferior to her younger brother in all respects. She was hurt by the distinction made by her mother. After his death, her mother almost cursed her and held her responsible for his death. She was aware of her mother's hatred towards her. Her relationship with her mother was in a crisis. Her father did nothing to mend their relationship. He, though the 'master of the house', had been inactive, not to be bothered by any of the trivialities of daily routine and by the strained relationship between them. He was just a mute observer. He did nothing to protect her from her mother's fury and hatred. He even did not sympathize with her. Saru felt: "He never took any interest in my school or college. He left it all to her. And she never really cared. Not after Dhruva's death. I didn't just exist for her; I died long before I left home". (Deshpande 37). However, she was fortunate enough to complete her medical education only because of the support she received from her father. Tired of suppressed atmosphere at home, she defied her parents and married Manu, a young man of her choice.

Her marriage to Manu was the first step leading her towards the fulfillment of her dream to be free from the insecure and suffocating atmosphere of her parental home. She found a good-looking poet, orator and a director of plays in her husband. She was almost in the heaven with her husband enjoying love and ecstasy. About her marital home she says: ". . . if there is a heaven on earth it is this . . . It was heaven, in spite of . . . women with inquisitive, unfriendly eyes, men with lascivious stares. And we were happy". (Deshpande 40). They were happy in their world in which people around them did not exist for them, and they, too, did not exist for them. But after a few days, she began to realize that their happiness is short-lived. They began to travel in opposite directions. Their love for each other began to disappear with her gaining recognition and respect as a lady doctor. Instead of sharing her status and prestige, he became a jealous and sexually aggressive husband with his pride and ego hurt. Saru remembered what he said: "I'm sick of this place. Let's get out of here soon". (Deshpande 42). In order to hide his inferiority complex and to prove his strength, he began to sexually attack his wife like a wild animal. Was it not Saru's tragedy that there was nobody to save her from her mother's hatred and curse at her parental home, and from her husband's sexual attacks at her marital home? Both her parental as well as her marital homes were traps for her, depriving her of freedom and happiness.

On hearing the news of her mother's death, she returns to her father after fifteen years with a hope to share her failure, her frustrations and disillusionments, her unbearable pain and agony with him. She tells him everything about her sadist husband, about his marital violence. She expects her father to help and support her. She wants him to say: "Don't worry, I'll look after you". (Deshpande 204). She is eager to hear these words from her father. But instead of saying so, he expresses his helplessness and says: "What can I do? . . . I helped you then because you had made up your mind. You knew what you wanted to do". (Deshpande 204-05). If a woman is determined, in spite of her plight and predicament, to go on living in a clear-sighted and genuine manner, with courage and confidence, she can help herself. He wants to suggest to her that if she makes up her mind, she can help herself, and that marital problems are to be solved only by husband and wife through interaction. He, therefore, again and again, asks her to talk to her husband and not to run away from him. He says: "You can't run away this way, Saru . . . Are you scared of him? . . . Give him a chance, Saru. Stay and meet him. Talk to him . . . Don't turn your back on things again . . . I'm asking you, pleading with you . . . But now I'm appealing to you. Don't go without meeting your husband. Talk to him. Tell him what's wrong . . . Are you not sufficient for yourself? It's your life, isn't it?" (Deshpande 216-17). Her father makes an appeal to her again and again not to avoid her husband, not to run away from him, but talk to him. He is worried about her, cares for her, and is concerned for her and her marital life. His words, 'it's your life, isn't it?' bring out a total change in her attitude towards her life and she decides to face Manu fearlessly and to lead her life with hope, courage and confidence. She is determined to prove that a woman with her inner strength and confidence, her positive attitude to everything including her problems can mend her relationship with others, especially with her husband.

Saru's marital family, too, is a typical middle-class family. It is also, like her parental family, a small family with four members—Saru, her husband, and two children, Abhi and Renu, one boy and the other girl. Outwardly, it is an ideal, complete and happy family, true to the slogan, 'we two, and ours two', with Abhi's pains and complaints, and with Renu's silences and withdrawals. Renu reminds Saru of her own mother, and her relationship with her mother. To her father, she remembers, she proudly said: "Renu . . . my daughter. She stares at me critically at times . . . She does not talk much. She reminds me of a room whose doors are closed. Nothing emerges, neither her joys nor her sorrows. And I sense a lack of feeling, of sensitivity in her. But when she sits down with a paper and a pencil, it is as if she suddenly becomes articulate". (Deshpande 33). Instead of drawing pictures of sunny gardens, colourful flowers, cheerful sunrises and playing children, she draws fearful pictures reflecting the dark, gloomy and frightening aspect of human life, as if, being a girl child, she is aware of the plight and predicament of an Indian female who has been a prey of Indian patriarchal society since time immemorial.

A Brahmin family, to which Madhav belongs, too, is a typical large family with its characteristic features. Madhav, the first year college student, staying with Saru's father, has three brothers and a sister. His family is a typical patriarchal family dominated by his father, who is a priest and a very learned but orthodox type of man, struggling to run his family with the help of his earnings. There is a strained relationship between Madhav and his father because he wants Madhav to follow his footsteps, but Madhav has his own plans and he is thinking of studying Accountancy as he likes figures and calculations. The aim of his life is clear to him. His brother, Satish, on the contrary, is crazy about films. He is interested in the world of fantasies. His father knows nothing about his craze for the filmy world, but his mother knows about it. He is deliberately kept in the dark about this because all the family members are afraid of him. There is a tense and suppressed atmosphere in his family. Madhav's mother, being a typical Indian woman, who faces her lot in an inevitable silence, is worried about Satish and others. His father wants Satish to learn Sanskrit and also to give up his schooling so that he may follow his footsteps in his life, but he does not like his father's idea. He, being a son, as a rule, fights his father to prove himself, and that, too, without directly talking to him. He threatens to run away to Bombay.

Madhav's father's expecting him to follow his footsteps, his expecting Satish to stop his schooling and to learn Sanskrit, his looking for a bridegroom for his daughter without consulting her, his giving little importance to his wife, his wife's silent suffering, her concern for her children and her helplessness, almost everything affects and reduces a personal space to be given to the family members to minimum, and imposes restrictions on individual dreams, aspirations and expectations. The growth of an individual becomes highly difficult in such type of a family in which personal and individual ideas and thoughts are suppressed. Madhav says: "He acts mild and obedient when father is around, but he's terribly wild really. And mother is scared he'll really run away . . . I'm wondering whether I should go home for a day or two . . . But what's the use? Father will scold me for wasting money on bus fare, Satish won't listen, and I can't talk to father, either. None of us can talk to him. There's Mrinal. She's between me and Satish. She's unhappy too . . . Father is looking for a bridegroom for her, but he'll never think of consulting her or asking her what she would like". (Deshpande 122). There is a strained relationship between father and sons as there is no communication as such between them. Sons almost hate their father. Madhav solemnly says: "I hate him. He sees only himself. Others don't exist in his world". (Deshpande 151).

This is a typical middle-class Indian family in which family members are living under one roof with their individual problems, with their own suppressed ideas and dreams, with its members not speaking freely with the head of the family, with sons and a daughter having a sense of remorse for their father, with their mother always silent and scared, with the members living together without understanding, co-operating and consulting one another. Every member of a family seeks to have his or her own mini world within one family. This is a conventional family with a tense, suppressed and strained atmosphere, a family with heavy pressures and tensions. This is a family in which the wife is required to live under the dominance and control of her husband. She also considers it her only responsibility to tolerate her husband's authority silently and ungrudgingly. Both Madhav's mother and Mohan's mother in, *That Long Silence*, did the same thing throughout their lives.

3.3.2 A Familial Discord in a Joint Family in 'Roots and Shadows'

Roots and Shadows is a projection of quarrels, debates, misunderstandings, conflicts, discords, issues and problems in a modern joint family in India. A familial discord is a by-product of an attempt to evolve a new type of a pattern of human relationships within a family on the part of its various members living together with no trust, no co-operation, and no co-ordination with one another. In the process of trying to evolve a pattern of new human relationships, many new problems related to intra-familial relationships have been created unknowingly, and these problems within a family are at the centre of the novel. Indu, the protagonist of the novel, lives in a joint family with her kakas, and atyas. This is the family to which she was brought as a fifteen days old motherless child. Akka, a dominant person in the family, has been ruling over the house since her coming to this house as a childless widow with her property and old uncle. This is the family that depends more and more on the domination of a matriarchal head of the family, Akka. The family, consisting of Indu's grandfather, his younger sister, Akka, and their cousin, Old Uncle and his daughter-in-law, Saroja who had a keen interest in music and her only fatherless son, Naren who, according to other family members, is good for nothing, is a typical Indian joint family with its merits and demerits.

Indu's grandfather has six children—Narmada, Anant, Govind, Madhav, Vinayak with his wife, Kamala and three daughters, and Sunanda Atya, a pure female creature, with her husband, Vasant and five children. Narmada Atya, the eldest in the family, had had a very hard, tragic and unfortunate life. She was a childless widow. She was ill-treated by her in-laws after her husband's death. She was brought to grandfather's home where she worked hard from morning to night. She expected nothing for her in her life. In spite of her household work, she always found time to give Indu and other babies their bath out of pure affection, to give a hungry child something to eat, soothe and comfort a crying child, or to relieve a tired, irritable young mother of her burden. She did all these things with a smiling face. She was ever ready to help all the members of the family. Sunanda-atya was yet another family member, who, like Anant-kaka, was against the break-up of the family, and who, as a girl, was slim, long-faced and long-eyed. She had a pallid and slightly concave face which seemed to have given her a fair complexion. She had a look of virginal innocence.

She got married at the young age of sixteen. She was called a lucky girl when she gave birth to her first baby boy. She made herself a complete and eternal female by adapting herself easily to her surroundings and circumstances. Though cunning, greedy, devious and unscrupulous, she, being the female, was neither assertive nor demanding.

Though from the same family, there was an eternal feud between Kaki and Sunanda-atya. The credit of keeping the battle within a family alive goes to them. Sunanda-atya, knowing that the home was her security and refuge against her miserable life with her jobless and irresponsible husband, had a genuine emotion for the house. As a child, Indu had witnessed minor skirmishes, guerilla warfare, pitched battles and a full scale war being fought on grandmother's silverware. Sunanda's grandmother was supposed to have promised her silverware on the birth of her first son, Krishna. But her grandmother had died before keeping her promise as Krishna was born after her death. Kaki did not hand the silverware to her on Krishna's birth. And since then, there was a war between Kaki's determination and Sunanda-atya's persistence. Her attitude to Kaki and her family was hostile. She was not happy with Mini's would-be husband. For her, it was not at all a suitable match. She, mockingly, said: "And now she thinks she's achieved something great by fixing up this match . . . It isn't at all a suitable match. Our grandfather and our father were not ordinary people. And all my brothers are so educated and well placed. None of those people ever went to school, and now they behave as if they're doing us a great favour by consenting to marry Mini . . . Mini is like my daughter and I'm speaking out of genuine affection for her . . . Instead of spending so much money on that marriage, wouldn't it be better to spend it on this house . . . our father's house? . . . And now they talk of pulling it down . . . I can't bear to think of it, Indu". (Deshpande 133-35).

Anant Kaka had four children: Hemant with his wife, Mangala and two children, Vishwas and Sanju, still a baby, Sumant, Padmini about to be married and excited by the idea and thought of marriage itself, a kind of achievement for her as well as her mother, and Sharad who wanted to be a doctor. Compared to Indu, Anant kaka's two elder sons, Sumant and Hemant were failures. Sumant was a graduate while Hemant was not. Akka wanted Hemant to take up a job and start earning, instead of running after a degree. He took up a job with which he was not happy. He did the job because, he thought, he had to look after his wife and two children. When Indu asked him to give up the job of a clerk if he hated it, he scornfully said: "And do what? . . . Don't forget I have a wife and two children. The way these women pestered me to get married then! It's a trap . . . that's what marriage is". (Deshpande 60). For Indu, the family with its members glaring hatred at one another was no more than a cage. There was a kind of unfriendly relationship between Indu and Sumant who was never easy and comfortable with Indu. She feels: "We had never been close, though there was scarcely a month between us. But there now was actual hostility, positive unfriendliness in his tone. It was not difficult to guess why. A failure? I hesitated to use the word; but yes, if success meant having a certain income, a certain way of life, both of Kaka's elder sons were failures. And I . . . by that standard I was a success". (Deshpande 37).

Anant Kaka was not at all pleased with his sons. His sons, too, were not in good terms with each other. They always complained against each other. Once, Anant-kaka burst out: "The hell with them! Complaining, complaining! One son of a bitch complaining about another. I'm sick of it". (Deshpande 53). Though, Hemant had a good job, though, he stayed with his parents, though, it was cheap and convenient for him to stay there, he was not happy, he always grumbled, and his wife, too, always nagged. In a response to Hemant who always said that he had to shoulder all the responsibilities in the family, Sumant, his brother said: "Hemant is lucky. No expenses, no problems". (Deshpande 53). Anant Kaka was tired of his sons' complaining and grumbling against each other, of the burden of duties and responsibilities, of family quarrels, debates, and problems. He received no support and co-operation from any member of the family including his sons to run the family.

Upset and dejected, he, too, complained: "Who didn't give Hemant a good education? Me. Who didn't help Sumant when he wanted some money after his marriage? Me. Who can't give Sharad money for entering a medical college? Me. I have a lot of money piled up, haven't I? . . . Look at this house . . . I can't even afford to pay the taxes on this now". (Deshpande 53-54). Though, it was very difficult for him to manage everything on his own, he never lost his courage. Being the eldest, he was shouldering the responsibility towards the family, he was struggling to keep the family with diverse pulls and conflicting feelings, interests and ideas united. He was struggling to keep the fabric of the family intact.

Old Uncle and Anant-kaka with Akka's cohesive force behind them had something in common. They did not have a sense of 'yours' and 'mine', but of 'ours'. This sense of 'ours' gave them strength to suppress their 'self'. They knew that if all members of the family asserted their selves, it would be difficult to keep the family together. Anant-kaka was not happy with a new generation represented by his sons and nephews. His sons were not interested in farming and agriculture, they all wanted cosy and comfortable office jobs. Indu had a sense of sympathy for Kaka who grumbled: "When father was alive, he just had to go there and the fellows would fall at his feet. Now, they've become too big. They know they have the upper hand. They're arrogant, disrespectful . . . Once this Padmini and Sharad are off my hands, I'm free. Your Kaki wants to go to Kashi and Badri and what not. Let her go and earn merit for both of us. I'll go and stay with my rich niece, a life of luxury and comfort". (Deshpande 54-55). He was hurt by the younger generation's indifferent attitude to the elders. He could not understand their changed way of life. It was difficult for him to adjust with a new generation represented by his sons. He was not happy with his wife, too, who always complained and grudged. He had a very bitter approach towards women in the family. Once, he said to Indu: "These women are so small-minded; they'll spoil the cooking to starve those they dislike. They don't care if they starve themselves in the bargain. She grudges the fact that the burden of the family falls on me.

She thinks it's because we live here. But tell me, Indu, can it ever be otherwise, wherever we live? I'm the eldest. I can't get away from that. And it isn't true that the others never help. Madhav helps whenever he can. And Vinayak? How can I expect anything from him? He isn't earning very much, and he has three daughters of his own. Your father has helped out once or twice. We brothers, we understand one another, but the women? God, how they dislike one another!" (Deshpande 136).

Kaki was worried about her daughter, Padmini's marriage. She preferred her daughter's happiness to the happiness of the entire family. She preferred the man chosen by Akka to Naren as a life partner for her daughter. She proudly said: "Look at that family, that house, it's even bigger than ours . . . My daughter will be mistress of all that. He's the only son, you know . . . It's my daughter I'm thinking about . . . if we let go this chance, we may never get one half as good again. And the house . . . It goes. You think I'll shed a tear? Since I came into this house, my lot has been work, work, and yet more work. As long as we live here, there'll always be parasites. People come and stay here as if they have a right over this house. As if they have some claim on us. Is it our duty to entertain these people and their families all the time? . . . The others get fat salaries and come and stay here like big lords. But when it comes to simple things like paying the taxes or the electricity bills . . . oh, let Anna pay. After all, he's the one staying in the house, isn't he? None of them even share the work. Am I everyone's servant? And, after slogging for all of them, what do I get? . . . Has anyone ever asked me what I want? That's why I'm telling you . . . ask Mini what she wants". (Deshpande 120-21). There was a kind of bitterness in her behaviour because of her son, Hemant, who had been filling up her mother with stories of how he would buy a new house as soon as they got their share of money from the sale of the house.

Sharad, Anant Kaka's youngest son, everyone's pet, did no work in the house. However, he got everything by flattering his mother and Akka. He was a different breed altogether. He took interest in arguing almost with everyone except Akka.

He was scared of Akka, and that, too, because he hoped to get money from her to pay the donation to enter a medical college. Anant Kaka was of the view that he was hopelessly spoilt by his mother. He was doubtful about his doing medicine. He said: "If you ask me, it's not so much the profession he's interested in; he imagines the 'Dr' before his name, himself driving a new car, and patients waiting in rows with their fists full of money. Pooh! The fellow won't even work to realize his dream. He got a third class last year". (Deshpande 46-47). His family was a burden for him.

Indu was a motherless child of Govind, who had parted leaving Indu, a fifteen-day-old baby with the family he hated and despised and who had not even come to see her until she was more than a year old, and that too, because she was a girl. He was totally indifferent to Indu. He had been a wanderer after his wife's death. He avoided his responsibilities towards his motherless daughter and his family. Even Indu's Kaki complained against him and his irresponsibility. Once she said to Indu: "I don't want to hurt your feelings, Indu; after all he is your father but—how often I had heard this sentence—I think it's too bad the way he avoids all responsibilities. Is this house only ours? Are these duties only ours? . . . There's Sumitra and Madhavrao. They never came even after they heard of Akka's death. They write they'll be coming for the thirteenth day. Yes, they'll come, after we've slogged like slaves getting ready for the ceremonies. Can't get leave, they say. That's a good excuse for him, but what about her? Is she working, too? And your father . . . he could easily have come if he had made up his mind. But he's never taken any interest in family matters. Is that fair?" (Deshpande 42). Kaki's attitude to Indu's father was so bitter and aggressive that even mild Narmada Atya could not defend him for his indifference and irresponsibility. Atya felt sorry for Indu. She said: "I always ask myself . . . why God couldn't have let your mother live! When he got married I was just like the rest. I didn't like the idea because she wasn't of our caste. What difference did it make? She could have made him happy. Look at him now! Ever since he lost her, he's been a wanderer. And with his brains, he could have gone far". (Deshpande 43). Indu tried to seek love and affection from the other members of her family, especially, from her kakas and atyas.

Akka was so dominating that nobody had the courage to rule out her words. She enforced very rigid rules and restrictions on all the members, on girls, in particular. She could not tolerate Indu standing alone with the boy in the library. Trying to be gay and whimsical, Indu said: "But Akka, that's the library . . . And we were just talking. Is that wrong? It's not as if we were holding hands, or touching and kissing . . . I haven't done anything wrong". (Deshpande 74). She was bold enough to face Akka and her conventional world. She was shocked to learn from Akka that her father was a quiet boy until her mother trapped him. She thought: "Ever since I had known it, there had been to me something sacred in the love between my father and mother, who had overcome the then almost insurmountable barriers of caste and lived a tragically short but intensely happy life together". (Deshpande 74-75). She decided to follow her father's footsteps. The same day she wrote to her father about her plans of leaving. She, unable to bear this suffocating atmosphere in the family, decided to leave her parental home out of her hatred for Akka. She, like Saru, in *The Dark Holds No Terrors*, who was full of hatred for her mother, hated Akka like anything, and married Jayant, a man of different caste and left her parental home. She was happy to see her Kaka and her happy and delighted father who defied Akka for the first time by attending her wedding. To attain freedom, she sought marriage as an alternative to the suppression of her dreams and desires at her parental home.

For Jayant, Indu's father was a wonderful person, and for Naren, a complete person. There was no piece missing in him, no piece in the wrong place. He was the "most wonderful thing to come out of the family . . . to be so detached and objective with your own daughter . . . it's a rare gift . . . Perhaps we should make it a rule that children should be brought up, not by their parents, but by strangers. Perhaps that's the only way of ensuring better relations between parents and their offsprings". (Deshpande 164). It was very strange that Govind and Jayant, father-in-law and son-in-law, two dissimilar men, appreciated each other. Govind was untidy, indifferent, careless, irresponsible and hopelessly confused about everything but his work, Jayant, on the other hand, was methodical, practical, elegant, and particular about doing things in the right way. Govind was wonderfully excited by the way Jayant did his work while Jayant showed a great enthusiasm in Govind's work. Indu knew nothing about her mother as she had lost her mother at her birth. No one in the family had ever spoken about her; no one even had mentioned her. Indu was totally ignorant, totally blank about her. It was from Old Uncle that she had heard of her mother for the first time at the age of six.

Madhav and Sumitra have three children: Sunil, Lata, and Geeta. Madhav was a top ranking civil servant. His wife was a daughter of a Civil Surgeon and Director of Medical services. Being educated in a convent, she, most of the time, spoke English. She considered herself superior to other members of the family. Her life was deeply rooted in pride, hypocrisy, affectation, empty platitudes, artificiality and superficiality. She lived her life with the assurance of being different and exclusive. Her children were trendy, mod and sophisticated. She couldn't bear her clothes getting mixed with those of others. She seldom used public toilets. She boastfully said: "I have no choice. I can't bear my clothes, getting mixed up with everyone else's . . . Oh, Indu, do you use these public toilets? Aren't you afraid of getting some infection? . . . I never use any public toilet. And if I'm forced to, I manage to avoid touching anything there . . . I've been spoilt from childhood, I suppose. My father, he never travelled except by First class and somehow I've got used to it . . . Tell me, Indu, how do you like this idea of Mini's marriage? . . . I think it's stupid . . . God, he looks like an idiot! No education, of course. And the whole of them . . . so terribly uncultured . . . And for that boy they're willing to pay ten thousand rupees as dowry . . . Plus all the wedding expenses. I thought Akka had taken leave of her senses. When I tried to say it to her, she said I was jealous. Me! Jealous of that! My girls can get better matches any day. Why, there was an offer for Lata a few months back, very well-to-do people with a prosperous family business. They were dead keen on Lata . . . But I . . . we refused. They may be rich, but they don't belong to our class. They didn't have any kind of culture". (Deshpande 63-64). She exposed herself, her vanity, bitterness, jealousy, nature, temperament through everything she said to Indu.

However, Kaki's version of the story brought out the truth that Lata's marriage was broken for dowry. They were the rich people who wanted twenty thousand rupees, the amount which Madhav and Sumitra could not manage. Instead of helping them with money, Akka was heard to have said: "What's wrong with you people? Your husband has been earning a good salary all along. Don't tell me you haven't saved up even for your daughters' marriages! Expenses! Don't talk to me of expenses! If you had spent less on saris and paints for your face and lips and nails . . . you wouldn't have had to ask others now". (Deshpande 65). Sumitra could not control her anger when she learnt that her family members thought that Lata's marriage broke off only because of dowry. She poured out her anger: "Dowry? What nonsense! . . . My God, the way these people spite us. It's unbearable . . . They can't bear the fact that we live comfortably, that our children are well educated . . . I tell you frankly, Indu, it's because of 'him' that I'm patient . . . And I shouldn't speak ill of the dead, but Akka's tongue was just poison". (Deshpande 65). Sumitra did not consider herself a member of that family. She had no attachment and affinity for the family. Actually, she did not seem to belong to that family. Her concept of a family moved only around her husband and children. She, with her very strange, self-oriented and egoistic views; her attitude to her large family with its members, her views on culture, marriage and on Mini's would-be husband, her hatred and jealousy for others, her superiority complex, her pride, hypocrisy, affectation and everything peculiar to her nature and temperament, was an obstacle in the way of strengthening relationships within a family. The family, therefore, ceased to be a single entity; a complete family, united by a strong bond, a common concern and loyalty.

Old Uncle, one of the two anchors of the family, the other one Anant Kaka, was only a poor teacher who had to retire on account of his bad health and come to live with the family as a poor dependent. Though dependent, he, being a man of experience, was one of the pillars of the family. He had been worried and concerned for his grandson, Naren. Naren's father was fond of music. His mother, Saroja, who came from a descent family, too, was wanted to learn music, but she could not because Akka was against her learning music. However, her husband wanted her to start learning music. Before they could realize their dream, after Naren's birth, unfortunately, both of them died. Old Uncle, since then, had been very soft with Naren. He very well knew that Naren was not accepted as a family member in that family, and nobody loved him. Nobody in the family except Indu had any concern for him. He was an unwelcome member of a family. He had chosen his own way of life. He was very happy in his own world, detached from others as if he preferred detachment to attachment. He did not ask for anything. He came to the family only to visit his grandfather; he stayed there for a day or two, if he was in a mood, and went away and stayed away from the family at a stretch. He did no harm to any member of the family. He was a kind of harmless and happy-go-lucky person, very happy with himself, with his music and his devotional songs. He was not a comfort even for Old Uncle, his grandfather. Once, to Indu, he said: "He's become old, and frail, and cantankerous. And I'm no comfort to him. A waster of a grandson...he's ashamed of me, No I'm wrong. It hurts him to see me like this. But this I can't change, can I Indu? A person has to go his own way". (Deshpande 27-28).

For Sumitra Kaki, a cultured peacemaker with pretence of soothing others, Naren was a difficult person. When he had a job, when he was earning, he was welcome. But when he gave up his job, he became a difficult person. Old Uncle, who was hurt by Sumitra-kaki's words, said: "Oh yes, when he had a good job, yes, then he was welcome . . . Why, he was even eligible even to become a son-in-law, wasn't he? But once he gave up his job and showed he wasn't interested in getting another like that . . . then, he became a difficult person!" (Deshpande 166). Sumitra-kaki, who had never done anything for anyone except her husband and children, realizing Old Uncle's angry mood, suddenly changed her attitude and said: "I'm sorry, Old Uncle, if I've hurt your feelings. But you know my nature, I'm frank. I can't pretend. And I must say Naren has one wonderful quality . . . he's never been a burden on anyone else". (Deshpande 166). Old Uncle held himself responsible for spoiling Naren and his life. He admitted: "And may be, it's my fault. I spoilt him, I know. Never forced him to do anything he didn't want to. Now, he is incapable of living by any rules. It's as if he has no ballast, gives up good jobs for no reason at all, wastes his time doing nothing.... We have very little to say to each other. I find him an enigma and he finds me a bore". (Deshpande 109). He cared for Naren and was worried about him.

On her return to her ancestral home ten years after her marriage, the home where all the family members have come to perform Akka's last rituals after her death, she is aware that her ancestral home is a place known for intrigues, groups within a family, schisms, jealousies, rivalries, barbed tongues and malicious words. All the family members, including Naren are jealous of Indu whom Akka leaves all her money and property after her death. Naren accusingly calls her an opportunistic and mercenary young woman. He says: "I'm accusing you. You leave home swearing eternal enmity against the old woman. And she hates you too. And then you come home after ten years and suddenly she dies, leaving you all her property". (Deshpande 85). Indu, for him, is a new guardian of the family after Akka's death, and she is to dominate the family as much as Akka did. She also feels that she is on the brink of adventure and she has got a chance to prove herself a true successor of Akka. She believes that Akka has made her her successor because she is strong enough to bear the burden of responsibility of the family. She accepts the challenge and decids to take up Akka's burden and to prove her strength by living up to Akka's expectations by fulfilling all the obligations she has towards herself and her family as well. She is determined not to turn her back on her ancestral family.

She changes her attitude to Akka who is not with her now. She feels she was not merely a dominating and interfering old woman, but something more than that. She admits that Akka was a sound and strong pillar of the house, and that she acted according to her beliefs. Indu realizes: "She was a prop, one of the strong pillars of a family. A family . . . it's like any other group. There are the strong and the weak. And the strong have to dominate the weak. It's inevitable. And Akka thought I was one of the strong ones. That's why she put the burden on me. And now, it is an obligation. I have to carry the burden . . . This is my family. These are my people. And yet . . . I hate them. I despise them. They're mean and petty, trivial and despicable". (Deshpande 159-60). Though, she decides to dominate discriminately and judiciously, not according to her likes and dislikes, but according to merits so that she can free herself of all doubts and pressures, she fails to do so because she is not as strong as Akka was.

However, Akka's decision to choose Indu as her successor and the guardian of her money and property is the beginning of a modern *Mahabharata* in her family. From the controversial discussion and debate in the family meeting, she learns that the wants and requirements of her family members are never-ending, their love is unreal and hypocritical, and their affection is rooted in pretence, hatred, envy and jealousy. The family members are eager to discuss and settle all the money and property matters in a family conclave, a typical conference filled with the atmosphere of secrecy and exclusion, the raised voices behind the doors and the whispered and subdued hissing of the female members of a family. They are blinded, possessed and haunted by the thought of money and property. For them, money is the only thing that matters in life. Familial relationship, unfortunately, fails to stand in front of money. Money becomes the root cause of misunderstanding, debates, quarrels and conflicts in the family. She is tired of her people, her own people quarreling, conflicting, debating and fighting among themselves. The home is made a battlefield by them.

She is frustrated by the battle going on regularly in her family. She remembers Arjuna's words addressed to Lord Krishna on the battlefield, *Swa-janam*, my people, our people, fighting among themselves.

Indu remembers her father, Govind, who has always been detached and objective not only to his motherless daughter, a rare gift, but to the entire family. He, though, one of the family members, to Akka's disgust and displeasure, always feels shy at such family meetings. To the surprise of the family, he, too, is present at the meeting. He is excited at his daughter's becoming a rich woman stepping into Akka's shoes, a new guardian of the family. He fails to hide his excitement and says: "Why, Indu, I never thought of that. It's all yours now, Akka's money and property. Why, you're a rich woman". (Deshpande 94). Indu's family fails to digest Akka's giving all her money, all her property to Indu, married to Jayant, who is even not treated as a part of the family. Akka is accused for this and that too after her death.

Vinayak-kaka, a father of three daughters, begins an argument by pouring out poison: "As a matter of fact, it's so unlike Akka, I'm wondering whether she was in her right mind. She had been sick for some time. Who knows how that affected her mental balance?" (Deshpande 83). For him, it is not fair to give everything to one person only, and that too, to the woman who has been married away. Anant-kaka's Hemant, too, calls Akka a partial, malicious, trouble-creating and trouble-loving old woman. Kaka does not like their accusing dead Akka like this. Madhav-kaka and Sumitra-kaki's son, Sunil, unable to control himself, suddenly bursts out: "I think it's a damned affair. Why should all of Akka's money go to Indu? We have as much right to a share as she has, if not more. She has no right at all, if you ask me. She isn't a part of the family now, is she?" (Deshpande 93). Sharad expresses his agreement by clapping his hands in his appreciation. For Madhav-kaka, too, Akka has been unfair to most family members, to Anna, to Anant-kaka, in particular. He says: "All this is a sheer waste of time. What's done is done. We don't discuss that any more . . . let's go on to the next thing . . . And before I do, let me make my own stand clear. I think Akka has been unfair, especially to Anna. He's the most affected . . . She had promised to finance Padmini's marriage . . . Now it all rests with Indu . . . marriage can take place if Indu keeps Akka's promise . . . Anna can't really afford to maintain this place. Akka was helping him. Now, who will? I can't. I have my own family to think of. I have two daughters to be married". (Deshpande 94-95).

It becomes a typical middle-class family where there is a conflict between old generation and young generation, where people don't understand one another, where people don't help and co-operate one another, where people hate and envy one another, where people are selfish and narrow-minded, where people distrust one another, where people are worried about their own selves, where people are in a hurry to have their own share of property, where people are not emotionally attached to one another, and where self-interest matters most. All the members of the family, except Anant-kaka and Sunana-atya, have no desire to save the ancestral house from the sale. Anant-kaka does not want to sell it to Shankarappa, who is now a respectable, rich businessman and who wants to demolish the house and build a hotel at the place. In anguish, he says: "Sell it to him. Let him demolish the house. What do we care as long as we get our share of the money? And what about us, old people? What are we supposed to do? Lie down by the roadside and die? Or will someone put us in the cattle pound? Or sell us to the butchers? Who cares? Yes, sell it, sell it". (Deshpande 95-96). It is unbearable for him even to imagine seeing the house demolished. He is frightened by the thought of the house that ceases to exist. Indu is terrified to know Kaka's bitter reaction to the idea of the sale of the house. Indu fearfully thinks: "The wall would crumble, the roof would crash down . . . But what of the feelings, the emotions, the passions the house had sheltered? Would they not linger here, where they had been born and nurtured? If not, where would they go? I had been a fifteen-days-old motherless infant when I had been brought into this house. I had lived eighteen years in it". (Deshpande 96).

Indu's family members fail to realize that homes are made by the people who live together in peace, happiness and harmony. For them, emotions, feelings, passions and relationships that develop in the house do not matter at all. It is unfortunate that long before the sale and demolition of the house, it ceases to be a home, a place of love and shelter. For Indu, the happy home implies: "The enchantment of waking up in the morning . . . birds chirping in the windows, a child crying . . . the tinkle of cups and saucers, Akka singing . . . women sitting at ease for the first time in the day, stretching out their aching legs in front of them . . . story-telling time . . . children lying with heads pillowed on warm laps, listening with a drowsy intentness . . . men returning home, shedding their slippers, washing their feet, and settling down with large contented sighs, the feeling of ease, contentment and indolence embracing the whole house . . . an aura of warmth that didn't have to be said in words, smiles, dinners and drinks. This was home, where one lived, not stayed". (Deshpande 96-97). This is Indu's dream home. Old Uncle gives Indu his idea of a family. He says: "Then, what's a family, Indu? A husband, wife and children? But what when the children grow up and go away, as they are bound to do? Is it only a husband and wife? But that too need not last forever? So, what's left? An individual? Is that what we should live for . . . one's own self? Isn't that the ultimate truth? That's what really matters . . . one's own self". (Deshpande 104-05). Old Uncle, a man of experience, tries to highlight the ultimate truth of life, the truth that every family member is an individual who always lives for his own self.

Indu is intelligent enough to know that she cannot please all her family members at a time. She also knows that her family, now, has become a large amorphous, heterogeneous group of people with conflicting interests. She fears that quarrels, conflicts in the family, and most importantly, self interest and self-centredness on the part of every member of the family, may kill the very spirit, peace, happiness and harmony of the family. It is very difficult for her to deal with all the conflicting individuals from her family. She envies Akka, the head of the family, who held the family together successfully. To Naren, she opens the door of her mind and says: "You know, Naren, I can almost understand Akka now. I mean, when they cringe and fawn and talk like they do, I feel I could rub their noses in the dust. And it's a wonderful feeling, holding all the answers in my hand . . . Ask Indu. Only Indu has the answers to all these questions". (Deshpande 86). She is haunted and possessed by never-ending questions, discussions, debates and conflicts.

She comes to the realization that the house is to be sold, Kaka's house, their house. She has a sense of sympathy for her Kaka. She understands: "Kaka has been finding it difficult maintaining the house. And the others refuse to help . . . And now Akka, who used to contribute, has gone. And there is a good offer for the house. Everyone is eager to sell and get his or her share or the pound of the flesh". (Deshpande 88). Anant-kaka is the only person who is breaking his heart over the house. He hopefully wants her to help him out. The family wants her to do something and to take the decision that pleases each and every member of her family. She becomes the most important person now. She looks at them all, Madhav-kaka in a mocking mood, Vinayak-kaka hostile, Anant-kaka appealing out of his eager eyes, and her father anxious and troubled. She feels restless and helpless. Though confused, she knows that the old house is a trap and it is better for her to come out of it as early as possible. She, therefore, decides to sell the house and to go back to her marital home, the home where she lived with Jayant, her own home. She says: "To think otherwise would be to take the coward's way again. I would put all this behind me and go back to Jayant". (Deshpande 186-87). She begins to believe that the home, the family has been a trap binding her to the past. She, therefore, decides to set herself free from the trap by selling the house and to go back to her husband to start her life afresh.

However, everything is over for Old Uncle and Anant-kaka. Anant-kaka tries to hide his helplessness, uneasiness and suppressed feelings when he says: "So, that's over . . . And now the vultures can come to pick at the flesh, vultures? No, they're not even that, just crows". (Deshpande 184). Indu, instead of responding to him, thinks to herself: "It was not my fight any more. I was out of it. Let them squabble over their shares, their dues. I owed them nothing. I had already decided what I was going to do with Akka's money". (Deshpande 184). With these thoughts and decisions, she frees herself from her responsibility in her ancestral family and decides to go back to Jayant. She comes out of the emotional struggle and decides to live a new and meaningful life with her husband. She comes to the realization that it is necessary both for the husband and wife to make adjustments and compromises in their marital life. She rightly chooses security through reconciliation with her husband. After rejecting the ancestral family, her own faceless people, she draws a magic circle around Jayant and herself.

The house is left to Shankarappa and his demolition squad. Indu does not stay to see the end of the house. Old Uncle is fortunate enough to die before the house comes down. Kaka and Kaki go to stay with Hemant in a small rented house. Indu feels that the family has every reason to hate her for her action of disposing off Akka's money, the action that arouses no rancor in any one, except Madhav-kaka's Sunil, who never speaks to her, and Sunanda-atya, who will never forgive her. Others are reconciled; they do not mind getting nothing so long as the others get nothing, too. Indu remembers Madhav-kaka's words: "I wish, Indu, you had kept the money exclusively for own people, if we don't help our own people, who will?" (Deshpande 11). She wants to respond with the questions: "Our own people? Who are they? Where do I draw the boundary?" (Deshpande 11). But, she does not because she knows that he has no answers with him.

She thinks over her decision and action: "When I had sworn that none of Akka's money would go to the family, when I had decided that I would give it to strangers instead. I had done so in a fit of pique, perhaps, of hatred against the family. But now I wonder whether what I did was perhaps for the best, even for the family. There's Sharad, Kaka's spoilt Sharad, who was all set for a career of parasitism, now thriving in his new job . . . Atya, however, is not pleased. She is shocked at the thought of her nephew, no, her father's grandson, rather, going into the hotel business . . . To her, there are still very few respectable careers . . . the law, teaching, working in a government office . . . medicine and engineering . . . I cannot convince her that Sharad would have suited none of these . . . But Atya cannot understand me. She lives in her own world and cannot grasp the rules of this strange one. She came to live with Jayant and me when the old house came down. It was not a choice made with determination. She had no other option. She had been listless, apathetic. A childless widow, knowing she had no claim on anyone. The house had been, perhaps, her own security . . . And at first, she was very unhappy in my house . . . She gets on well with Jayant. I had wondered how Jayant would accept her with her regulated widow's way of living . . . her rituals, her fasts and her self-deprivations . . . I think of my own childhood and of how I got affection from Kaka, understanding from Old Uncle and loving care from Atya; and I know why there is a faint tinge of pity in me for the small families of today". (Deshpande 12-13). She, however, fails to keep the joint family intact after Akka's death. She feels sorry for the death of her joint family.

3.3.3 Relationships within a Family in 'That Long Silence'

That Long Silence is a realistic projection of Mohan's parental family, the family in which Mohan's mother suffers a lot due to a deep patriarchal structure of a typical Indian family. Mohan's mother has been a silent sufferer throughout her marital life. Mohan, to Jaya's surprise, considers his mother's silence as her strength, and, therefore, he praises her as a tough and bold woman. Though an eye witness of her mother's mental torture and harassment by his father, instead of blaming and condemning his father, he admires his mother as a strong and virtuous woman. His relations with his parental family members, being projected in the novel, are normal and natural. The tie and bond between Mohan and his parents is sacrosanct. He has been dutiful and responsible member of his family. Jaya remembers: "Even in our worst days, he had dutifully sent his father some money in the first week of the month, whatever our problems may have been. But there was more than just duty in Mohan's theory. To Mohan, parents loved their children and children loved their parents because they were parents and children". (Deshpande 78). Though surprised, she appreciates her husband's fastidiousness and his passion for neatness and order. She remembers the home in Saptangiri, in which Mohan lived as a boy, the home which is known for chaos and disorder, the home in which all the family members except Mohan used to throw their clothes without folding them. Jaya is amazed to notice the only common thing between them as husband and wife, i.e. their love and passion for neatness and order.

Rahul, Mohan's only son, is never in good terms with his father. Though, Mohan never accepts it, Jaya feels that there is a kind of hostility between them. She says: "It seems to me that hostility towards our children is deeply ingrained in us, warring with the self-love that parades as parental affection . . . for each step the son takes into adulthood, into an active involvement with the world, pushes his father further back into obsolescence and decrepitude". (Deshpande 79). Mohan retorts Jaya when she, in order to soften Rahul's hostility for his father, says: "After all, every son must fight his father to prove himself, every daughter her mother". (Deshpande 9). Rahul is interested in nothing including his studies. He takes some interest in cricket for a while, then, his interest shifts to music and then to comics. For him, everything in the world is boring. He seldom opens his books. When his father is around, he opens his books and just stares at them blankly. After having seen his report card, Mohan loses his temper, and he makes a typical complaint of Indian parents: "I begged, I borrowed money for school and college, I studied whenever I could get a few minutes, wherever I could find a bit of space, and I never got anything less than a first class. And this boy! He has everything he wants, we deny him nothing, and look at his marks! I'm ashamed that my son should do so badly". (Deshpande 49). Mohan is truly worried and concerned not only about Rahul, his studies and his career, but also about his daughter, Rati, and his wife. Though, there is a strained relationship between them, Jaya unsuccessfully tries to keep their relationship normal and healthy.

Mohan is a typical Indian husband and a father in the best sense of the term. He is always ready to do anything for the happiness of his family. But he commits a mistake when he believes that happiness in life depends only upon money. His ambition to be a wealthy person opens the door of the trap of the scandal in which he is caught. He does not blame himself for the scandal. He says that he did it for his wife and children. He says: "It was for you and the children that I did this. I wanted you to have a good life, and I wanted the children to have all those things I never had". (Deshpande 9). In order to prove his innocence to his wife, he blames Agarwal for everything. He said: "I'm finished. Both Agarwal and I are finished. Agarwal deserves it, he's been doing these things ever since he became Secretary, he got into this, he got more out of it than I have done, he's responsible for the whole thing, not I". (Deshpande 9-10). A gap begins to develop between Mohan and his family members because of the absence of communication between them. Jaya is helpless in dealing with her husband involved in the scandal, her despairing son and a gloomy daughter. She is unable to cope with them, with her husband, in particular. She totally fails to know and understand not only her husband, but her children as well. She feels: "We had been like two clumsy amateurs, novices playing the roles of mother and child. And now, fifteen years later, we were back at the same point. And there was Rati, mocking at me, jeering at me from behind the cardboard cut-out figure of my daughter I had propped up—a girl, grave, serious, independent, understanding". (Deshpande 173). Though, she tries to maintain peace and harmony in her family, she fails to do so.

Jaya, being a typical middle-class woman, blindly follows the tradition of her mother-in-law and sister-in-law by silently performing the role of a loving and devoted wife, and a caring and dutiful mother. She gets absorbed into the tradition of her marital family in such a way that she becomes a stereotype of a woman who is silent, nervous, incompetent, tolerant and dependent. She always tries her level best to please her husband. She even sacrifices her dreams and aspirations, her 'self' and 'individuality', almost everything for her husband. But she is shocked when she realizes that her husband doesn't understand her, her emotions and feelings. She is totally upset when she comes to know that her husband is not emotionally attached to her, and they are just two persons, a man and a woman who are living together just to fulfil their physical needs. Hers is a small family with a man and a woman, married for seventeen years, a couple with two children, a couple going in different directions, strangers to each other. She finds her family life intolerable with boredom of the unchanging pattern and monotony. There is nobody who is safe, secure, assured and confident in her family. Jaya, too, deceives her husband by aborting her child without his knowledge, and by getting involved with Kamat. In spite of this, she remains true to her role of a dedicated and devoted wife. In the end, she realizes that she is required to assert her individuality, and she decides to do as she wants and desires.

Mother-daughter relationship, too, occupies a place of importance in the novel. There is a very curious relationship between Jaya and her mother, who has been enjoying domination in her brother's home for about twenty years. But her power and domination is now started to be questioned and challenged by aggressive Vanitamami. She is afraid of losing the battle. She is looking for a place she can retreat to. Both Dinkar and Ravi, her sons, are not ready to shoulder their duty and responsibility towards their family. They escape leaving the responsibility to Jaya. Jaya's mother becomes childishly possessive. Her world now moves around Jaya. Jaya wonders: "She, who had never seemed to bother very much about my activities, was now prying, curious and resentful, about any part of my life that took me away from her . . . When I had passionately wanted her love; she had ignored me and concentrated on her sons . . . When I got married, she had been unperturbed, there had been not even a pretence of tears when I had left home". (Deshpande 106). Now she wants Jaya to look after her, to give her emotional support, as her sons, Dinkar and Ravi are selfishly involved with their families, Dinkar with Geeta and

Ravi with Asha. Jaya is expected to look after two families, her parental family and her marital family.

Though, she is named 'Jaya', the name that stands for victory, she is shaped and moulded as a weak, passive, silent, and submissive creature in her parental family itself. She is taught that the feminine virtues in her will protect her in her life. She is always made aware that she is a girl. The process of silencing on her part begins in her childhood itself. She has been a silent sufferer right from her childhood. She is made to nurture a sense of shame as she fails to respond to and appreciate classical music. Her grandmother always scolds her for her inquisitive nature. Her Ajji teaches her two games, one the game of silence, and the other that of waiting patiently. She is also trained to believe that a husband is a sheltering tree for a woman, and that happiness and success of a woman depends only and only upon her male counterpart after her marriage. She is also trained to be neat and clean. She is reminded of her ancestral homes. She remembers: "In our home in Saptangiri objects had cheerfully strayed away from their places, if they ever had any, and nobody had minded: not Appa, so uncaring and unnoticing of trifling details, nor Ai, always indolent and slapdash. The other two homes I knew had been just as bad. The town house in Saptangiri, where Ajji lived with the Kakas, Appa's two brothers, and their families, was austere and bare, pared down, like Ajji's own life, to the essentials. And Ai's home in Ambegaon, where other Ajji, Chandumama and Vanitamami lived, was chaos with its rarely made beds and clothes piled on to the large clothes-horse until it threatened to collapse". (Deshpande 12). Jaya grows up among these things and people, and that, perhaps, makes neatness and order an inseparable part of her life.

It is impossible for Jaya to forget 'a family tree' prepared and sketched by Ramukaka, her paternal uncle. He said: "Look, Jaya, this is our branch. This is our grandfather—your great grand grandfather—and here's father, and then us—Laxman Vasu and me. And here are the boys—Shridhar, Jannu, Dinkar, Ravi . . .". (Deshpande 142). Jaya is surprised not to find herself in that family tree. It is from Ramukaka she comes to know that she does not belong to that family, but to Mohan's family. However, she gets no answer to the question, why Kakis and Ai have no place in that family tree. She is one of the three children of her parents, the other two being, Dinkar, her elder brother, and Ravi, her younger brother. To Jaya, Ravi is conspicuous even in a crowd, the best-looking of the three, with Appa's height and sharp features, and clear complexion, and an accomplished hand at deceit. His lies are calculated and premeditated. Jaya cannot prove herself to be Ravi's protective and loving elder sister. She can not have a link of shared childhood with him, the link that she can have with her Dada, Dinkar. She can remember his maddening tenacity as a child, the way he fought his own battles on his own without anger and hostility, not bothering about anything but acquiring what he wanted at any cost. And it is because of this, perhaps, he frequently quarrels with Asha, his wife. Nobody takes their quarrels seriously.

Both Dinkar and Ravi, instead of shouldering their responsibility of the family, cunningly escape after their marriage. Jaya wonders: "Ravi, of course, was fluid and irresponsible . . . But Dada? Yes, they had had hopes of him. I myself would never have been able to imagine that he would escape so wholly . . . Now it was clear that he would never return". (Deshpande 104-05). Both Dinkar and Ravi have changed completely. They are deliberately staying away from their parental family. Jaya remembers Vanitamami's complaint against him and his family: "Dinu has changed, hasn't he? And then, it's his wife, of course. She tries to keep him and the children away from us . . . As if we can't understand. And Dinu doesn't say a word to her. But the boy was always like that, he never quarreled with anyone, a simple boy". (Deshpande 105).

When the family needs support after Appa's death, Dinkar keeps his mother at a distance from him. He does not care for his mother, and also for his younger unmarried sister. He is not worried, not concerned about his mother and others. Jaya is angered by her brothers' leaving her behind with their mother. Jaya's mother wants, as if frightened, to be very close, to be attached to her daughter. Even after Jaya's marriage, she expects a lot from her. Jaya is caught between two families, her parental family and her marital family, as if she is a connecting link between these two families. She expresses her anger when she speaks to Ravi: "I suppose she'd like me to abandon my husband and children, or may be she'd like me to be abandoned by my husband like Kusum, so that I can go and stay with them for months". (Deshpande 103-04). She finds it difficult to look after both the families with undue wants, demands, requirements, and expectations, baseless doubts, and misunderstandings. She realizes that without Appa and Ajji the Saptagiri home has ceased to be the home, the place known for love, trust, understanding, safety, security, peace, harmony, happiness, assurance and confidence. She is not happy with the nature of relationship that exists in her parental as well as in her marital home. She, therefore, says in disgust: "It's only with the dead that we can have a perfect relationship. There are no knots, no awkward tangles here. We can mould the dead to our desires, to suit our purposes". (Deshpande 151).

3.3.4 Intricate Relationships within an Extended Family in 'A Matter of Time'

A Matter of Time explores the intricate relationships within an extended family, encompassing four generations of men and women who are the inhabitants of the Big House. Aru, who is struggling to understand her father, Gopal's desertion and her mother, Sumi's indifference, is at the heart of the novel. When Gopal walks out on his wife for reasons even he cannot articulate, Sumi, his wife, returns with her three daughters, Aru, Charu, and Seema, to the shelter of the Big House called *Vishwas*, where her parents, Kalyani and Shripati, live in a strangely oppressive silence. They, though living under one roof, have not spoken to each other for more than thirty-five years. As the mystery of this long, strange, unbearable, oppressive and unpredictable silence is unraveled, a horrifying and frightening story of loss and agony is laid bare, a story that seems to be repeating itself in Sumi's life. The canvas of conflict in human relationships is expanded in space and time through the history of family with four major women representing four generations in the focus; Manorama, her daughter Kalyani, Kalyani's daughter, Sumi, and Sumi's daughter, Aru.

The name of the house, a living presence in the novel, is not derived from the abstract quality of trust, but it is after an ancestor, Vishwasrao, the man with whom the family history begins for Kalyani, the man who came down South with Madhavrao Peshwa on one of his expeditions to the Karnataka, and the man who established his family there. The house, which is built just to endure, stands for the meaning of its name and its solidity. It is clear that it was built by a man not just for himself, but for his sons, grandsons and grand-grandsons. The house is unique, the only one of its kind in the neighbourhood, the thing of pride for its inhabitants. Kalyani, who is proud of the house, is never tired of saying in its praise: "People used to come just to look at it. There was no house like it in the city". (Deshpande 5). Vishvasrao, with whom the family history begins for Kalyani, found a stone idol of *Ganapati* while taking his bath in the river Kaveri. The significant event of finding the idol of *Ganapati*, the Peshwas's family deity, totally changed not only his life but the life of his family as well. He was asked to install that idol in a temporary shelter and to stay there as its guardian. In addition to this, he was granted all the lands surrounding that area as a reward and incentive. Since then he and his family have been staying on there and enjoying the power of landlords. He, undoubtedly, the hero of the family document, a clever and ambitious man, did not miss any opportunity to retain and spread his power in the area. Since it was the family document from India with its patriarchal set-up, women had no place in this family document. According to Gopal, this family document is not true as he has not been able to find Vishwasrao's name in any of the records of the expeditions.

Vishwasrao was gifted with adventure that made him give up his family lands and follow the Peshwa on his expeditions. As there was enough family spirit in him which allowed him to share his property and prosperity with two of his brothers who joined him later. Though he was not a soldier, to Gopal's surprise, the family record makes frequent mentions of his courage and bravery. Gopal doubts how a Brahmin family takes a pride in claiming heroic and martial qualities. Vishwasrao and his family did not remain loyal to the Peshwas after Madhavrao's death. In order to survive in the foreign land, they had to compromise with the local rulers and to be loyal to them. When the *Marathas,* Haider and his son, Tipu, the *Nizam*, the local Mysore *rajas* and the two foreign powers were fighting for control and power, the family remained loyal to their caste, status and their ideas of themselves. The generation after Vishwasrao's sons gave up the pretence of soldiering and settled down just as landlords. They were cunning enough to know that their being the guardians of the temple gave them all the privileges, a status and a position in the region. The family, thus, took its roots, settled and prospered in the village called Ganeshkhind.

When Gopal visited the family house, it was almost in ruins and no member of the family lived in the village. The family moved to Bangalore where Narayanrao built another family home and the temple as well. Kalyani and Goda, now, speak of the prosperity of the family with pride and nostalgia. Kalyani, in particular, is proud of the history and the prosperity of the family. She feels proud to be a part of the interesting story of her family. She tries to modify the history of her family out of carefully chosen material, deliberately leaving out everything that is dark and discomforting. Aru, for the first time, hears the story of her own past, the story of her own ancestral family, the story "of Madhavrao Peshwa and Vishwasrao, of the finding of the idol, the building of the temple and the family settling down around it". (Deshpande 114). Unaware of the fact that the story, in a way, is connected to her and that the people Kalyani is speaking about are a part of her life, Aru is startled and confused.

For Kalyani and Goda, Vithalrao and Manorama's marriage itself is a myth, a miracle; it's a story of love, the love of a man and a woman. Manorama is a daughter of a poor village Brahmin while Vithalrao is an educated and intelligent son of a well-to-do man from Bangalore. For Kalyani, all the characters including Vithalrao and Manorama, the hero and the heroine, in the drama of marriage are the unusual people. Vithalrao's father, a modern man, in its true sense, after having noticed the girl's confidence, self-assurance and intelligence, does not hesitate to do what can have damned him in the society he lives in by making an offer to the girl's father for his son. Manorama's parents, her mother, in particular, too, are modern in the sense that they take a bold decision of sending their daughter to Yamunabai's school at a time when education for a girl is treated as an obstacle in the way of her marriage prospects. It is Yamunabai who changes a poor girl with a running nose and a younger sibling constantly sliding down her skinny hips, a girl in a patched and shabby dress, a girl trapped in the drudgery of household work into a confident, self-assured and intelligent girl attracting the attention of the visitors from Bangalore. Manorama's mother is an honest woman who persuades her husband to write a letter to Vithalrao's father to let them know that Manorama has grown up. Manorama's father, a poor man even by the standards of time, has four daughters, of whom Manorama was the oldest. He writes a letter to the groom's father and immediately after Vithalrao and Manorama get married as has been planned. For Kalyani and Goda, the marriage is like the ending of a fairy tale. Charu mischievously says: "And they lived happily ever after". (Deshpande 119).

Manorama's natal family remains behind the curtain after her marriage. She does not continue with her relationship with her parental family. She takes a strange decision to deprive herself of love and emotional support the woman gets from her parental home even after her marriage. She rejects her family, her mother's home, a fountainhead of care, love, affection and emotional support. Her mother's death just a year after her marriage makes it possible for her to distance herself from the family. However, she does not break her ties with it completely. She gives every possible help to the family, especially during the crisis. She rarely goes to her parental home. Her brothers and sisters, with the only exception of her younger sister, are never invited to her marital home. She has a soft corner for a motherless boy, who lost his mother at the age of one.

He is the only one of her siblings to visit her marital home. Vithalrao, who sees ambition and intelligence in this silent and withdrawn motherless boy, decides to help him. He sends him to a good school, later to a good college, and after he completes his law, gets him a job in the office of his friend, a renowned lawyer in Mumbai. When he starts his career as a lawyer, Manorama does not have any uncomfortable feeling to selfishly and cunningly remind him of what he owes them, what he owes her, his elder sister. She persuades him to marry her daughter, Kalyani. Though, Vithalrao is not happy with what his wife does, knowing her determination, he cannot stop the marriage.

Kalyani's mind goes back to the earlier part of her life. She feels that there was no more to her life than her being a daughter. She does not have any happy memory of her life as a daughter. Her mother, who wanted to have a son, was not happy at the birth of a baby girl. There was a strained relationship between Kalyani and her mother. She received no love, no affection from her mother. Being a girl, she could enjoy no liberty. Though she was as clever as her father, she was not allowed to continue her education. She once said: "I was a clever girl. I was very good at Maths like my father. He wanted me to become an engineer". (Deshpande 128-29). But in spite of her interest in education, she was not allowed to complete her education. Her mother was the obstacle in the way of her education. She was taken out of school and cunningly married off by her mother to her own brother, Shripati. Her mother felt happy and secure as she succeeded in keeping the family property in her family itself by making Shripati marry Kalyani. Even after her marriage, Kalyani has a sense of regret for having no freedom to have education and for her lost education. To Goda, she once said: "I envy these girls, don't you, Goda? They are so free". (Deshpande 150). It is difficult for Kalyani to forget her mother's disappointment, anger and cruelty with her. She has to carry the heavy burden of this memory throughout her life. She becomes a visible symbol of her mother's failure to have a son.

Her mother did not like her coming back home as a rejected and deserted wife. She felt that it was a disgrace to her family. She was totally destroyed. She gave up everything and never participated in public activities since the day of her return. Vithalrao did not like the way his wife treated their daughter. He tried his level best to bring Kalyani and Shripati together. Unable to tolerate the strained relationship between Kalyani and Manorama, and between Kalyani and Shripati, he had a stroke for which Kalyani was held responsible by her mother. Kalyani, who was concerned about her father, looked after him as if he was a younger sibling, patted his hand and sat silently by his side until he recovered. He felt soothed and comfortable in her presence, and it was something that filled his wife with an angry grief. She could not tolerate this tender relationship between father and daughter. A few days before his death, he kept repeating some words nobody could understand. It was Kalyani who understood what he wanted to say. He wanted someone to put him down on the floor. When Manorama was away, Kalyani, unable to bear her father's agony, placed him on the floor. She could see a happy and peaceful look on his face. He died in a short while in peace. She was held responsible for his death. During Manorama's illness, too, it was Kalyani who looked after her. Kalyani was the only person who knew what she had to bear throughout her life. Manorama in the last days of her life was not only tyrannical but also doubtful and fearful. She even charged Kalyani with trying to kill her. Immediately after Shripati's return to the Big House, she died unforgiving.

It is difficult for Kalyani to forget the way she was treated as a daughter as well as a wife. However, she herself is a miracle, a wonder, two women existing in one, Kalyani who was caught in a trap of her mother's cruelty in her pre-marital life, and Kalyani who has been compelled to live her marital life in a strangely oppressive silence. Though, Aru tries her level best to connect and relate these two women, she fails. Suffered and tortured throughout her life both before and after her marriage, Kalyani does not give up her stubbornness and mulishness. She refuses to wear her mother's diamonds or saris, and "the furtive air with which she mends clothes, as if expecting her mother to come upon her and say, as she so often had, 'Haven't you anything better to do than this beggarly occupation?'" (Deshpande 153). However, she, her mother's despair, a weak and feeble creature, succeeds in defeating her mother with the help of her mulishness.

Gopal, who is a teacher in the University, gives up his teaching job. He gets affected by the students' attack on him in the University. Feeling defeated and frustrated, he deserts his wife and three daughters and stays scarcely a few miles away from his marital family in the house of Shankar, one of his old students. Since his coming to Shankar's house, he dreams of his father and his parental family which is a complex and mysterious web of intricate familial relationships. He thinks to himself: "Since coming here, I have been dreaming of my father. How do I know that the man I see in my dreams is my father? I was only eight when he died and nothing of him has remained with me, neither his face, nor his voice, nor his manners, nor any memory linking the two of us together, just a blank . . . And yet, I am certain that the man who visits me in my dreams is my father . . . Knowing nothing about him then, except that he had married his brother's widow who became my mother . . . A man who sinned against his brother by loving his wife, the brother dying of grief and the man marrying immediately after . . . a kind of man moved by pity to marry his brother's widow, to make that brother's daughter his own. A Lakshman-like younger brother, keeping a promise made to his dying elder brother to look after his young widow and child". (Deshpande 41-42). He immediately corrects himself. How can he compare his father, who married his brother's widow after his brother's death just out of passion, with Lakshman, Lord Rama's brother from the epic, *The Ramayana*, who even never looked at Sita's face? After having read Shakespeare's *Hamlet*, the most terrible version of his parent's story comes to his mind. For him, his father now becomes a man succumbing to his passion for his brother's wife and finally marrying her after his brother's death. He firmly believes: ". . . my father was never a father to me—not after

I knew their story. He was my mother's guilty partner, he was Sudha's uncle, her step-father, he was my mother's husband . . . And now I dream of this kindly man, as if we have, through the years, achieved a kind of peace in our relationship, as if, like any son with a loving father, we have finally, after a long struggle, achieved a harmonious relationship". (Deshpande 43).

He is not disturbed by his dreams of his father and his family. He thinks that these are the things of the past which have nothing to do with him now. Sudha, both Gopal's step-sister and a mother, who is absorbed by her young children, has freed him from the tug of her concern. Ramesh, the son of P. K., a man known for his sense of duty and responsibility, Gopal knows, will not despise or hate him for his deserting his wife and daughters. The strong bond between them will help him to make up his mind to take on the responsibility of his family, Sumi and his daughters, on himself. When he goes to the Big House to see Sumi after Gopal's desertion with his wife, Chitra and their twins, Jai and Deep, he is surprised at Sumi's serious question: "What kind of a man is he, Ramesh? . . . Sometimes I think you know him better than any one of us does. Sudha was more like a mother than a sister to him; you're a kind of brother, not a nephew. He was closer to you than anyone else I know". (Deshpande 22). Sumi feels that there has been a close relationship between them and that they know each other well. But he too does not know much about Gopal and his strange behaviour. Nobody knows why he left his parental home before his marriage, and his wife and daughters, his happy marital home after his marriage.

Sudha has been a cheerful, vigorous, healthy and confident girl even after the death of her parents. Gopal believes that after the death of his parents, Sudha is the only link that ensures the continuity of his life and soon after there is P. K. as well. But the very foundation of his life is shaken when he comes to know that Sudha and Gopal do not share a father. He feels that he is caught in the trap of betrayal. He, therefore, decides to set himself free from the so-called bond of a parental family. It is difficult for Sudha to accept his decision to leave his parental family. He tells her that he is going to Shivpur, the place his parents have come from. He, accompanied by Sudha, goes there. Gopal then speaks out his decision: "I'm not going back to Bombay with you, I'm staying on here, and I'm joining college here". (Deshpande 53). They begin to quarrel, and the quarrel goes on and invariably ends in her desperate sobbing. P. K. successfully persuades her to let Gopal have his way in his life, and makes her agree to go back to Bombay without Gopal.

Kalyani's marital family, with her husband, Shripati and two daughters, Premi and Sumi, and a lost son, Madhav, is a middle-class Indian family. Kalyani and Shripati live in a strangely oppressive silence and they have not spoken to each other for more than thirty-five years in their marital life. Their daughters get greatly affected by this long and oppressive silence between their parents. They are never free and comfortable with their father, in particular. Premi is reminded of herself as an infant, a frightened child, the moment she comes to her parental home, with a fair intention to give her help to Sumi, a deserted wife. She envies the existing close and intimate relationship between Aru and Charu. She regrets: "Sumi and I, we were never like this. Sumi was always ahead of me and I was forever trailing behind, never able to catch up with her. And it makes no difference that I am now a successful professional, mother of a seven-year-old son, wife of a prosperous lawyer. The moment I come home, all this dwindles into nothing and I can feel myself sliding back into adolescence, getting once again under the skin of that frightened child Premi who's always waiting here for me". (Deshpande 17). She remembers herself as a frightened child "who, heart thudding in fear, had climbed the forbidden stairs, opened the door and met the blank stare, the question: Why are you here?" (Deshpande 18). There was a kind of dead and fearful silence between Shripati and his daughters. She remembers her father never spoke to her until she was ten. She also remembers her father who really spoke to her when she completed her medical education only to tell her that she was getting married to Anil.

She has preserved a dark picture of her father in her mind, a father staying in his room upstairs, never coming out, and never speaking to the family. She knows that going to his room has been only a formality she has observed during her every visit home. This time climbing the stairs slowly and unwillingly, she thinks that it will be the same thing this time too, and to her surprise, it is exactly the same. Nothing has changed. Her father asks her about Nikhil, speaks of Anil and of his father, but not about Gopal and Sumi. Angrily, she thinks to herself: "Nothing has changed, nothing ever changes here. I was a fool to imagine I could do something that I could be of any use". (Deshpande 19). Her love and concern for her sister with her daughters has brought her to the Big House. But her conversation with Sumi conveys the message that her help and solace is not needed any more. She tells Aru: "I think I'd better go. I'd stay if I thought I could help, but there's nothing I can do . . . Any time you need me, for anything, even if it's not important, just ring me up and I'll come right away". (Deshpande 19).

Sumi is confident enough to live her life independently. She decides to face the challenge of looking after her daughters on her own. Her daughters are the very stuff the fairy tales are made out of. Though, not free and comfortable, they begin to adjust themselves in the Big House. They understand the importance of the adjustment in life. Aru, in particular, develops a sense of responsibility, the sense that began when she was only six years old, with her habit of babying Seema when Sumi was ill and unable to look after a new-born baby. She has been looking after Seema since the day Gopal brought the baby back from Kalyani. She is still the same girl, anxious, worried and puckered, trying to soothe and comfort her younger sister, making her bed, ironing her clothes and what not. Charu charges her and says: "Why do you make Seema's bed, why do you iron her clothes? You're spoiling her". (Deshpande 35). However, her charges are very rare, and she, like the rest of the family, accepts the fact that "Seema is special, isolated not only by the five-year gap between them but by something else that none of them can spell out". (Deshpande 35). Aru wants to shoulder all the responsibilities in the family. She, in a sense, wants to be a man in the family. She shows maturity in leaving Charu free for her studies. She tries to steer her mother and sisters through the stormy passage of change in their life. Kalyani does not want her granddaughters suffer because of their father. When she goes to see Gopal, she remembers her parents. She says: "Look at me, Gopala. My father died worrying about me, my mother couldn't die in peace, she held on to life though she was suffering because of me, she didn't want to leave me and go". (Deshpande 47). She earnestly requests him to think about his wife and daughters. Trying to control her anger she says: "What about your daughters? Have you thought of them? . . . Have you thought of what have you done to them?" (Deshpande 47-48). It is unfortunate that she fails in her attempt to save Sumi's marital family.

Charu's approach to her father and his desertion is sharp and bitter. She does not want even to speak with him. When Aru comes back after having seen her father, she says: "It's no use; it's no use talking to him. I could have told you that. Listen to me, Aru, let's not get involved in their hassles, and let's get on with our lives. All these are not important . . . They're important, if you let them be. I won't. They can't mess up my life. I'm going on with what I want to do . . . As long as I can complete my studies, I don't care where the money comes from. I'm not like you and Ma". (Deshpande 58). Like Madhav, in *The Dark Holds No Terrors*, she does not allow anything to be an obstacle in the way of her education, and she wants to go on with her life without bothering about her father. Sumi feels uneasy to notice a great change in her daughters. She has a very odd feeling that the house is accepting them as it accepted Kalyani and her daughters, making them its part a few years ago. She sees her daughters lowering their voices so that they are not heard by their grandfather upstairs. She thinks to herself: "I don't want my daughters to live with a hand clasped over their mouths, like Premi and I had to". (Deshpande 59).

Hrishi, Charu's classmate, a daily visitor to the Big House, calls the Big House, a *zenana*, the place with too many females. His words remind Sumi of Gopal who had said: "It's not easy to be the only male in a family of females . . . you feel so shut out". (Deshpande 60). Premi calls it a cursed family, a cursed home. In her talk to Gopal, she says: "We're a cursed family, Gopal. I'm frightened for our children". (Deshpande 137). Sumi, too, agrees with both Gopal and Hrishi when she thinks: "They're right, both Gopal and Hrishi, there's something wrong about a house with only females—or males. It's too lopsided, not balanced enough . . . There's none of the tension that's necessary to make us feel alive, to give us the excitement of living". (Deshpande 60). She is now worried about Aru who is becoming conscious of the tense situation in the house, of the strange relationship between her grandparents. She has never spoken to her daughters about the long oppressive silence between them. But as they are living in the house, they cannot get away from the strangely oppressive atmosphere in the house. Though, things have changed since Sumi's childhood, though, Shripati is not the same to his granddaughters as he was to his own daughters, the oppression of his unseen self makes itself felt in the house as if that atmosphere is a part and parcel of the Big House. She is sure that in the house, where Kalyani is a victim of oppressive silence, a rebellious girl like Aru cannot forget what Gopal has done to his wife and daughters.

Aru, in her childhood, was excited and fascinated by the idea of a complete family. She felt that even without the son, theirs was a complete family. She treated her family, the unit as something that was intact and forever. She had never imagined a time when it would no longer be in existence. Now with Gopal's going, to her, "it has not meant merely an empty space in the family, but the disintegration of it. There is no family left. We are five separate individuals, all of us going our different ways, five units that don't add up to a whole". (Deshpande 184). It is difficult for Aru either to accept the disintegration of her family or to understand it at the young age of eighteen. She suffers from a sense of having lost her support and footing in the world with different members going in different directions. She thinks that things are going wrong, they will go wrong and they won't be put right again. She is filled with indignation when she looks at her grandmother who has been suffering a lot in silence. She cannot speak openly even to her mother because of her silence. Sumi does not allow anybody to have a glimpse of her vision of her mother as a hysterical and self-punishing woman. She has put this vision away in her chest of rejects, never letting it come to the surface.

Now looking at Kalyani moving through the house with confidence, she is surprised to see Kalyani with her complex and intricate net of relationships with so many people. Watching Kalyani, she is reminded of the spider she had seen one morning, scuttling from point to point, drawing silken threads out of itself, weaving in the process a web with a beautiful design. She, a wife of Shripati Pandit, a renowned lawyer, has gained courage and confidence. She is proud of her name, Kalyani. She, with the look of a pleased child, says: "My father chose it. My grandfather thought of it actually. It seems that when he was told of my birth, he said—it's a good day for us then. And he recited: Shreyasam, Shivam, Bhadram, Kalyanam, Magalam, Shubham . . . And my father said—right, we'll name her Kalyani". (Deshpande 210). However, the irony of her life lies in the fact that she was destined to suffer in her pre-marital life as well as in her life after her marriage. Her silence, an inevitable part of her life, is deep, dense, mystirious and inexplicable.

Gopal is of the opinion that any relationship within a family can be kept intact, not by the rules or by the law, but by human emotions. In a response to Surekha according to whom it is the legal responsibility of the husband to look after his wife and children, he says: "We can't always live by the rules, can we? Even lawyers know that. There are things like human emotions". (Deshpande 213). Though, Surekha agrees with him, she adds: "Yes, and that's where the law comes in. If your emotions damage someone else, the law takes account of that. People speak of the law of the jungle, but that's some kind of a law too. It's lawlessness that's destructive and leads to chaos". (Deshpande 213). She means to suggest that the husband and the wife, going in different directions, are responsible for the destructive and chaotic situation in the family.

He is astonished to learn from her that his daughter, Aru, who accused him of being a coward, blames herself for his walking away from the family. He also learns that Sumi does not want Aru to take her father to the court. Sumi's concern for Aru makes her say: "Making what has happened in our family part of the war between men and women—no, I don't like that. The truth is, Gopal, I want Aru to go with her life . . . I want her to enjoy the good things in life, I want her to taste life, I want her to relish it and not spit it out because she finds it bitter". (Deshpande 220). However, the question still remains. How can Sumi want her daughter to go on with her life, to make her life easy and comfortable, to enjoy the good things in life and to taste and relish her life, with her father who has already left the family and with her mother who is about to leave the family? Sumi has no answers to all these questions with her. She and her husband do not realize that the life of their daughters have been made difficult and chaotic by their parents themselves. Knowing Sumi's decision to accept a job in the residential school and to leave the family with her younger daughter, Seema, Aru firmly believes that her family life is over. But as man proposes and destiny disposes, before Sumi can do something in her life on her own, she dies in an accident with her father, thus leaving two women, two faces, one old and the other young, linked by a curious resemblance to live their life together.

3.4 Extra-marital Relationships

The attainment and enjoyment of sexual pleasure and freedom by an unmarried woman before marriage, and by a married woman outside marriage does not have a social sanction in India. Social norms and culture in India do not allow the woman to get involved in any sexual activity apart from marriage. Widows also are not allowed to get involved in such type of relationships. However, a married woman, unable to free herself from an unhappy marriage, is tempted to get involved in extra-marital relationship. She ceases to confine herself only to the marital relationship. Being frustrated in her marital life in which she is deprived of true satisfaction and denied liberty and individuality, she, willingly, opens the door of the world that leads her to extra-marital relationship.

She deceives her husband by getting involved in extra-marital relationship just out of a sense of resentment and revenge. She gives herself to the other male with a desire to defy her husband. Simone de Beauvoir writes: "If conjugal love-making has excited the wife's curiosity without satisfying her senses, she is likely to finish her education in some other bed. If her husband has succeeded in awakening her sexuality, she will want to enjoy the same pleasures with others because she has no special feeling of attachment for him". (Beauvoir 563). Deshpande's women protagonists experience complete sexual pleasure and gratification during the initial years of their marriage. But very soon they realize that their male-counterpart becomes a brute that always satisfies his sexual desires without consulting their opinions, without considering their desire and feelings. Her female protagonists; Saru, Indu and Jaya, in a state of frustration, turn their backs on their husbands and get involved in extra-marital relationships.

3.4.1 Sarita's Extra-marital Relations in 'The Dark Holds No Terrors'

Saru's frustration and failure in her marital life makes her look for refuge in her relationships with Boozie and Padmakar Rao. Boozie, a doctor, is a dark but handsome and masterful man. His language, accent, stride and pride, his swift movement through the wards, his banter with his patients, his humour, perfume, clothes, and his fondness for pretty girl students, almost everything is special, exceptional and uncommon. Though, he is from a mediocre middle-class family, he behaves as if he is born to possess all the things in his life, including beautiful, attractive and intelligent girls. But he is a good teacher. The beginning of a relationship between Boozie and Saru is dreadfully unpromising. Saru remembers his shouting at her: "I don't want incompetent, clumsy uninterested females cluttering up this place. Go home and play with your pins and knitting needles. Even a moron could have done this simple thing. Why do you come here when you're not interested?" (Deshpande 89). As he shouts at her, she feels insulted and humiliated. She thinks somebody has torn off her clothes in the public thereby displaying her nakedness to the world.

However, slowly, he begins to take interest in her. From the moment he takes her out for a cup of coffee, Saru, too, begins to give him positive signals. She admits: "It took me a long time to realize that his interest in me was as a woman, not as a student. It was not innocence that deluded me but my feeling that because I was married, I was out of bounds for all males. I thought no male would take 'that' kind of interest in me. Yet, here was one. That was soon obvious, even to me. It was only the 'Why' that remained a mystery". (Deshpande 91). She allows herself to be attracted towards him. She cheats her husband by making him believe that there is just a teacher-student relationship between them. She learns a lot from him. She is shaped, moulded, chiseled into something more polished, nearer perfection. She wonders: ". . . God, how fast I learnt things, apart from Pediatrics I mean, from him. It was he who taught me to dress with elegance and simplicity, who taught me how to speak good English, who improved my accent, who taught me how to enjoy good food, how to read and what . . . oh everything". (Deshpande 91).

She develops a physical relationship with Boozie as she is tired of her shabby way of living with a frayed sari she cannot replace, a movie she cannot see, an outing she cannot join in. Without money, she knows, her life with Manu is petty and dreary. With a hope to fulfil her finale of a middle-class dream, a well-furnished house of their own, she gives herself to 'please' Boozie, who can make things easier for her. Within a few months, he gives her work in a research scheme that gives her very badly needed extra money, and most importantly that keeps her away from Manu for longer hours. She becomes the registrar in a year, passes her MD in less than two years, and gets appointment as an Assistant Honorary at a suburban hospital, with a consulting room of her own in the midst of other well-known busy consultants in four years. Manu never questions his wife about Boozie and his giving her money, his putting his hand on her shoulder, his slapping her on her back, his holding her hand or his hugging her. Saru is resentful towards Manu for his neglecting Boozie's display of his affection for her in the public at the inauguration of her consulting room. The true nature of a relationship between Saru and Boozie, is, in fact, known to Manu who is helpless and can do nothing. Saru uses Boozie as a key that opens the door of success, respect, recognition and popularity for her.

Sarita, unexpectedly, meets Padmakar Rao, one of the few college boys with whom she felt very comfortable, perhaps, on account of his feminine name 'Padma', the name that deprived him of his manliness. He always used to say: "I say, don't call me Padma, Call me Rao". (Deshpande 125). Initially during her college life in Bombay, she was never comfortable with any male student except Padma, who was her partner. He was so tactless that he became very unpopular student in the batch, especially among the girl students, whom he regarded with an ingenuous critical curiosity. His remarks on their clothes, the way they talked, and the way they walked made him their immediate enemy. His tactlessness of saying the wrong things made him flunk in his viva and practicals. Though, he was fairly intelligent and wonderfully sincere, he failed twice. He was a kind of bookish, theoretically a very sound student destined to be an academic. Sarita is surprised when she learns from him that he is a GP practising in the heart of one of Bombay's worst slums. Now he speaks to her about his practice, about his earning money and what not. His interest and concern seems to be in making money through his knowledge of medicine and ignorance of the poor workers dwelling in slums.

Now their meetings have been very frequent. He is always eager to meet her either for tea or for lunch. He begins to enjoy her company. He enjoys meeting her, talking to her. He gets innocent happiness and pleasure out of these meetings. He is not happy with her orthodox and traditional wife who is only interested in talking about her servants and children. She is a typical Indian wife who never takes food until her husband goes home and has his, cooks just what he likes, never calls him by his name. She is, for Sarita, a good wife and a good mother. During one of such meetings, he urges her to have their lunch together, but for that she has no time. He appeals: "But Sarita . . . You have got to come . . . I've been waiting here for so long. I never imagined you'd say no. You can't refuse". (Deshpande 130). He takes her acceptance for granted. She holds herself responsible for this. She thinks to herself: "It was my fault. I had listened to him as perhaps, no one ever had. I had talked to him, smiled at him, given him that which was most precious to me . . . my time". (Deshpande 130). When he presses her for lunch, she feels trapped, hating the panic which overcomes her. She gets scared at the thought of a man being interested in her. She admits: "And now I knew it had not been thoughtless on my part. I had done it deliberately, coolly, with calculation, because, foolishly perhaps, I had imagined it would give me an escape route, something that would lead me out of my loveless trap. Wasn't it always the solution for a woman who found no happiness with one man to try and find it with another?" (Deshpande 132). Padma's taking interest in her is misjudged and miscalculated by Saru. He is interested in childlike and innocent relationship with her. He, like Boozie, does not see her as a woman. Disillusioned in her marital life, she considers Padma a temporary substitute for her unfulfilled marital life.

3.4.2 Indu's Physical Relationship with Naren in 'Roots and Shadows'

Indu, in a confused state of mind, enters into a physical relationship with Naren, her childhood friend. He, according to Indu, has been one of the restless persons in the world but sometimes he seems to be completely at ease and peace with himself. Indu appreciates his free and simple way of living, his not wanting to belong, his not wanting to be envied, his not wanting to be admired, his living his life as he feels to live, as he desires to live. She is quite free and comfortable with him. She remembers what he said about his needs and requirements. He said: "My needs are simple, two sets of clothes, two meals a day, apart from tea and cigarettes. I'm quite cheap to maintain really". (Deshpande 85). She experiences and enjoys a taste of freedom, completeness and excitement in Naren's company. She likes his detachment; his completeness and she wants to be like him. She is very free and bold when she speaks to Naren. She does not hesitate to use the words like 'kiss, rape, deflowered, sex, orgasm, in her conversation with him. She, who is tired of working in a women's magazine, opens the door of her heart and asks Naren: "What the hell shall I write about?" (Deshpande 78). She doesn't know whether to write about women's lives and their frustrations, about a family life and domestic quarrels, about love, about marriage with the ultimate happy end or about menstrual pains, the pangs of childbirth and the ecstasy of orgasm. She feels limited, restricted and hampered by her gender. She is resented by her womanhood because, she feels, it has closed so many doors to her. Naren advises her not to fight against womanhood, but to accept the fact that she is a woman.

She tells him everything about her strained relations with Jayant, everything about herself, her writings and her failures. She is full of complaints about her husband. She says: "It's not that he doesn't care . . . we're on different planes . . . It humiliates me . . . and Naren, it was I who proposed to him . . . You know the word 'deflowered' they use for girls . . . I thought of it when Jayant touched me for the first time . . . I felt as if my body had burgeoned into a flower of exquisite felicity . . . And Naren, my response to him was so natural, so much beyond me and outside me . . . and now I know . . . it shocks him to find passion in a woman. It puts him off". (Deshpande 82-83). The way she speaks to Naren about her husband, about their touching each other, about her passionate love for her husband, about almost everything throws light on her relationship with Naren.

Her close friendship with Naren makes her aware of her natural impulses. She is caught in a trap of passion and willingly offers herself twice to Naren thereby making a crime of wronging and deceiving her husband. She remembers; "Naren pulled me down so that I lay on the carpet beside him, his face close to mine, so close that I could not see him at all . . . he laid his hands lightly, teasingly on my breasts . . . they moved downwards to my waist, my hips. I gazed at him unflinchingly while he went on . . . and moved his face, his lips towards mine . . . I lost all my senses except one, it was so magnified, as if little nerve ends had sprung up all over my body. And I was, yes, responding to him with ardour and warmth when I realized who it was". (Deshpande 79-80). Indu, all of a sudden, comes to her senses and realizes that it is not Jayant, but Naren. She controls her passion, controls herself from this temptation, the enemy of both, man and woman. She, who considers herself essentially monogamous, angrily pulls herself away from him. She wants to prove herself to be a pure and faithful wife.

Naren is unpredictable, perverse and sometimes terrifying. Indu calls her an egoist as he is always involved with his own self, not interested in what happens with others around him. He does not bother about issues and problems in the family, and about demands and expectations of the family from Indu. He, too, wants something from her. He, shamefully but cunningly says: "What do I want, Indu? . . . Maybe it's you, you, with all that money thrown in. Why go after the eggs? I'll settle for the golden goose itself . . . Imagine getting you, all that money, and seeing the family turn green. No, not green, black, with hatred. But I told you I was the big bad villain, didn't I? . . . Take me seriously, young woman. I have my eyes on you". (Deshpande 86-87). Undoubtedly, it is Indu who takes an active and leading role in developing a physical relationship with him by keeping her husband in the dark.

Indu feels like a desolate, deserted and abandoned child when she learns that Naren is going back to his work, rather he is going away from her. She cannot tolerate the idea of his going away. She is astonished at his affectionate, loving, soft and gentle voice when he says: "What is it, Indu? (Deshpande 147). She feels: "Indu. My name. And yet, the way he said it, it could have been 'my darling', or 'my love' or any other endearment . . . Endearments were only for babies and very young children. But adults? . . . I had learnt to take everything in my stride. Endearments, kisses, caresses, even foul abuse . . . nothing could shock me anymore. And yet, at Naren's words, at the sight of Naren's face as he looked at me, the response of that prim, ignorant child came back to me". (Deshpande 147). It seems that Indu is eager to offer herself physically to him, and he, too, is very anxious to accept her offer. Both are passionate to physically 'meet' each other in the true sense of the term.

Indu, who considers herself true and sincere to her husband, intentionally exposes herself by offering herself physically twice to Naren. When she gives herself to him for the first time, she is partly afraid and partly happy and excited. She remembers every minute detail with crystal clarity and precision: ". . . he came closer and put his arms around me. Now I could no more see nor think, but only feel . . . I lay down impelled by his thrusting body, feeling at first a passive languor . . . An ecstasy filled my body and I could not be still any more . . . I clung to him convulsively, marveling that I did not have to hold myself back. And when it was over, we lay back, both of us, exhausted and shuddering". (Deshpande 151-52). She does not feel guilty for her sexual relations with Naren. On the contrary, she pretends to be bold enough to say that she has not committed any crime. Though she says so, her conscience goes on pricking her. She feels nervous and thinks of what she has done. Her mind is burdened with the thought of sin or crime that she did. She loses peace of her mind. She thinks of the gravity of her sex with Naren. She thinks to herself: "Adultery . . . what nuances of wrongdoing . . . no, it needs the other stronger word . . . what nuances of sin the word carries. I will now brood on my sin, be crushed under a weight of guilt and misery. But, instead, perversely, my mind began, coldly, analytically, to think of what I had done. I thought of all this with a kind of remorseless logic, a detached objectivity, as if I was thinking of some other person". (Deshpande 155). With these thoughts she goes to bed reassured. After seeing a confusing dream, she wakes up to find herself at home, the home which she alone has the power to save, the home for which she has something to do.

She gets hopelessly confused and frightened. In a confused state of mind, she again goes to Naren to physically 'talk' to him upstairs. She recollects everything: "He was there. How had I missed him? He sat up immediately as if he had known I would be coming and had been waiting for me. I went to him and he put his arms around me wordlessly. And knowing him for what he was . . . irresponsible, unreliable, fickle, amoral, I clung him as if he were a pillar. It was years since I had cried that way . . . a soundless, violent shuddering. At last it was over and Naren gently eased an arm away . . . He covered me with his blanket, Old Uncle's shawl, with the gentle carefulness of a doting mother, and lay down beside me, close, but not touching. His body was already familiar to me . . . its odours, its contours, its feel". (Deshpande 156). How can Indu call Naren fickle and amoral? It is not Naren who goes to her, but it is she who goes to him. She herself is responsible for everything that happens between them. She allows herself to be caught in Naren's trap.

There is little chance of love between them as Indu has no belief in love. She says: "I don't believe in love . . . there's no such thing . . . not in real life, anyway, only in books and movies . . . It's a big fraud, a hoax, that's what it is. They tell you it's the greatest thing, the only thing in life, and you believe them and fall into the trap". (Deshpande 157). She does not agree with Naren for whom love is a beautiful trap. She strongly believes that sexual instinct, maternal instinct, self-interest and self-love are the only basic truths in human life. There is no such thing like love. She feels pity for Devdas who died for love. The very idea of a grown-up man moaning and crying for love, pining for love is ridiculous and disgusting for her. Her negative and cynical approach to love seems to be responsible for her plight and predicament. Love, she feels, has no role to play in a marital life. She tells Naren about her relationship with her husband: "I told myself, I loved him . . . I had surrendered to him, step by step . . . I realize now that it was not for love, as I had been telling myself, but because I did not want conflict . . . I had clung tenaciously to Jayant, to my marriage, not for love alone, but because I was afraid of failure". (Deshpande 158-59). Saying so, she bursts into a storm of weeping. Naren tries to console her. Weeping, a kind of medicine with a cathartic effect, makes her calm, quiet and clear. Now in a peaceful state of mind, she speaks freely to Naren about everything. She remembers: "Exhausted, I leaned against him, silent. Gently he put his hand on my hair. And this time he did what he had once said he would. He loosened it with the solemnity, the earnestness of a priest performing some rite. What was happening between us was complete in itself. It needed no commentary, no explanations". (Deshpande 160).

She is very passionate about her relationship with Naren. She again and again proves herself to be dishonest and disloyal to her husband. She feels guilty of having cheated her husband. She thinks to herself: "For Naren and I . . . it was no infatuation. Naren was still Naren to me . . . Twice, briefly, our flesh had touched. But that had, oddly, created no new bond between us. It had not been so for me with Jayant. Then, with his touch, I had felt as if I had lost not only part of myself, but the whole". (Deshpande 171). Naren is tempted to be physical with her for the third time. However, she decides to drive out the private devil in her by not allowing herself to offer physically to him. It is perhaps because of Indu's decision to go back to her marital home that Naren, who is afraid of water as both his parents were drowned, kills himself by drowning deliberately. She experiences a sense of utter grief and loneliness when she sees Naren lying there dead, detached, remote far removed from the living and their emotions. When Old Uncle wants her to tell him everything, she just thinks to herself: "Everything? . . . Can I tell you we made love? Not for love, nor lust either, but for motives of our own . . . No, that's too easy an explanation . . . It cannot explain the feelings between us . . . It cannot explain how the darkness inside me was banished, replaced instead, by a gentle, kindly dawn". (Deshpande 179). She considers the days that she spent with Naren as something complete in themselves.

3.4.3 Intense and Mysterious Relationship between Jaya and Kamat

Jaya, deeply rooted in Indian context, is a typical Indian wife who has sacrificed her life for her husband and children. She accepts her husband as a sheltering tree. Following her brother's advice, she tries to be as good as possible with her husband but she fails to keep her relationship with her husband intact and normal. However, her marital life becomes dull, mechanical and routine. Marriage has changed Jaya; it has swallowed her with her dreams and aspirations, her 'self' and individuality. She considers herself a poor idiotic woman. She feels trapped and insecure and believes: "I know better now. I know that safety is always unattainable. You are never safe". (Deshpande 17). She feels lonely and unsafe.

Frustrated in her life with Mohan, she develops a secret relationship with Kamat, a lonely man in her neighbourhood. The emptiness and nothingness in her life draws her towards Kamat, who, unlike her husband, does not have male-ego. It is Kamat who offers her badly required emotional support and shelter, makes her believe that she has sacrificed almost all her principles, scolds her for being such a coward in facing life to save her marriage, and tells her to take herself and her life seriously. It is Kamat who warns her: ". . . beware of this 'women are the victims' theory of yours. It'll drag you down into a soft, squishy bog of self-pity. Take yourself seriously, woman. Don't skulk behind a false name". (Deshpande 148). He helps her to know the causes of her failure as a writer. He gives her necessary courage and confidence to accept the truth that she has stopped writing because she has been afraid of failing. She is haunted by Kamat's words: "The fact is you're scared, scared of failing". (Deshpande 148). He wants her to express her anger, personal views and vision of life in her stories. He inspires Jaya who believes: "There's no room for anger in my life, no room for despair, either. There's only order and routine—today, I have to change the sheets; tomorrow, scrub the bathrooms; the day after, clean the fridge". (Deshpande 147-48).

The relationship between Kamat and Jaya is not intense, but mysterious. Kamat is the only man who talks very freely and naturally with Jaya. Jaya wonders how a man and woman can talk so freely. Jaya says: "But this man...it had been a revelation to me that two people, a man and a woman, could talk this way. With this man I had not been a woman. I had been just myself—Jaya. There had been an ease in our relationship I had never known in any other. There had been nothing I could not say to him". (Deshpande 153). She is more free and comfortable with this man than with her husband. She gets emotionally involved in him. In his presence she talks about her parents, about her father's death, about everything she never spoke even to her husband. Once as she speaks to him, Jaya remembers: ". . . and this time he held my face lightly within his palms, so light a touch that I had scarcely felt his hands . . . and passed his fingers lightly over my face. And the touch had meant nothing. But this time . . . his eyes had looked steadily, almost dispassionately at me. And my body had responded to that look, that voice, that touch. I had almost felt his body on mine, becoming a part of mine, I had felt his mouth on mine; I had almost been able to smell and taste his lips . . . At that moment, however, I had instantaneously rejected the body's response. I had moved away from him, from that scarcely touching grasp, I had left him without a word". (Deshpande 157). Jaya, thus, annihilates her husband by responding naturally to Kamat and his body.

A Middle-Class Indian Woman: A Creature Made by Beliefs and Superstitions

CHAPTER 4

4.1 Role of Mythology and Philosophy in Shaping Indian Sensibility

Indian beliefs, legends, mythology, epics, films, fairy tales, culture and philosophy have a deep impact, both positive and negative on Indian way of life. Deshpande highlights the impact of these on the life a middle-class Indian woman in her novels. It is true that Deshpande is not an aggressive and revolutionary kind of a feminist who believes the male to be the only cause of women's sorrows and sufferings, their plight and predicament. She admits that a woman herself, to a large extent, shapes her life and destiny to suit the convenience of her male counterpart. Her character itself is her destiny. In addition to this, her move towards liberty and modernity is hampered by Indian beliefs and superstitions, orthodox, customs, conventions and traditions. Some Indian women eat food in the unwashed plates used by their husbands. Most Indians believe that if you utter the name of 'Rama', the mythological king of Ayodhya, the immortal soul of the dead goes to the heaven. An Indian woman has a strong belief in the power of a *tulsi puja*. It is also believed that a *tulsi puja* performed by a married woman helps her live as a *Suhasini* and helps an unmarried girl to have a good husband. Practice of certain rites and rituals for a birth, a marriage and a death, matching of horoscopes believed to be necessary to arrange marriages, playing post-wedding ceremonial games, observing fasts, performing *pujas*, applying *haldi* and *kumkum* as a symbol of wifehood, celebrating *hartalika*, *mangala gouri*, *Bhau-bij*, *Raksha bandhan*, *Diwali* festival, *Ganapati* festival, birth and death anniversaries of the near and dear ones are a few of the inseparable parts of Indian conventions and traditions.

Simple living and high thinking, Ramu Kaka's favourite axiom, are the words Jaya, in *That Long Silence*, has heard very often as a child. When any of his family members asks for something, he advises them: "It's not how you look, what you have or what you wear that's important". (Deshpande 60). Gandhi had a strong desire to change human nature with the help of his principles, the principle of truth and that of non-violence. Is it not the irony of his life that the man who practised the principle of non-violence throughout his life was assassinated? Jaya remembers what she told Mukta: "When we were children, my father was in the *Hindu Mahasabha*. And after Gandhi died he had to go into hiding, you remember how they were persecuted then because of Godse? And one day a mob came to loot our shop . . . And they called themselves Gandhians, those men who were after men like my father. Poor Gandhi, he thought he could change human nature, but people don't change". (Deshpande 180). The followers of Gandhi, who called themselves Gandhians, didn't hesitate to violently attack the members of the *Hindu Mahasabha*, and loot their property, thus proving themselves to be far away from the teachings of Gandhi.

The generation represented by the people like Old Uncle, in *Roots and Shadows*, is inspired by the great Indian heroes like Tagore, Gandhi, Vivekananda and many others with their philosophy, principles and teachings. Old Uncle, with a sense of pride, asks: "Tell me, Indu, who are your heroes? I don't mean you personally, but all of you, your generation. We had Tagore and Gandhi, Vivekananda, Aurobindo . . . and so many more. Who are yours?" (Deshpande 100). Indu, who has no answer to the question, only says that she and her generation do not have any heroes and it is the time of anti-heroes. Old Uncle intends to suggest that people need to have certain heroes to give a proper direction to their life, that life can be shaped and guided by certain beliefs, and that success and happiness do not depend only upon money. He says: "People had different things at different times, things to believe in . . . Since people began to think, there have been so many 'isms' as well. For us, it was patriotism. Now, what have you got, child? Do you believe only in success? One must earn so much; spend so much . . . is that all that matters?" (Deshpande 105). Indu fails to understand Old Uncle's concept of success.

Jaya, in *That Long Silence*, has been a great admirer and lover of Indian film music, in general, and the songs of Rafi and Lata, in particular. She even enjoys the advertisements when she goes to see a movie with her husband. Advertisements create an illusion of a happy married life in her, an illusion of life without sorrows, sufferings, defeats, failures and disasters. She is happy to follow the footsteps of the mythological characters, Sita following her husband into exile, Savitri following death to reclaim and win back her husband, and Draupadi stoically sharing her husbands' travails. She desires to be an ideal Indian wife by following her husband blindly like Gandhari who bandaged her eyes to become blind like her husband in the epic, *The Mahabharata*. She believes in the story of the sparrow and the crow, the story in which the sparrow is happy and comfortable with her home and babies. She is inspired by the song children used to sing when they were little. It was a kind of game, something about a mulberry bush, a game in which we imagine we are moving, getting on, going ahead, but we are just going round and round, coming to the same point again and again. It is this song which makes her believe that the only purpose of her life is just to go on living life. Jaya's sensibility has been shaped by Indian myths, fables and philosophy.

Human life is moulded even by the ideologies of different political parties. Jaya knows that her son, Rahul, as a child, was in a confused state of mind. He used to ask questions just out of curiosity. When, as a child, he saw a street brawl between two political parties, he ran to his parents with a question: "Daddy, what are we? Daddy, are we the *Red Flag* or are we the *Shiv Sena*? Mummy, what are we? Mummy, tell me what are we? (Deshpande 50). His parents were irritated by his questions. Her mother's answer, 'we are nothing' was taken seriously by him and he considered and made himself nothing since then. Jaya still remembers the girls in the hostel, standing in the balconies, watching the road-lining crowds waving the flags in their hands, and hearing the loud cries of *Hindi-Chini bhai bhai*. Something went wrong and the war broke out between India and China thus affecting lives of the people from both the countries. It is true that a way of life is affected by the clash and conflict between political parties as well as between neighbouring countries.

There has been a two way relationship between films and human life. Films, to a large extent, mirror life, on one side, and men are tempted to imitate film life, on the other side. Men struggle to know the meaning of their life in the light of films that they watch and songs in them. Sumi, in *A Matter of Time*, forgets herself when she hears the clown's song; *Jeena yahan, marna yahan, iske siwa jana kaha*. She watches the movie until the end, when the clown, a tragic and doomed victim, dies. The clown with his tragic end troubles and tortures her. She begins to consider every individual a tragic and doomed victim. She puzzles over the meaning of the words of the song. Moving from one interpretation to another, she interrogates herself: ". . . what do they mean? That this world is all we have and therefore there is nowhere else for us to go? That we have to live here and die here? Or does it mean; this is what we have, this area of action is enough for us, we live here and die here, we need no more?" (Deshpande 9). She feels that she has perceived the truth of human life, the truth that we have to live here and we have to die here.

She is so much under the influence of movies that it is she, who, after watching Satyajit Ray's *Charulala*, chooses the name for her second daughter after the heroine. Saru's younger brother, in *The Dark Holds No Terrors*, is named after Dhruva, a mythological character, the child, who was pushed off his father's lap by his stepmother, and who, full of anger, sorrow and humiliation, became the constant North Star by giving himself up to a steadfast meditation. During his meeting with Surekha, the lawyer, Gopal, too, remembers Hindi film songs when he speaks about his dead parents. He says: "My parents died when I was eight, they were crushed by a bus . . . They died together. You know all those Hindi film songs about living together and dying together? When I think of them, it is of my parents I think and of how their bodies were so fused together in death that they could not be separated . . . Well, what I'm trying to say—our journeys are always separate, that's how they are meant to be. If we travel together for a while, that's only a coincidence". (Deshpande 212). He interprets this philosophy in his own way and tries to relate it to the songs about living together and dying together.

Saru, in *The Dark Holds No Terrors*, gets dazzled by Manu's friends, a new world for her, an escape from her dull and uninteresting world of lectures, patients, examinations and results. The new world is charged with excitement and enthusiasm. She remembers Vasu speaking of a movie he has just seen, a movie in which the heroine is a pure-minded dancing girl. He seems to be greatly impressed by her acting. In ecstasy he says: "You remember the gesture of hers, when she's dancing before the man who wants to buy her? One graceful gesture . . . one gesture, but, my god, so full of coquetry, disdain, femininity, pride, and those eyes behind the veil . . . A man would give away kingdoms for such a gesture, such a look". (Deshpande 154). His approach to the dancer, her gestures and look is exceptionally romantic. Saru feels that he fails to understand the ugly truth of prostitution and exploitation, the sordid reality behind the veil of romanticism. She seems to be impressed by endless conversations, arguments and discussions, unlimited cups of tea, plates of fried stuff, readings of plots of stories, articles, plays, half-written poems and what not in that new world.

However, her initial excitement and enchantment begins to fade slowly and gradually as she realizes that their approach to all these is ridiculous. She thinks to herself: "They often reminded me of cocks pecking in the field of literature and the arts. They would never get anything out of it but the small unwanted grains . . . Their facility with words, which had fascinated me initially, had now begun irritating me. Words, words, words . . . Sometimes, they can obscure the meaning of life. They can hide the fact that there is nothing behind them. They will spend all their lives talking; these people, and never reach anywhere. But they are not failures". (Deshpande 155). Indian movies and songs, poems, literature and other arts play their roles in shaping and developing Indian sensibility both positively and negatively.

In *A Mattre of Time*, after Gopal's desertion, Aru, with the feeling of hostility for her father, goes to see him. She uses her hostility as a weapon, as a sword. With the intention of knowing the reason behind his desertion, she shoots questions, Yaksha's questions, at her father. She asks: "Is it because of something Sumi did, something she said? Is it because of us, because of me? Is it because I was rude to you, because I always argued with you? Is it because of what I said to you when you decided to resign? Is it money?" (Deshpande 50). On hearing these questions, he is reminded of Yaksha and his questions. Aru's anger reminds him of Sumi and her anger which is sharp; one clean cut and it's over. Aru, on the contrary, hits with a blunt weapon, uncaring of where the blow falls, even getting herself hurt in the process. Gopal's desertion breaks a kind of war, rather creates a war-like situation in the family. When Sumi goes to meet Gopal, he says that Aru is on her mother's side. She immediately flashes out at him and says that this is not a war and she doesn't want the children to take sides. In a response, Gopal says: "It's inevitable. Don't you remember Yudhishtira's words, 'we are five Pandavas against a hundred Kauravas. But when an enemy comes, we are a hundred and five against the enemy?' I'm the enemy now. She can't help seeing it that way". (Deshpande 83). Gopal compares his family with that of Pandavas in *The Mahabharata*. However, for Sumi, his life, now, is tantalizingly disjointed, scattered bits and pieces, difficult to be put together, as senseless as the room where she stays.

Sumi, feeling uneasy and restless, leaves Gopal and his room in silence. For others, she has changed. Gopal thinks to himself: "I could only sense her distress; something had happened, but she did not, perhaps she could not, share it with me . . . Sumi has changed . . . Changed from what? Is there one inviolate self, deviation from which becomes change? It was Sumi who made me think of this when, laughing at her own idea, she spoke of Draupadi's disguise as Sairandhri, the queen's maid. Don't you think this was something she had often wanted, to be by herself, to sleep alone, to be free, for a while, of her five husbands? . . . What about Arjuna becoming Brihannala? Yes, that was easy; Arjuna, tired of the male world of war and violence, of relating to woman only as lord and conqueror, became Brihannala, the eunuch, so that he could enter the gentle world of women, of music and dancing and become an insider in this world". (Deshpande 86). Like these mythological characters in disguise, Gopal can see different roles locked in Sumi. Life is nothing but a story in which we play different types of roles. We, like Vyasa, the creator of *The Mahabharata*, cannot write the story of our life.

The higher truth relating our life is always beyond our realization and perception. Our belief in the strength of Indian mythological characters, the belief that Meerabai drank poison and yet lived, that Purandaradasa was converted by God in the guise of a mendicant, that Saint Tukaram's poems, rather his *abhangas* remained safe and sound and emerged intact from the river Indrayani after thirteen days, that the marriage of Shiva and Parvati was a magical and awe-filled story of love of a man and a woman, are the inseparable part of our lives. The very fabric of Indian sensibility has been kept intact by these beliefs. In a response to Premi's question, 'why did you do it, Gopal?' Gopal is once again reminded of the Yaksha's question to Yudhishtira. To Premi, he says: "You remember the Yaksha's question to Yudhishtira: What is the greatest wonder in this world? And what Yudhishtira's answer was! We see people die and yet we go on as if we are going to live forever. Yes, it's true, that is the greatest marvel of this world . . . In fact, it's the secret of life itself. We know it's all there, the pain and suffering, old age, loneliness and death, but we think, somehow we believe that it's not for us. The day we stop believing in this untruth, the day we face the truth that we too are mortal . . . it will become difficult, almost impossible to go on . . . It happened to me. I stopped believing . . . I could no longer believe that there is a meaning to my life". (Deshpande 133-34). His belief that his life has no meaning makes him leave his wife and daughters.

Saru, in *The Dark Holds No Terrors*, too, believes that we have to go on living until it is time for us to go. She is reminded of the parable of Buddha with his trust in the ultimate truth that death is an inescapable human condition, that it is certain and inevitable. Gopal considers Aru's desire to put the world right itself a problem. To Surekha, he says: "When I was her age, I wanted to put the world right too. I was sure the revolution is the answer . . . My father told me to read the story of Nahusha. I didn't know it then, I didn't even know it was in the *Mahabharata*. I read it much later, after my father's death, and now I know why he wanted me to read it. It tells us that every revolution carries within it the seed of its own destruction. One oppression only replaces another . . . I am a feminist, oh yes, I am. I am on the side of women. I know that we're all of us in this awesome game together, but the rules are almost against women. I believe things have to change . . . But until patriarchy is thrown out as a whole, we still need to see that the rules are observed". (Deshpande 214). The story of Nahusha makes him aware of the fact that the seeds of destruction are in the revolution itself.

While thinking about the play to be written for a school competition, Sumi remembers a story of the king and his much-loved and beautiful daughter who used to eat rice and curds everyday. The tree grew in the backyard where she washed her hands after every meal. She declared that she would marry the young man who could identify the tree. The gardener's son, who saw her washing her hands at the spot everyday, identified the tree as 'Rice and Curds' tree and won her hand. The story has been interpreted in a variety of ways. Sumi wonders why the princess insisted on such a strange declaration and condition. She begins to interpret the story in her own way. She thinks to herself: "Had she fallen in love with the gardener's son . . . plotted the whole thing, knowing this was the only way she could get him? . . . Yes, she must have been a clever young woman, indeed, and, perhaps a passionate one. Had she watched the gardener's son at work, noticed his muscles gleaming in the sun and decided she would have him for her husband?" (Deshpande 157). She gets excited at the thought that she is a clever young woman who used man's own weapons against him. She remembers Kausalya and her promise given to her husband. She thinks to herself: "Would Kausalya have sent her son Rama into exile because some time, long ago, she had promised a man she would give him any boon he asked for? What a dangerous weapon such a promise was! Things change with time, people change, circumstances change; nothing is constant". (Deshpande 157). She gets haunted by these ideas and the story of the gardener's son and decides to write the play based on this fairy tale. She also decides to end the play with a happy note, with the word *Shubham* leaving the princess and her husband to enjoy the fruits of their marital life.

The fairy tale makes her look at her strained marital life through a new angle. She knows that it is the love that plays a vital role in marital life. She also knows that it is not only Shakuntala and Dushyanta, Romeo and Juliet, but common people, too, have been pledging, consummating and dying for the thing they call love. The success of the play on the stage motivates her to keep the darkness of her life behind and the idea of the second play keeps knocking at her door. The play enables her to forget the sordid reality of her marital life. She now decides to write about Surpanakha, a mythological female character from a great epic, *The Ramayana*, the demon sister of the demon king Ravana, who was in love with the Aryan prince Rama. It was an unpleasant story in which the two brothers Rama and Lakshmana mock and ridicule her, and finally mutilate her by cutting off her nose. Sumi's sensitivity leads her to an altogether different interpretation of Surpanakha's love for Lord Rama. Sumi believes that women are ashamed of owning female sexuality; they cannot speak of it, not even to their own selves. But, she feels, Surpanakha, a woman charged with sexuality was not frightened to speak of her sexual desires. She, in a sense, gives a lesson to meek and silent women to speak out their desires without any fear.

Indian life, to a large extent, has been moulded by the two great epics—*The Mahabharata* and *The Ramayana*; and other Indian myths and stories and by the thoughts and philosophy of Indian thinkers and philosophers as well. Indian children are being told the stories from the Indian epics. Indu remembers the story Old Uncle had told them as children, the story of Bhishma lying heroically on the bed of arrows made by Arjuna. On her return to her parental home as a frustrated wife, She is reminded of a Krishna-Sudama story and the photographs of Gandhi and Nehru and of Krishna as a crawling infant in *The Dark Holds No Terrors* take Saru back into her childhood. She, later, learns from her father that her mother who was on her death bed wanted him to read *The Mahabharata* and *The Ramayana*. She wanted him to read the episode of Duryodhana waiting for the Pandavas to come and kill him. The episode gave her the courage to face her death with courage.

Indians, being Indians, look at the concept of retribution and punishment in their own way. Saru feels that she has been punished in the form of her sorrows and sufferings because she has done wrong to others. She admits: ". . . I deserve it after all. Look what I've done to him. Look what I did to Dhruva, and to my mother. Perhaps if I go on suffering . . . It's because I wronged her that I'm suffering now". (Deshpande 204). Jaya remembers how her grandmother used to frighten children with her dire pronouncements: "Tell lies now and you'll be a lizard in your next life, steal things you'll be a dog, cheat people and you'll be a snake". (Deshpande 128). Jaya is mature enough to know that people do not have to wait for another life for punishment and that an act and retribution follow each other naturally and inevitably in one life only. She knows and believes: "Dasarath killed an innocent young boy whose parents died crying out for their son. And years later, Dasarath died too, calling out for his son". (Deshpande 128). Old Uncle, in *Roots and Shadows*, has his own philosophy of crime and punishment. He says: "We have to pay for the sins of our ancestors". (Deshpande 137). Sunanda Atya believes:

"But you always pay for your wrongs. That's why I say. And it's true. Look how much trouble they had getting Mini's marriage fixed up". (Deshpande 133). She means to say that it is difficult for Mini's parents to fix up her marriage because of their wrong doings. People, who go to take a bathe everyday in the tank near the Shiva temple, blindly believe that sins can be washed away by taking a dip in the tank. It is Naren who says: "To wash away my sins . . . what else? I have a ritual dip every day like a good Brahmin. Hold your nose, loop up your sacred thread, and wash away your sins". (Deshpande 172).

Indians are in the habit of blaming others for their failures. Sunanda-atya, an Indian woman, who is proud of her son, Krishna, does not hesitate to blame others for her son's failure in examination. She says to Indu: "You know he failed his SSC twice . . . He did, and it isn't his fault. He's really a clever boy and he worked hard. But they failed him by just a few marks. It's shameful. So many boys, not half as good as him, passed. But what can you expect these days when you're a Brahmin?" (Deshpande 137). Indu is shocked to hear it from her that they deliberately failed him because he's a Brahmin. Since her return to her ancestral home, she has been hearing her own people say: "They refused us jobs; they refused us promotions; they refused us admissions; and now 'they' were failing us in our exams. 'They' had become the scapegoats for our failures, our weaknesses, and our faults. Injustice . . . yes, it does exist . . . And one thing was clear to me . . . it is the weak, the incompetent, the undeserving who sit and moan". (Deshpande 137). Nilima, in *That Long Silence*, a fatherless child since her birth, a dark baby, a crow in a family of fair-skinned swans, has been always a disturbing factor for her grandmother who always mutters: "How can the child be so dark? . . . None of our people are dark". (Deshpande 62). But Nilima, though a female child, is strong enough to plant herself sturdily in front of her fair-complexioned grandmother. Nilima once tells Jaya with vicious malice: "They call me a crow too, just because I'm dark. Who cares! I like crows anyway. They're so sharp, aren't they, auntie?" (Deshpande 63).

4.2 *The Dark Holds No Terrors*: A Mirror of Indian Beliefs and Superstitions

The Dark Holds No Terrors mirrors the impact of Indian myths and legends, beliefs and superstitions, conventions and traditions on Indians and their way of life. It also mirrors the practice of rites and rituals, fasts and *pujas*, inseperable part of the life of most Indians. Sarita, knocking on the door of her parental home, is reminded of the Krishna-Sudama story from the epic, *The Mahabharata*, the story in which Krishna and his queen Rukmini run happily to greet a poor, rugged Sudama standing at the gate of the palace. Standing at the door of the house, she is tempted to compare herself with Sudama. For a moment she sees her mother, her dead mother standing in front of *tulsi*, with her eyes closed, hands folded, lips moving, as if praying *tulsi* for her death as a *Suhasini* before her husband. An Indian woman desires to die as a *Suhasini* with her husband still alive when she dies. She believes that her performing *tulsi puja* will help her to die as a *Suhasini*. She has full trust in the strength of *tulsi puja*. Her parental home is a typical home of a Hindu family where she sees three faded photographs, the first of her grandfather whom she had never seen, the second of smiling Gandhi and Nehru in a burst of patriotism and the third of Krishna as a crawling infant, chubby, solemn, with a hint of a smile in the eyes and a real peacock's feather stuck on the infant's head.

Saru's room is given to Madhav, the first year college student, who has been staying with her father for more than two years. Her father asks her to lie down for a while in the *Puja* room, which is an inseparable part of a typical Hindu home. She lies down there with her eyes closed, enjoying smells of oil and camphor, incense and flowers. The room is bare now, but the pale ghosts of the old odours, the tarnished silver mango leaves hanging from the top of the doorway are the only indications that this had been a *puja* room once. She is surprised to see mealtime rituals very strictly followed by Madhav. She curiously observes: "He had removed his shirt and sat down on the plank, legs crossed, sacred thread prominent on his chest. Before starting on his food, he did all the things she had almost forgotten. Water in the cupped palm, the drops around the plate, bits of rice on one side of it". (Deshpande 30). She has a negative approach towards, almost a sense of hatred for these meaningless rites and rituals, customs and conventions.

However, she too used to go for *pujas*, fasts, rituals and mumbled prayers with some hope before her marriage. She remembers as a growing girl she had looked at herself in the mirror on the door of the almirah, hoping to see herself to be pretty and attractive. As she opens the almirah now, there are all those things which were splendid treasures to her as a child. She finds a few glasses, one water container, small bowls, an *attar* tray, a rose-water sprinkler which had been regularly taken out each and every year on the special occasion of *haldi-kumkums*. This was the occasion when she became more important than her brother, Dhruva. It was the occasion when she was the daughter of the house who could apply *attar* to the backs of women's hand. She also finds the *Benaras* sari her mother used to wear for *haldi-kumkum*, wedding and thread ceremonies. Her mother had a strong desire to have the *Chanderi* sari for Dhruva's thread ceremony. But after Dhruva's death there was neither the thread ceremony nor the *Chanderi* sari. There were no *pujas*, no *haldi-kumkums*, and no weddings. She finds another bundle of squares of cotton and silk which were used as traditional token of auspicious gifts given to married women on ceremonial occasions. She remembers being invited by a friend to a ceremony held in the eighth month of her pregnancy. The mother had done all the traditionally prescribed rituals for the pregnant daughter, ending up with the gifts of sari and blouse piece, given to the girl along with a coconut, *paan-supari* and grains of rice. It has been an Indian tradition that newly married girls are invited with their husbands to their parental homes during the *Diwali* festival. Sarita who married against the wish of her parents, was not fortunate enough to be invited to her parental home during festivals.

Celebration of various festivals such as *Diwali* festival, *Dussehra, Ganapati* festival, *Gudi Padwa, Makar Sankranti,*

Holi and many others have been an inseparable part of Indian culture. *Diwali* festival is the festival of lights while *Holi* is a popular festival of colours. *Gudi Padwa* is celebrated as the New Year's first day. The day of *Dussehra* is considered the auspicious day. The formal opening of Saru's consulting room took place on the auspicious day of *Dussehra*. She remembered little processions of *Ganapati* immersion going past their house, accompanied by the ringing of a brass bell and children's vociferous cries: "*Ganapati bappa morya, Pudchya varshi lavkar ya*" (Deshpande 147). Saru's family, too, celebrated this festival. After *Ganapati* immersion, there was *puran-poli* and a light still burning in front of *Ganapati*'s niche where a coconut took the place of the idol until the next morning. Saru's mother stopped celebrating *Ganesh* festival after Dhruva's death, but she retained the other gods in the *puja* room and performed her *puja* in the morning regularly. She had full trust in her *puja* and worship which was a kind of religion for her.

All these are the social festivals which bring and connect people together. Indians are interested not only in these festivals but also in casual meetings. They casually meet one another with no specific purpose or intention. Saru remembers one of such casual meetings with a colleague of Manu's and his wife. About a casual meeting Saru, often, thinks: "It's like a ballet or *Bharat Natyam* dance, these meetings between couples, between families; not with the beauty and rhythm of the dance, but all its rigidity. It's as if we move on chalked lines, no deviations allowed at all. The men slap each other on the back, feigning a greater intimacy than there really is while the females smile and simper, talk of children and servants, and, if the children are there, coo at them. And then, saying to one another with equal insincerity . . . Do visit us, you must come . . . we part, the smiles falling off our faces with remarkable rapidity, the women slipping smoothly into criticism and invective". (Deshpande 111). However, though, stupid and idiotic drama, such casual and harmless meetings have been a very common Indian way of life.

There is no society in human history which does not believe in religion in one form or the other. Religion has always played a very important role in the life of Indians. Indian people believe in religion and to worship gods and goddesses is a kind of religion for them. Religion is something that controls and governs human life. R. M. MacIver and Charles H. Page write: "Religion, as we understand the term, implies a relationship not merely between man and man but also between man and some higher power. Hence, it normally invokes a sanction which may be called 'suprasocial', whether it be primitive ghost fear or the present 'wrath of God' or the penalties of an afterlife of torture in hell or merely the sense of being 'out of tune with the infinite' when its supposed laws are disobeyed". (MacIver and Page 168). Man's belief in gods and goddesses, his frequent visits to the temples and other religious places, his going on pilgrimages, his worshipping God in the form of *puja*, his participation in religious activities and his celebrating different types of rites and rituals help him to experience peace of mind.

Saru used to go to the temple every Friday with her mother who carried the brass tray with flowers, coconut and the *haldi* and *kumkum* containers. She was never allowed to carry the brass tray with *Devi*'s offerings for the fear of her dropping it. Dropping down *Devi*'s offerings was believed to be a heinous crime, a sacrilege and a catastrophe. It was also believed that the woman, who dropped the tray with *Devi*'s offerings, would be cursed by *Devi Mother*. Saru was uneasily fascinated to hear this about *Devi* and her power. On her visit to the temple, she enjoyed the ringing sound of the temple bell, the fascinating echoes of the sound of the bell, the smell of oil, camphor and flowers, the cheerful babble of the female talk in the temple. She could feel and experience the sameness of women's talk, their attitudes, their responses, their sensibilities which could be easily predictable. One day she had a frightening but memorable experience in the temple. She saw a middle-aged woman worshipping *Devi* with holding her tray of offerings in one hand, and applying *kumkum* to *Devi*'s forehead with the other. Suddenly the tray fell out of her hands, and the woman looked like a creature with a frightening mask-like face and popping eyes staring at *Devi*. She then began to gyrate, turning round in a slow and peculiar motion. She went on with her feet thumping, hands flailing, sari loosening, and hair flying round the awful face with frightful eyes. One of the women from the temple moved forward to apply *kumkum* to the rotating woman's forehead. Other women including Saru's mother did the same thing. With *kumkum* and sweat mixing together, her face became bloody red.

Saru, as a child, was terrified by her appearance and ran out to the open courtyard where women used to gather in the evenings to listen to the man in the red shawl reciting the *puranas* in a singing tone. She sat by the black stone bull in the centre and touched the tiny stone bells round his neck. The bull, too, was applied *kumkum* and offered flowers between his dainty feet. After some time, her mother came out and gave *prasad* to her. Saru saw the same woman again, leaning against the pillar, her legs stretched out in front of her, her face relaxed and empty, the *kumkum* on her forehead wiped away except for the usual mark between the brows, a symbol of wifehood. She was given rock sugar as *prasad* by that woman now with a gentle and smiling face. She was confused as she failed to understand the woman, who, according to her, was divided into two different beings. She even could not understand what her mother meant when she said: "The *Devi* entered into her". (Deshpande 103). It was very difficult for Saru to accept the belief that Devi enters into the woman.

There are the people who believe in epics, myths and parables. They allow their lives to be guided by these literary writings. They enjoy the parable of Buddha highlighting the certainty and inevitability of death. Buddha once told a grieving and mourning mother of a dead child: "Get me a handful of mustard seeds from the house which has not known death . . . learn the truth and be comforted. Death is an inescapable human condition". (Deshpande 77). The mother was comforted to learn the truth that death is certain to all. She also learnt that we need to move on until we take our last breath; we need to go on living until there is time to go. Great epics like *The Mahabharata* and *The Ramayana* have the capacity to console the suffering and afflicted. When Saru's mother was on her death bed, believing that she was certainly dying, she wanted her husband to read something from these epics. She used to lie quietly, sometimes falling asleep in the middle of a sentence. Saru remembers her father who said: "In the last few months, she almost stopped speaking. She liked me to read to her . . . *The Mahabharata* and *The Ramayana*. It seemed to comfort and soothe her . . . But one day I saw that she was listening very intently. When I finished reading, she said . . . Read it again. It was that episode of Duryodhana . . . at the very end of the battle . . . When the Kauravas are defeated and when Duryodhana finds he is almost the only one of them left, he leaves the battlefield and goes into a lake. He waits there for the Pandavas to come and kill him". (Deshpande 195). She died peacefully as a *Suhasini*. Saru was surprised to know that her face was peaceful when she died, and there was no struggle, no bitterness on it. *Mavshi* considers Saru's mother a lucky woman because she died as a *Suhasini*. She believes that her death gave a full stop to her plight and predicament. However, *Mavshi*, who is not happy with her widowhood, asks: "But tell me, you're a doctor and know all about dying and living . . . Saru, why am I, a fat, old, unwanted woman left alive when he, so useful, so much wanted was taken away? Why am I alive when he is dead?" (Deshpande 77). She feels lonely and incomplete without her husband. She considers herself an unlucky woman who is destined to live the life of a widow.

4.3 Depiction of Indian Beliefs and Superstitions in *Roots and Shadows*

Superstitions are deeply rooted in Indian society. Superstitions, social ills, refer to any belief or practice which is not explained by any logic. Any faith or practice which is not questioned and challenged on the basis of facts or truth is a superstition. Since superstitions don't allow the people to think logically and rationally, their strange irrational and illogical behaviour leads them to heavy losses in terms of money, health, and peace of mind. Though, Indian society is fast progressing, there are many Indians who nurture superstitions. Most Indians, like Saru's mother and many other Indian women, regularly visit temples, churches and other religious places to pray and worship God with the hope and belief that God will help them to realize their worldly needs and requirements. It is believed that if an unmarried girl worships and prays *tulsi*, she gets a good husband and that if a married woman does so, *tulsi* will keep her husband safe and sound. Indu got irritated when she was told that if she called her husband by his name, it not only showed disrespect but also shortened her husband's life. She could not control herself and exclaimed impatiently: "That's just to frighten the women, to keep them in their places. And poor fools, we do just that. What connection can there be between a man's longevity and his wife's calling him by name? It's as bad as praying to the *tulsi* to increase his life span". (Deshpande 32). She was surprised to see women piously circumambulating *tulsi*, devoutly standing in front of it with their folded hands and closed eyes. The conversation between Atya and Indu in the novel (Deshpande 32), speaks a lot about the beliefs and superstitions of Indian women:

> What's it for?
>
> You'll understand when you get married,
>
> What'll happen then?
>
> You'll have a husband. And the tulsi . . . if you pray to her . . . she'll keep him safe.
>
> Didn't you pray, Atya?
>
> I did, child. But it was not written on my forehead that I should be so fortunate.
>
> What's written on mine, Atya?
>
> Lots of good fortune, my darling.

Indu did not fail to understand what Atya meant by good fortune. She knew: "Lots of good fortune. To Atya that meant that I should not survive my husband and that I should die before him". (Deshpande 32). Fortune of the woman is believed to be determined by *tulsi* and its prayer by the woman.

Anant-kaka was in a hurry to get rid of his daughter, Mini whose horoscope had a flaw in it. Indu considered him a poor man whose family, Mini, in particular, was a burden for him. He was pleased with the man chosen by Akka for her. According to Akka it was a perfect match for Mini. Anant Kaka, too, said: "It's a good alliance . . . Yes; I think we've been lucky. Considering the family, status and all that, we've been quite lucky . . . He has two legs, two arms, two eyes, two ears . . . I'm just telling you he's a normal human being. So what if he's little dark? So what if he's not too bright?" (Deshpande 47-48). Indu was shaken with laughter to learn Kaka's list of his would-be son-in-law's qualities. According to the horoscopes it was a perfect couple. Madhav-kaka had a different opinion. He said: "Not perfect . . . But what couple could be perfectly matched? Tell me, Indu . . . you chose your own husband. Are you a made-for-each-other couple? . . . Marriage itself is a difficult enough business. For two people to merge into one identity, it's . . . almost an impossibility. But given certain things in common, languages, customs, rituals, backgrounds . . . all this makes it easier". (Deshpande 98). He meant to suggest that common language, common customs, common rituals, common background ultimately lead to a happy marriage. Indu, however, did not agree with him and his concept of a happy marriage. A happy marriage, to state the truth, depends upon trust and understanding on the part of a couple. It is a matter of sharing and respecting emotions and feelings of each other. It is ridiculous, irritating and superstitious to give importance to the castes, communities, customs, stars, *gotras*, and matching of the horoscopes in a marriage. Like superstitions, Indu thought, the caste-system has been another social evil in India.

Indian tradition believes *kumkum*, green bangles, black beads to be the symbols of wifehood; considers wifehood auspicious while widowhood inauspicious. Mini, a bride, is excited at the very thought of marriage. It's a great achievement for Mini's mother that she is getting her daughter married. Indu is surprised to see the change in Mini when Kaki lifts the saris out of the trunk. Looking at her beautiful and glowing face, Indu thinks: "I knew she was fulfilling her destiny. To her, it was the marriage that mattered, not the man". (Deshpande 4). Marriage ceremony is organized with great pleasure and excitement. The home is crowded with invitees. Indu is mystified by a happy sense of participation on the part of the relatives who have kept aside earlier animosities, misgivings and conflicts. The home is filled with the smell of flowers, food and incense sticks. Kaka has been enjoying his role of a genial host while women have been working continuously in the kitchen. As ritual follows ritual, there are ripples of excitement with an undercurrent of tension. Indu recollects: "In the afternoon, all the women in the family were equipped with green glass bangles. Mini's delicate wrists, loaded with bangles, looked like the symbol of the change in her. They lost their girlishness and seemed heavy with womanhood. Mini herself was aloof, as if caught up in some private dream of her own. She seemed to be conforming to the romantic image of the blushing bride dreaming of her bridegroom". (Deshpande 3). Indu rejects a romantic image of a bride dreaming of and eagerly waiting for her bridegroom. She believes that the image has always been false not only for Mini but for most brides in India. She does not seem to be happy with marriage, a turning point in the life of a girl.

Indu remembers a little gift given to her by her Kaka and Kaki on her wedding. She recollects: "Kaka . . . the only one in the family who had come for my wedding, apart from my Father, of course. Perhaps it was the first time Kaka had defied Akka. But he had said nothing about that. On the day, however, he had awkwardly pushed a small packet into my hands . . . I had opened it and found a piece of green silk, green bangles, packets of *haldi* and *kumkum*, all the symbols of a happy wifehood. I had been incredibly touched". (Deshpande 40). Indu, like Saru, in *The Dark Holds No Terrors*, considered herself unfortunate as she and her husband, Jayant were never invited to her ancestral home during the festivals only because she had married Jayant, the man from a different caste, against the wish of Akka. Anant-kaka once asked Indu: "How does it feel to be back, Indu? You don't know how happy I feel to see you home. I felt guilty we never asked you to come home with your husband. The first Diwali . . . I did think of it. But Akka . . .". (Deshpande 46). Anant-kaka wanted to invite them but he could not because of Akka, a matriarchal head of the family.

Indu was away from her parental home for ten years. She knew that it was not easy for her to forget the pattern of life that she had experienced before her marriage. She was trained to brush her teeth and wash her face before having a cup of tea. She went to the tap near the raised washing stone in the backyard. She preferred it to the bathroom with its slimy stone floor and huge copper vessels which were rarely cleaned. She thought: "When had they last been cleaned? There had to be an eclipse or a Diwali for the bathroom vessels to get a cleaning". (Deshpande 34). This has been a common practice followed in Hindu families. She remembered her friend, back from abroad, told her: "You know, Indu, even there, I used to remove my stockings and shoes and wash my feet in the bath tub before going to bed". (Deshpande 34). This, according to Indu, has been an Indian way of life. It is difficult for Indians to escape the compulsions, conventions and traditions. Indu knew: "We flatter ourselves that we've escaped the compulsions of the past; but we're still pinioned to it by little things. If not, why do I hesitate to have a cup of tea before washing and brushing? Why do I dislike the thought of a meal before I've had my bath?" (Deshpande 34). Jayant sarcastically called it her natural fastidiousness. With a smile, he said: "You're the same after all. Same taboos, same fetishes, under a different name". (Deshpande 35). Indu, a member of a typical Indian household with cups without ears, saucers that never matched, with no spoons, and the household, follows a few of such compulsions and conventions.

However, Indu, being revolutionary, was against certain baseless conventions and traditions. She did not like the same traditional pattern of serving the meal. Once when she tried to change it, the result had been disastrous. She remembered: "Since childhood the right method of serving food had been drilled into me. Salt here, chutney and pickles below it, vegetables on the right, *dal* in the centre, *ghee* only after serving the *dal*. The pattern was rigid and there could be no deviation from it. Once in a contray mood, I had purposely changed it. The results had been catastrophic. I had fled to Old Uncle, always my refuge then, and I cried out, 'Why can't we do it in any other way?'" (Deshpande 14). She also reacted against certain rites and rituals when she said: "A birth, a marriage, a death . . . We Hindus have elaborate rituals for all of them. They seemed meaningless to me, the rituals that Akka's husband's nephew, Shridhar, performed . . . Yet I knew it was unavoidable. Your religion claims you at last, however little you believe. We try to fool ourselves that we are not like other living things. For us, we think, death is not the end. It is the beginning of something else . . . But they don't really go anywhere, our dead". (Deshpande 58-59). After Akka's death, as her body had been taken away for her funeral rites, Indu remembered: "Outside I could hear the shuffling sounds of bare feet on the floor. They were leaving. Someone began to moan as a hoarse voice uttered the name with which Akka would be speeded on her way to heaven. *Ram, Ram, Shri Ram.* Atya clung to me conclusively . . . And then they receded . . . the footsteps, the murmurs, and the smell. We were left in silence". (Deshpande 21-22).

The woman, as we know, who dies before her husband is believed to be fortunate and a widow, who does not shave her head after her husband's death, is treated as a second class citizen. Indu was shocked to see Kaku's uncovered head. Kaku, a widow, felt pride to have two good, holy and sacred names, Ganga, the name given to her by her grandmother, and Kaveri, the name given to her by her mother-in-law. She proudly said: "Ganga . . . That was my name in my father's house. Actually, it was my grandmother who chose it. She had just returned from Kashi. What a welcome they gave her! . . . Going to Kashi was a real pilgrimage in those days. Now, you just sit in a train and reach Kashi. What merit is there in such a pilgrimage? . . . Another holy river, the Kaveri, my mother-in-law chose that one, both good and holy names". (Deshpande 118). So saying she began to weep, but she controlled herself and wiped her eyes with the end of her sari. In the process, she exposed her head which was "the bare skull, with its short hairs, looked somehow, not only indecent, but obscene when bared". (Deshpande 118). Indu then understood why Anant-kaka had strongly resisted the idea of Narmada-atya's becoming a shaven widow after the death of her husband. Indu knew: "She was now a second class citizen in the kingdom of widows. The orthodox would not eat food cooked by her". (Deshpande 118).

The woman has deliberately been kept away from the *puja* room during the periods. Indu's ancestral home, too, had a typical *puja* room. She was irritated by the convention of not allowing the unclean woman to get into the *puja* room. She was raged against the rules which make her an outcast for three days in a month. She, in a fury, had once said that she would not be a girl then. But she knew she could not break the rule of nature. She remembered Kaki complaining: "It's so difficult to know these days . . . Nobody observes the rules any more. Even Sumitra . . . whenever she comes here, she always says, 'I just finished'. You can fool people, but you can't fool the family gods". (Deshpande 119). These and many more such customs and conventions, beliefs and superstitions have been deeply rooted in Indian society. We cannot do away with all the rules and patterns, all the customs and conventions. It was from Old Uncle Indu learnt that we need to have some rules so that life can have direction and discipline, grace and dignity, and that we can always find measures of freedom within these rules. She was greatly inspired to see Old Uncle's love for and trust in gods and the great Indian heroes like Swami Vivekananda. It was, perhaps, because of Swami Vivekananda, his hero that he chose his grandson the name 'Naren'.

4.4 Reflection of Indian Rites and Rituals in *That Long Silence*

That Long Silence projects the image of a typical middle-class Indian wife accepting her husband, Mohan, as a sheltering tree. Jaya, a product of Indian customs, conventions and traditions, follows her husband silently and ungrudgingly, to suit Indian context. After their marriage, Jaya and Mohan, as per Indian convention, are initiated to play a post-wedding ceremonial game. The one who finds the coin first in the post-wedding ceremonial games rules the other at home, Jaya is told by Mohan's family. She has been moulded in such a way that she deliberately accepts a secondary role to be ruled and dominated by her male counterpart just by moving her fingers in a mound of rice in a plate, and by allowing her husband to find the coin first and win the game with the intention of having a delicately balanced relationship between them. She herself decides to accept a secondary role in her marital life. She considers herself a trodden worm. An Indian woman rarely wants to see her husband defeated in any game. About the post-wedding ceremonial game that she plays with her husband, Jaya remembers: "As we had begun, a mound of rice in a plate between us, I had deliberately dawdled, my fingers scarcely moving, while his had scrabbled frantically through the grains, groping for the coin. But it was I who had found the silver rupee first . . . Ours has been a delicately balanced relationship, so much so that we have been sniffed off bits of ourselves to keep the scales on an even keel". (Deshpande 6-7). It is her sensibility developed in Indian patriarchal set-up that makes her accept defeat in that game.

Vanitamami, another typical Indian woman, performs her early morning *tulsi-puja* almost daily. *Tulsi-puja* becomes an inseparable part of her life. Jaya recalls that moment vividly: ". . . and Vanitamami herself, with a tray of *puja* things in her hands. She was returning to the house after her early morning *tulsi-puja*; perhaps it was that which made her say what she did. 'Remember, Jaya,' she had said, 'a husband is like a sheltering tree". (Deshpande 31-32). She has full trust in her fasts as well as in her ritual circumambulations of *tulsi* plant, and of the peeple tree with the hope of attaining her aim which, in reality, is beyond her reach and attainment. Mukta also has more days of fasts than the days on which she has her normal and regular meal, with the purpose of avoiding widowhood, the basic purpose of Hindu women's fasts. She feels a sense of pride when says to Jaya: "I'm fasting today. *Hartalika*. I made this *shira* for Nilima. She wanted it and Mai got into a temper. 'The girl should be fasting today, not eating sweets,' she said". (Deshpande 133). It has been a traditional belief that a young girl gets a good husband if she fasts on *Hartalika*. Nilima scolds her mother, Mukta and remarks: "All your fasts are so stupid. Give them up, Ma, you're really horribly old-fashioned". (Deshpande 68). Nilima, truly, reacts bitterly against age-old beliefs and convictions which are not in favour of Indian women. Vimla, who is eager and desperate to be a mother, too, performs *Mangala-Gouri puja* with the hope to have a child.

Applying *haldi* and *kumkum* on the forehead, wearing green bangles and a green sari are the signs of wifehood in most cases in India. These are considered the ornaments of a married woman. When Jaya goes to her husband, Mohan's father's home, she sees the photographs of the mother and daughter which have been put up on the walls. Jaya sees the mother who "looks like any other woman of her time, staring blank-faced at the world, the huge *kumkum* on her forehead blotting out everything in that face but the 'blessed woman who died with her husband yet living . . . and Vimala? . . . I can see something in common between them, something that links the destinies of the two . . . the silence in which they died". (Deshpande 38-39). The crow is believed to be an inauspicious bird. It is also believed that the crow comes to the *pindas* of the dead who has left nothing undone in his life, and if the crow does not come to the *pindas*, it is believed that all the desires of the dead are not satisfied. It is believed that a confused cry of a bird predicts someone's death. Jaya recollects: "In Saptagiri . . . sometimes, even at night, there had been a confused cry of a bird, a cry that, for some reason, had terrified Ai. A woman full of portents and omens, she always claimed that it was this unnatural sound that had given her a premonition of Appa's death". (Deshpande 55-56).

4.5 *A Matter of Time*: A Projection of the Woman as a Puppet in the Hands of Destiny

A Matter of Time is a multi-generational story that moves around the plight and predicament of Indian women whose lives are deeply rooted in Indian beliefs, superstitions, conventions and traditions. When Gopal walks on Sumi, she is brought back to the shelter of the Big House with her three daughters. Her eldest daughter, Aru is not happy and comfortable in that house. She, with her inner sense of order, does not intend to be a part of that house. She realizes that a deliberate attempt has been made to conceal Gopal's desertion from the people. She is mature enough to realize that none of the family members have visited them, even not Goda, a sharer of Kalyani's joys and sorrows, or her daughter, Devaki, Sumi's special friend, or Ramesh, a regular visitor to the house. They know everything about the incident, but they stay away deliberately. Only Nagi, who has worked with Kalyani for more than ten years, does not show such scruples. Aru is irritated by her body language and her clucks of sympathy for 'poor things'. In a response to Aru, who exclaims in anger: "Stop staring, Nagi . . . Have I suddenly grown an extra nose", Nagi reacts: "What's the use of getting angry with me? It's all our luck, it's written here; we can't escape it. Look at my poor Lakshmi, we thought he was such a good man and he left her for that other woman". (Deshpande 14). She is a typical Indian woman who believes that a man is a helpless puppet in the hands of luck, and that everything happens as per the destiny written on his forehead. She intends to suggest that Gopal's deserting his family is an onslaught of fate. But Sumi does not think so. She knows that the reason of his deserting the family lies inside him; rather the reason is Gopal himself.

While looking at the two photographs, one of Kalyani and Goda, and the other of Kalyani and Shripati, bride and bridegroom, she remembers Gopal's words: "Destiny is just us". (Deshpande 25). She has a very strange and uneasy feeling when she looks at the photograph of husband and wife, groom and bride, her parents. She sarcastically remarks: "Destiny is just us . . . Yes, their future is here, it can be seen in this picture, clearly, what is to happen to them, to their marriage. We don't always need astrologers, palmists or horoscopes to give us a glimpse of our future lives. They lie within us . . . Destiny is just us, and therefore inescapable, because we can never escape ourselves. Certain actions are inevitable because we are what we are. In a sense, we walk on chalked lines drawn by our own selves". (Deshpande 26). She knows that it is very strange to talk about living life on chalked lines. For her, life is a magician's bag, full of odds and ends, put your hand in the bag and you never know what you get out of it. Nothing is predefined; nothing is predetermined. A magician, being an entertainer, she knows, does not take the risk of something ugly, something frightening taking out of his bag. But this is not possible in human life. We are destined to accept everything without making any selection like the magician. She, therefore, believes: "So Gopal's theory fits better after all. Destiny is just us. And yet, if Gopal's life is shaped by his being what he is, what about us, the girls and me? We are here because of his actions: how does this fit in? . . . But I have no desire really to pursue these thoughts". (Deshpande 27). Sumi has heard Kalyani blaming fate or destiny for the milk boiling over, for a sudden and untimely death, almost for everything. She has never taken the word 'fate' seriously. For her fate is something harmless, something innocent, a kind of domestic pet in her home. But Gopal's use of the word 'destiny' gives it a different and deeper colour.

Gopal becomes restless at Aru's question as to why he got married at all. He is reminded of Kalyani who said: "It was fated. You were meant to come here, to live with us, to marry my Sumi". (Deshpande 65). Everything in human life seems to be fated, destined and preordained. Man, as Thomas Hardy believed, is a plaything in the hands of destiny. Gopal is tempted to believe in what Kalyani says. He thinks to himself: "If it was indeed pre-ordained, it means that my leaving Bombay, my studying in Shivpur, my getting a job in Bangalore, coming to know about the outhouse behind Kalyani's house—all these were part of it . . . Why did I marry Sumi? Because I met her—it's as simple as that . . . I should have walked away from her then . . . A predesigned pattern we can not see because we are part of it? I remember trying to explain to Sumi that football is not just a mindless game as she thought it; it's not just a lot of grown men kicking a ball about, as she said. I tried to tell her that there is a plan behind all that aimless kicking, the seemingly haphazard passing. That all those actions which seemed futile and unconnected were in reality part of a plan, a working towards an end—a goal". (Deshpande 65-66). He believes that the aimless kicking of the ball in the game of football has a definite plan behind it. Similarly, no action in human life is aimless. Every action in human life is a part of the plan which works towards an ultimate goal.

Gopal knows that we have a very complex relationship with the past. It is the past, in one way or the other, knowingly or unknowingly, reshapes our present life, our dreams and desires. The truth is that human life can be lived forwards, but it can only be understood backwards, and that the present is modified by the past. It is their preoccupation with the past which has brought Gopal and Kalyani, Gopal and Sumi together. However, Kalyani and Gopal look at the past in different ways. For Kalyani, everything in the world is pre-ordained and we are mere instruments in the hands of destiny. To her, even Bhagiratha's bringing the river Ganges down to the earth is not, as it is to Gopal, a magnificent human act, the act of human determination. Yamunabai, a daughter of a well-to-do landlord, who has a strong desire to work for the realization of her vision, her vision of doing something constructive for girls and women who live with nothing more in their lives than the slavery of endless drudgery and childbearing by giving them education, too, like Kalyani, believes: "We must never forget that we are the only instruments". (Deshpande 188). She believes in her *mantra*: "*Nimittamatram bhava Savyasachi*'—be thou only the instrument, Arjuna. The end is not us, it is outside us, it is quite separate from us". (Deshpande 188). Gopal believes that past and present are inseparable. He strongly believes: "Yes, we need to know our beginnings. Without that we are forever exiles, forever homeless . . . But we don't really have to go out in search of our beginnings; it lies in us . . . Karna didn't need the armour Kunti had put by him when she abandoned him as a baby; the knowledge of his *Kshatriyahood* was part of him, it was through this knowledge that he reached an idea of himself . . . It's a fool's game trying to escape". (Deshpande 217-18). Sumi, too, believes that it is a cycle, nothing comes to an end, things go on coming back again and again, they are all connected.

Indians, generally, are the people who believe in idols of gods, *pujas*, fasts, rites and rituals. Though, Kalyani's father, Vithalrao was neither a religious man nor a believer in idols and rituals, he brought and installed a *Ganapati* idol in the niche above the front door of the house he was building. Kalyani's mother was not happy with this installation because it was too high to perform its *puja*. However, she performed her *puja* twice a month with the help of her servant who used to climb a ladder to clean it and offer some flowers to the idol. The tradition of performing *puja* is continued by Bora. Sumi knows: ". . . he cleans the idol with Nagi assisting and Kalyani watching. He wipes it with a wet cloth until the god emerges glossy and shining, clear of his filmy veil of dust and cobwebs, his pot belly gleaming, one leg daintily crossed over the other. Finally, putting a dot of *kumkum* on the forehead, Bora tucks a hibiscus behind one ear and another in the loop of the trunk. Then climbing down the ladder, he looks with satisfaction at his work before folding his hands reverently". (Deshpande 115). Kalyani, too, imitating her mother whom she must have seen performing such kind of *puja* as a child, continues her tradition, folds her hands and mutters: "Look after us, *Ganapati*, protect us". (Deshpande 115). It has been a common belief of the Indians who believe in God that He looks after and protects us. However, Sumi, to her own surprise, responds by saying that God does not do such a good job of looking after women who suffer. She feels that the idol is only a piece of stone after all.

Indians believe that life and death are in the hands of God. They believe in certainty of death and immortality of human soul. After Sumi and Shripati's accidental death, hundreds of people gather to attend their funeral ceremony. It is a strangely silent gathering of the people. There is no loud display of sorrow even from the family, either, with the exception of Charu. Aru and Charu watch their mother and grandfather leave the house never to return. They stand in an utter silence as their bodies are taken away. Gopal is staring at the river in which the ashes of the dead are mingled. He remembers and thinks over the word *Runmukta* uttered by the priest at the end of a small ceremony. He knows that the dead are free now, free of all human debts, human duties and responsibilities, free of everything. Human lives, the grief and mourning of the living for the dead, everything is ephemeral, everything passes, nothing remains. He believes: "Yes, Sumi is free, but at the cost of her body, of life itself. Is this freedom? You must not grieve for the dead. Yes, don't grieve, because they have not gone, they are still with us, they will always be with us . . . But Sumi's body has gone, there is nothing left of it . . . we live through our bodies, we relate to the world, to others, through our bodies . . . But there's P. K.'s theory that death only means that your role is over and you go backstage into the darkness while the play goes on . . . I want to believe in it . . . I will learn to live with the knowledge that Sumi is dead . . . And yet, if Sumi has truly gone . . . why do I, sitting by this river, see her clearly? I can see her floating in, her body weightless, her face serene, smiling at me. I see her sitting on the river bank, her child in her arms, her face gleaming and beautiful in the twilight". (Deshpande 237-38). He is haunted by Sumi's memory. He comes to the realization that nothing comes to an end, the dead leave their mark on the world, the mark that enables the living to live their life in this world. He thinks to himself: "If it is indeed true that we are bound to our destinies, and there is no point struggling against them, even then this remains—that we do not submit passively or cravenly, but with dignity and strength". He will carry this thought with him throughout his life.

A Middle-Class Indian Woman: A Victimized Creature

CHAPTER 5

5.1 An Indian Woman: A Victim of Social Evils

Deshpande's novels focus on the place and position, plight and predicament of a middle-class Indian woman who is treated as a subordinate member of a tradition-bound, male-oriented society. She is born and destined to bear everything—children, sorrows, sufferings, oppression, suppression, subjugation, torture, injustice and exploitation. Social issues such as male-ego and male-domination, gender-discrimination, urge for a male child, patriarchal attitude to a female being, caste-system, dowry, child-marriage and others have been hampering the growth and development of the woman's self and individuality. Though an Indian woman, to a large extent, is the architect of her destiny, she is a puppet in the hands of Indian patriarchal society with its ills and evils, age-old beliefs and superstitions, conventions and traditions. Her life is moulded by Indian milieu. Naturally, she is so fluid and flexible that you can pour her into any mould. Women all over India suffer from similar psychic disturbances on account of patriarchal attitude to them in a male dominated world.

5.1.1 Gender-discrimination: A Curse for the Indian Female

In connection with the difference between man and woman, Simone de Beauvoir writes: "One is not born, but rather becomes, a woman. No biological, psychological, or economic fate determines the figure that the human female presents in society; it is civilization as a whole that produces this creature, intermediate between male and eunuch, which is described as feminine". (Beauvoir 295). A woman suffers a lot on account of the issue of gender-distinction. Sandra Harding writes: "Gender difference is the most ancient, most universal, and most powerful origin of many morally valued conceptualizations of everything else in the world around us . . . As far back in the history as we can see, we have organized our social and natural worlds in terms of gender meanings . . . Once we begin to theorize gender to define gender as an analytical category within which humans think about and organize their social activity rather than as a natural consequences of sex difference, or even merely as a social variable assigned to individual people in different ways from culture to culture, we can begin to appreciate the extent to which gender meanings have suffered our belief systems . . . institutions". (Harding 71).

Though a little girl is as strong as her male-counterpart, she is treated as an inferior creature. She is treated as a live doll and is denied equality and liberty. Our customs, conventions and traditions do not treat girls as boys are treated. The treasures of feminine wisdom are poured into her ears and feminine virtues are thrust into her. She is not allowed to question, argue, think, and to fight. She is not expected to be clever and intelligent. Old Uncle, in *Roots and Shadows*, says to Indu: "For a woman, intelligence is always a burden . . . We like our women not to think". (Deshpande 33). She is trained to submit, wait, complain, weep and ultimately to surrender. She has no choice but to submit and to accept. It is Indu who says: "A woman's life contained no choices. And all my life, especially in this house, I had seen the truth of this. The woman had no choice but to submit, to accept. And I had often wondered . . . have they been born without wills". (Deshpande 6). She is made a timid and subdued creature. She is trained to stay at home; her comings and goings, her actions and activities are always watched and controlled by her male-counterpart. She is not encouraged to take charge of her wills and desires, amusements and pleasures, dreams and aspirations.

Women in India suffer a lot owing to the biased and patriarchal attitude to them. Surprisingly, women themselves, to a large extent, are responsible for the issue of gender-discrimination. Saru, in *The Dark Holds No Terrors*, is a victim of gender-discrimination, an issue kept burning by her mother. Her mother's biased attitude to her creates a sense of remorse and revolt in her. Her life has been rooted in nothingness, emptiness and uneasiness as a result of ill-treatment that she receives from her mother. Her mother always curses her as no mother ever should because she is a girl child. Her father, a typical Indian father, believes that it is the duty of a mother to look after her daughter. He seldom takes interest in her school or college. He has left it all to her mother who really never cares for her. She does not exist for her after Dhruva's death. She is held responsible for her younger brother's death. She has been disinherited and ignored by her mother. Her agony lies in the fact that she fails to answer her daughter, Renu's question: "Who is Dhruva?" (Deshpande 34). She does not know how to respond to her question. She thinks to herself: "Why do I never tell her . . . Dhruva was my kid brother who died when he was seven. He was drowned. I watched him drown. And my mother said . . . Why didn't you die? Why are you alive and he dead?" (Deshpande 34-35). She keeps her agony, pain and unhappiness suppressed in her. She is terribly shocked by what her mother said in one of her conversations with her:

> Don't go out in the sun. You'll get even darker.
>
> Who cares?
>
> We have to care if you don't. We have to get you married.
>
> I don't want to get married.
>
> Will you live with us all your life?
>
> Why not?
>
> You can't.
>
> And Dhruva?
>
> He's different. He's a boy. (Deshpande 45)

Saru has a strong desire to be a doctor. She does not want just to get married and end up doing just what her mother did.

She works hard, gives up all her pleasures and concentrates on her studies. She scores the first class in her Inter Science, a passport to a medical college. But her mother is against her medical education only because she is a girl. She wants to get rid of her by giving her away in marriage as soon as she completes her degree. She is considered a responsibility to be given away in marriage by her parents. She tells Saru on her face that they cannot spend money on her education as well as on her marriage. In this connection, Veena Das writes: "Daughters are comparable to something kept in trust for another (*anamat*). You have to care for them, love them, and you will be held responsible for them but you are destined to lose them. Once a daughter is properly married and goes to her own house, it is like a debt that has been paid". (Das 93). Saru's mother has this approach to her daughter. She says to her husband: "And don't forget medicine or no medicine, doctor or no doctor, you still have to get her married, spend money on her wedding. Can you do both? Make yourself a pauper, and will she look after you in your old age? . . . Let her go for a B.Sc . . . you can get her married in two years and our responsibility will be over". (Deshpande 144). Saru has been tortured by the grief of being unwanted, being ignored and ill-treated especially by her mother. She expresses her agony: "Nobody likes me. Nobody cares for me. Nobody wants me". (Deshpande 83).

In a response to her mother's 'no' to her medical education, she shouts bitterly: "I'm not talking to you; I'm not asking you for anything. I know what your answer will be. No, forever a 'no' to anything I want. You don't want me to have anything; you don't want me to do anything. You don't even want me to live". (Deshpande 142). A huge gap develops between Saru and her mother. Her mother dislikes and curses her. Saru believes that she is unhappy and destroyed because of her mother's curse. She remembers Prof. Kulkarni's words: "I always imagined no mother could ever dislike her own child. But Saru's mother seems to be an exception. She shocked me. Imagine saying . . . I will pray for her unhappiness. Let her know more sorrow than she has given me". (Deshpande

197). However, her father is ready to help and support her so that she can go ahead and do what she wants. He says: "You know my salary isn't very much. Oh yes, I can pay your fees and for your books and hostel . . . but nothing more. No luxuries. You'll have to manage with whatever I send . . . Will you manage without complaining?" (Deshpande 143-44). Her father's support signifies a victory for Saru. The most needed and welcome support that she receives from him gives her a golden opportunity to set herself free from her mother's trap of gender-discrimination and to realize her dream of going to medical education. Her joining medical college in spite of her mother, standing up against her, asserting her will against her, everything in itself has been a kind of miracle which is possible, Saru knows, only because of her father's support. She admits: "I won that time. But I was not alone then. *Baba* was with me. He helped me. Without him, I would have never succeeded". (Deshpande 139).

As a child, Indu, in *Roots and Shadows*, was often told to be meek and submissive, obedient and unquestioning. She recollects: "As a child, they had told me I must be obedient and unquestioning. As a girl, they had told me I must be meek and submissive . . . You must accept everything, even defeat, with grace because you are a girl, they had said. It is the only way, they said, for a female to live and survive . . . But still, I had laughed at them, and sworn I would never pretend to be what I was not". (Deshpande 158). Though she does not want to be meek and submissive, in the course of her life, she begins to believe that the only way for the woman to live is to be meek and submissive, to live her life according to the demands and requirements of her male-counterpart, to surrender to him, and to make compromises by shedding bits of herself along the way. Being a typical member of Indian society in which sons are preferred to daughters, Padmani is right when she says: "What choice do I have Indu? . . . Of course, I am marrying him because there's nothing else I can do. I'm not good at studies. I never was. I went to school because . . . I had to, and then to college because Akka said I must go. So I went. But I failed and it was a relief to give it up. There's only one thing I'm really good at . . . looking after a house. And to get a home, I have to get married. This is not my home, is it? . . . You know it isn't. Ever since we were small, we were told . . . 'You'll be going away one day to your own home'. They said it to you and me, never to Hemant or Sumant or Sharad or Sunil". (Deshpande 125). She feels as if she has committed a crime of being born as a girl.

Indian society has been following a son-oriented tradition. Indu thinks that her father left her as a fifteen-day old motherless baby only because she was a girl. He did not come to see her until she was more than a year old. Indu now feels that he would not have done so if she had been a son. She knows: "It was a tradition in our family that girls were left to their mothers; that a daughter was exclusively the mother's business. When his girls were in school, Madhav-kaka had never known what class they were in. But Sunil's education was so scrupulously and harshly supervised by him that Sunil had turned deceitful, with the connivance, of course, of his mother". (Deshpande 163). However, Vinayaka-kaka, to Indu's surprise, was the only exception to this tradition. He was fond of his daughters, his youngest daughter, in particular. He used to enjoy plaiting her hair and tying a bow in her sash. But women in the family did not like this deviation from the tradition, from the normal Hindu moral code. They were of the view that Kamala-kaki, his wife, was inadequate and incomplete both as a wife and a mother.

Deshpande highlights the social issue of gender-discrimination in her novel, *That Long Silence*, too. Though, Dilip and Kusum are born of the same parents, they are treated differently by their mother, Vanitamami. Even when Dilip failed in his matriculation examination, his mother fondly said: "Our Dilip is a non-matric . . . Everyone scared of our Dilip . . . He's the leader of the unions and the factory owners give him money to keep him pleased". (Deshpande 22). She never got tired of admiring him only because he was a son. Dilip was born for success whereas Kusum for failure and defeat. Kusum was neglected because she was a female. It was Jaya who could feel her anguish, fear and despair. When Kusum killed herself, no one felt sorry for her death. Jaya's mother wrote to her: ". . . but it was a good thing in a way. She was of no use to anyone after she went crazy, nobody needed her". (Deshpande 22). Her words, 'of no use to anyone' frightened Jaya, who thought: "Maybe her fate was sealed when she was born to those feckless, hopeless parents of hers. A father who cared for nothing but smoking and movies, who never worked a day in his life; a mother whose world centred round her youngest, the baby on her lap, while the rest of her kids ran around in wild abandon, unkempt, dirty, unfed . . . what chance did Kusum have with parents like that?" (Deshpande 22).

Female characters, minor as well as major, in Deshpande's novels, suffer a lot on account of the issue of gender-distinction. Manorama, Kalyani, Sumi, Aru and others, in *A Matter of Time*, are caught in a trap of gender-distinction in one way or the other. Sumi, being a married woman, feels that she does not belong to her parents' house. She feels a parasite in the house. She remembers she was not allowed to have male friends. She cannot forget restrictions imposed on her by her father. She recollects: "Yet, when I was at home, he disapproved of all my friends, boys, especially. He saw me once with a boy and said, 'Remember my dignity'. And then I found Gopal right here at home". (Deshpande 73). He now does not like Charu going on Hrishi's motorcycle. Kalyani, too, regrets her not getting permission to complete her schooling. She once said: "I was a clever girl. I was very good at Maths like my father. He wanted me to become an engineer—can you believe that? You will be the first woman engineer in the country, he used to say". (Deshpande 128-29). As Saru's mother was against her higher education, Kalyani's mother, Manorama was against her education. Saru was fortunate enough to complete her medical education as a result of the support she received from her father, Kalyani was not. She was not allowed to complete her schooling. She was taken out of school and married off by Manorama to her own brother, Shripati, thus giving a full stop to her education. Manorama was not at all happy with Kalyani only because she was a girl. Kalyani knows: "I was a great disappointment to her, not only because I was a girl, but because . . . I was none of those things she would have liked her daughter to be. I was not beautiful, not smart . . . I feel very sad sometimes to think that I gave her no joy at all. My mother didn't care for my children, either. Daughters again, she said". (Deshpande 226). Kalyani's approach to her daughters differs from that of Manorama. She is proud of her daughters and her granddaughters.

Deshpande's girls, with the exception of Saru, Indu, and even Sumi have no role to play in choosing their life partners. They do not have any freedom to take any decision on their own. Their marriages are arranged either by their parents or by their relatives. Sumi's sister, Premi tells Gopal about her marriage: "Do you know what the truth is, Gopal? When I came home after my finals, I didn't know it myself, that I was to marry Anil, I mean. Anil doesn't believe me, but that's the truth. *Amma* didn't know, either. I was the one who told her . . . It was the same about my going to Bombay to do medicine. *Baba* got the forms for me; he told me to fill them up and said I was to go to Bombay. I can't help thinking that *Baba* sent me away to punish *Amma*". (Deshpande 132). Both, Sumi and Premi have the same experience. Sumi's talk with her male friend is followed by her marriage with Gopal, and Premi, too, does not know that she is getting married to Anil. Being girls, they are not taken into confidence in any matter; rather, they have no role to play in decision-making. They are destined to accept the decisions made by their parents and to submit to the restrictions imposed on them in Indian patriarchy.

When Sumi decides to stop her search for a separate house for her and continue to stay on with her parents, she remembers Nagaraj, an estate agent who said: "That's a very good decision, madam, a very wise decision, safer for you and your daughters to be with your parents. The world is not a good place for women to be on their own . . . And this is your parents' property, I think you said . . . but some day it will be yours". (Deshpande 195). Sumi gets excited at the idea of the property belonging to her one day or the other. Her mind moves around the words: 'Some day it will be yours'. She feels and experiences a sense of attachment to the house for the first time. She thinks to herself: "Mine. No, ours. It will be Premi's and mine—or will it? Knowing *Baba*, it could well be Nikhil's. He's the only male in the family. Nikhil belongs to his father's family, he most clearly and emphatically does; yet, to *Baba* he may be the only possible heir". (Deshpande 195). Well aware of Indian conventions and traditions, according to which, the property belongs only to the male, she is angry with herself for these thoughts but they do not leave her. She is ashamed of herself for these thoughts but she can do nothing as they are deeply rooted in her mind. Kalyani, once, said to Aru: "Daughters don't belong. All three of you birds will fly away to your own nests". (Deshpande 198). She knows that from time immemorial the daughters are given away in marriages.

5.1.2 Indian Urge for a Male Child

Urge to have a male child is a social evil deeply rooted in Indian society. It is an irony of a woman's life that the woman herself has a strong desire for a male child. Saru has been hated and cursed by her mother only because she is a girl. Her mother is so blind in her love for her dead son that she holds her daughter responsible for his death. Her daughter does not exist for her. She regrets that she has no son to light the pyre. It is difficult for Saru to forget Manda and her parents' visit to her. She remembers Manda's mother who said: "We're staying with Suresh . . . he's in Andheri. And Manda got married two years back. Her husband is a lawyer. This is her first child, a son". (Deshpande 23-34). Manda's mother can not conceal her beaming and glittering face when she says, 'her first child, a son'. Manda is lucky to have her first child, a baby boy. Vinayaka-kaka and Kamala-kaki, husband and wife, in *Roots and Shadows*, blame and curse themselves for having only daughters, and for having no son. Akka, the head and the prop of the family, always had a soft corner for boys. Though, Sharad does not do a stroke of work in the house, he, being a boy, is everybody's pet. Nobody asks him to stop studying though he fails only because he is a boy. Padmani's mother prefers a fellow chosen by Akka as Padmani's husband only because he is the only son in the family; he is the only successor of the family wealth and property. She does not even think of the idea of giving her daughter's hands to Naren, who, according to her, is a good for nothing fellow. She says: "Really, Indu, how could you have imagined that I'd give my daughter to that vagabond, that fellow without a job, without money, without a home? . . . How can you even compare the two? Look at that family, that house . . . have you seen it? It's even bigger than ours . . . their lands? My daughter will be the mistress of all that. He's the only son, you know". (Deshpande 119-20). Sunanda-atya with her fair complexion, which gave her husband at the young age of sixteen, has been treated as a lucky girl only because her first child is a boy.

Kusum, a typical Indian woman, in *That Long Silence*, has been emotionally attached to her children. Vanitamami, much worried about Kusum, used to ask Jaya: "Why don't you take our Kusum to a lady doctor, a poor thing, she has three daughters, at least let the fourth be a son". (Deshpande 21). Nayana, a mother of four children, two girls who lived and two boys who died soon after their birth, now carrying her unborn child for the fifth time, a child-producing machine, passing her hand tenderly over her swollen abdomen, says to Jaya: "This time, . . . it is going to be a boy . . . Why give birth to a girl . . . who'll only suffer because of men all her life? . . . No, no . . . better to have a son". (Deshpande 27-28). Though she hates and curses men, her husband, her brothers, and her father as wasters, good-for-nothings, drunkards, she has a strong desire to have a son, who, she feels, would be her solace and support. Jaya is shocked to read an account of how baby girls were put to death, buried alive. She has a sense of bitterness for her mother who showered special affection on her sons, affection of which she was deprived. She regrets: "When I had passionately wanted her love, she had ignored me and concentrated on her sons . . . When I got married, she had been unperturbed, and there had been not even pretence of tears when I had left home". (Deshpande 106). When Anil, pregnant Mukta's husband, died, she was comforted by the thought that the child yet to be born would be a baby boy. But to Mukta's dismay, a baby girl, Nilima is born. Jaya's grandmother, too, who prefers a boy to a girl, gives all her jewels to Chandumama, who has no children, only because he is a male.

After Gopal's departure, Sumi with three daughters, in *A Matter of Time*, is brought back to her parental house. She feels an intruder in that home. She thinks: "We're interlopers, my daughters and I". (Deshpande 70-71). She remembers that it was Goda who sang the song at Nikhil's naming ceremony, a song full of joy, a woman sharing her joy on the birth of her son with her neighbours, friends and relatives. She has seen the adoration of the male child in her song: "A son is born to me, dear friend, a son is born to me . . . Nine months I bore the pain and now my house is filled with light". (Deshpande 71). The song makes her feel that the very purpose, the very reason of her existence is to give birth to a son. The house at the birth of a male child is full of joy and excitement. Being a boy, Nikhil's presence itself livens the family up. He is shamelessly pampered by everyone. Even Shripati does not mind his frequent visits to his room. Running up and down the stairs, he creates a link between the room and the rest of the house. In spite of the family's concern for her and Nikhil's special affection for her, Sumi with her three daughters begins to suffer from a sense of not belonging to the house. During her search for the house, she is shattered to pieces by the pain and agony of the woman, Ramchandra Rao's wife, who has lost her only son in an accident. The woman seems to have lost the very purpose of her life after the accidental death of her only son. The dialogue between the woman and Sumi, to Sumi's surprise, highlights the very significance of the son in the life of the woman:

> "How many children do you have?
>
> Three.
>
> Sons? Daughters?
>
> Daughters.

We have only one son. He died three months back in a car accident. He was returning from Mysore. We built the upstairs flat for him. He was to get married". (Deshpande 81).

Gopal, too, admits that life without a son has no meaning. To Premi, he says: "I could no longer believe that there is a meaning to my life, a happy culmination waiting for me at the end of it. Can you imagine what living with such a person would be for my children? For Sumi? . . . For you, it's Nikhil, isn't it? But not for me . . . No, Premi, the meaning has to be found in your own life". (Deshpande 134). There is every reason to doubt that he, a typical Indian husband, is pining for a son. Premi's spontaneous response to Aru's question, 'what do you get out of it?', 'There's Nikhi'. (Deshpande 138), underlines her pride to have a son. She frankly admits that her son, Nikhil is the outcome of her marriage. Moreover, how can one forget the truth that it is Shripati and Kalyani's lost son, Madhav is responsible for a strangely oppressive silence between them.

However, Vithalrao, Manorama's husband, is an exception to a conventional desire to have a son. He does not submit to any pressure either to marry again when his wife, who is denied a son, finally gives birth to a daughter after a series of miscarriages or to adopt a son, preferably one of his own grandsons. Rejecting both the pressures, he says: "Why should I leave my property to a stranger, to someone else's child, rather than to my own daughter, no, to my own two daughters?" (Deshpande 128). Manorama is disappointed with Kalyani, a concrete and visible symbol of her failure to have a son. She manages Kalyani's marriage with her brother, Shripati, a silent, withdrawn, intelligent and ambitious young man who was given support and co-operation by Vithalrao to complete his education and to get a job in the office of his friend, a renowned lawyer in Bombay. Kalyani, who has been a great cause of her mother's disappointment, can do nothing to please her mother except once when she gives birth to a baby boy. At the birth of a baby boy in Shripati's family, "there was a great rejoicing then. Vithalrao, joking, had called it a red carpet lying-in. It was literally that, for there was a beautiful red carpet by Kalyani's bedside for her to put her feet on, the moment she got out of bed. And the fire under the huge copper pot burned all day, so that Kalyani had hot water to wash even her little finger. The naming ceremony was memorable. The house was full of guests, fragrant with flowers, gleaming with silverware. The poor were fed and the dustbin in the street was overflowing with banana-leaf plates for two whole days". (Deshpande 151). The family proves to be a typical Indian family full of joy and excitement at the birth of a baby boy.

5.2 Plight of a Tradition-bound Indian Woman

An Indian woman is caught in the trap of beliefs and superstitions, conventions and traditions deeply rooted in Indian society. She, a caged creature, is deprived of justice, equality and liberty. She does not have a free and autonomous existence apart from her male-counterpart. She is controlled and dictated by the males before as well as after her marriage. She is not allowed to share the world in equality as the world belongs to the males. She is treated as an inferior member of her society. She has been facing suppression, subjugation, injustice and exploitation. Indian women novelists in English including Deshpande have been concerned with the projection of the image of an Indian woman struggling against the oppressive social norms of a male-dominated society. Deshpande's novels, in particular, carry the readers deep into the inner psyche of her women characters who are torn within on account of the tensions generated by the discord between the individual dreams and aspirations, and the oppressive social milieu.

5.2.1 'The Dark Holds No Terrors': The Woman's Fight for Survival

The Dark Holds No Terrors is a psychological journey undertaken by Saru in her quest for her self-realization and self-exploration. It is about her struggle to realize her dreams and aspirations, and to set herself free from the norms and restrictions imposed on her by Indian patriarchy. She is frustrated as a young girl as a result of the issue of gender-discrimination and the preference given to Dhruva, her younger brother by her mother. In order to set herself free from the hatred and tyranny of her mother, she decides to go to the field of medicine, to earn and to stand on her own legs, thereby proving herself as an independent individual. She marries Manohar against her parents with a hope to enjoy the fruits of freedom. During the earlier days of her married life, she reaches the zenith of love and security of which she was deprived in her parental home. Her husband showers love and happiness in the form of sex on her. Each act of sex has been a triumphant assertion of his love for her. She begins to feel that her problems are over after her marriage, and she finds herself almost in the heaven.

But very soon her marriage begins to lead her towards frustration. As soon as she gains recognition as a lady doctor, her celebration of love comes to an end. Her marriage begins to break under the weight of her success in her profession. Her husband's ego does not allow him to tolerate her success and popularity as a doctor. A traditional equilibrium of a superior husband and an inferior wife begins to be disturbed by her recognition as a doctor. He becomes a jealous and a sexually aggressive husband. He attacks her like a wild animal. She becomes a victim of his bestiality and brutality. She is terrified and totally shattered by the horrors of the marital rape imposed on her by her husband. She feels utterly humiliated at the thought of being used for her husband's sexual pleasure. Unable to bear the torture any more, and with the hope to free herself from that torture, on hearing about her mother's death, she decides to go back to her parental home, the home she had vowed never to come back to. She frankly tells her father about her sexually aggressive husband: "I never knew till then he has so much strength in him . . . I could do nothing against him. I couldn't fight back . . . I could do nothing. I can never do anything. I just endure . . . Yes, again and again and again and yet again. I've lost count". (Deshpande 201).

Marriage plays a vital role in the life of men and women, especially in the life of women. Ideally, it is a special kind of friendship, a special kind of partnership between husband and wife, the success of which depends upon trust and understanding, adjustment and compromise. Sarita herself said in an interview given to a woman's magazine: "It's all a question of adjustment, really. If you want to make it work, you can always do it". (Deshpande 118). However, she loses her faith in marriage and marital partnership. Her eternal female dream of finding happiness through a man remains unrealized. She expresses her feminine agony in her talk to the girl students. She says: "But if you want to be happily married, there's one thing you have to remember. Have you girls seen an old-fashioned couple walking together? Have you noticed that the wife always walks a few steps behind her husband? If he is an MA, you should be a BA. If he's 5′4″ tall, you shouldn't be more than 5′3″ tall. If he's earning five hundred rupees, you should never earn more than four hundred and ninety-nine rupees. That's the only rule to follow if you want a happy marriage. Don't ever try to reverse the doctor-nurse, executive-secretary, principal-teacher role. It can be traumatic, disastrous . . . Women's magazines will tell you that a marriage should be an equal partnership. That's nonsense. Rubbish. No partnership can ever be equal. It will always be unequal, but take care that it's unequal in favour of your husband. If the scales tilt in your favour, god help you, both of you. And so you must pretend that you're not as smart as you really are, not as competent as you are, not as rational as you are, not as strong either. You can nag, complain, henpeck, whine, moan, but you can never be strong. That's wrong which will never be forgiven. Don't struggle, don't swim against the tide. Go along with it; and if you drown nevertheless, well, that's an easier death after all. They will teach you about economic independence and an independent identity. Forget the words. If Draupadi had been economically independent, if Sita had had an independent identity, you think their stories would have been different? No, these are things that have been voluntarily surrendered, consciously abandoned, because that is the only way to survive, and what, in the long run, matters more than survival". (Deshpande 137-38). This has been a tragic and pathetic tale of an Indian woman from time immemorial.

Saru, a typical Indian female, grows and lives within the oppositional and conflicting structures of freedom and bondage, male-domination and resistance, a space within which she accepts and challenges the conventional norms and values of Indian family and society. She struggles to survive in the world totally dominated by the males. She suffers a lot in her pre-marital life as well as her marital life. She has a very bad childhood because of her mother who prefers her son to her daughter. When she hears of her mother's death, her first thought is: ". . . who lit the pyre? She had no son to do that for her. Dhruva had been seven when he died". (Deshpande 21). She has been a neglected and unwanted child. She is made to feel a stranger in her parental home dominated by her mother. Relationship between Saru ans her mother is deeply rooted in hatred. She knows her mother always curses her. Differentiation that her mother makes between her son and daughter hurts Saru's ego and cracks her identity. She remembers the smell of flowers and the atmosphere filled with joyous excitement on Dhruva's naming day.

She remembers the story narrated by her mother, the story of mythological Dhruva, the child who was pushed off his father's lap by his stepbrother, and who, full of anger, sorrow and humiliation, gave himself to a steadfast meditation as a result of which he became the constant North Star. Saru's younger brother was named after that Dhruva from a myth. She recollects: "There was always a *puja* on Dhruva's birth day. A festive lunch in the afternoon and an *aarti* in the evening during which Dhruva, as an infant, sat solemnly on *Baba's* lap, and as a child, by his side, cap on head, fatuous smile on face, while I helped my mother to do the *aarti*. My birthdays were almost the same . . . a festive lunch, with whatever I asked for . . . but there was no *puja*". (Deshpande 168-69). After Dhruva's death, there were no celebrations at home. Her birthdays were passed over in silence.

Her mother blames Saru for Dhruva's death. She is haunted by her mother's words; "She killed her brother. She killed her brother". (Deshpande 145). Saru fails to say: "I didn't. Truly I didn't. I loved him, my little brother. I tried to save him. Truly I tried. But I couldn't. And I ran away. Yes, I ran away, I admit that. But I didn't kill him". (Deshpande 146). She is accused of something she never did. It is impossible for her to bear the burden of the guilt. She can do nothing but to bear it. She can share her sorrow with no one. She is almost disinherited. She does not receive emotional support even from her father. She has a strong urge to confide, to talk to someone, but there is no one to comfort her. She considers herself a wronged child, an unloved daughter, a scapegoat.

Saru is sensible enough to know that she is not the only woman who is destined to suffer in her life. As a child, she had seen her grandmother who was deserted by her husband a few years after their marriage. Her grandmother's father had taken the deserted woman with her daughters to his house and got the girls married. Her grandmother had never complained and accepted everything with a belief that it was her fate written on her forehead. She was a young woman with two little daughters then, one of whom was Kamala, Saru's mother. It was *Mai-Kaki* for whom Saru's mother was a brave woman, a woman of courage who never complained, a woman who was immensely strong. Even when she was dying, she had a sense of hatred for Saru. When *Mai-Kaki* asked her to go to Saru, she said: "What daughter? I have no daughter". (Deshpande 109). Saru is too unfortunate to get motherly affection from her mother. There has been something unpleasant in the way she looked at her. For her, Saru is an ugly girl. Saru remembers her mother dispassionately saying: "You will never be good looking. You are too dark for that . . . I'll give you a certificate to say that you're beautiful. Will that satisfy you?" (Deshpande 61). Tired of unbearable tension and anxiety, her mother's dislike and hatred for her, Saru, in a fever of excitement, defies her parents, marries Manohar and unfortunately is caught in the trap of marital violence.

As a growing girl, on her way to school, Saru had often seen the woman on the doorstep seeing her husband off, their hands touching each other, a contact so swiftly ended that it was like a passing shadow. She was fascinated by their smiling at each other, oblivious of everything else. The world around them did not exist for them. Unfortunately, Saru could not find such type of a man-woman relationship at her own home. She saw the same woman after a few days, now as a widow with a bare forehead and a drab sari. Her eyes, lost and empty, were the symbols of her widowhood. She was frightened to see her eyes indicating that she was nothing without her husband. She was terrified by the thought of putting all of herself into another and then be left alone after her husband's death. She was tempted to compare herself with that woman. She was nothing even though her husband was alive. She was tired almost of everything—marital-violence, male-savagery and total submission. She was tired of monotonous pattern of her life which kills the emotional aspect of her life. She wanted to be alone, to sleep peacefully, to wake up without any pain, to live without any fear, and just to live without thinking and dreaming.

The woman, from time immemorial, has been content with a secondary and subordinate role assigned to her in various fields of life including literature. Sarita remembers Vidya, one of her friends, who was interested in acting and was very much absorbed in the theatre, and loved it with a great passion. On Shakespeare, she, once, burst out: "We all know he's the greatest dramatist of all times . . . But, shall I tell you men one thing? He has a very limited vision . . . What I'm saying is that his is a typical man's view of life—the man at the centre, the woman always on the periphery . . . Well, look at the way he made the women always subordinate to the men . . . He made the woman's personality merge into the stronger colours of a man's personality. Look at Hamlet, Lear, Othello; and look at Ophelia, Cordelia, Desdemona, poor, feeble shadows. And when you come to a conflict or a climax, the woman recedes into the background". (Deshpande 155-56). This has really been a sordid reality that the woman is made to move around the man and to live according to his desires and plans.

Saru knows Vidya had to give up her passion for acting and theatre after her marriage. She remembers her words: "Ashwin doesn't like the idea of my going on the stage. His family disapproves it too. They don't mind my associating with the theatre occasionally, but no acting, directing or anything like that". (Deshpande 156). Vidya is made to accept the old and traditional pattern of marital life which seems an oasis, a haven of peace, comfort and security, where the husband goes out to work and earn money, the woman stays at home, looks after it, looks after her husband and children, cooks and cleans, scrubs and sweeps. It is unfortunate that she is not allowed to dream of freedom, or to be more precise, she does not dream of freedom. The woman who desires independence is considered a wanton girl. Saru remembers an episode from Kalidasa's *Shakuntala* told by her friend, Nalu. When Shakuntala was rejected by her husband who was a king, she was advised to stay on in the King's harem, or as his slave, because he was, after all, her husband. When Shakuntala, weeping, shamed, humiliated, tried, in spite of this noble advice, to follow the ascetics back home, one of them turned round and thundered at her: ". . . What a wanton girl, do you desire independence?" (Deshpande 138).

Smita, Saru's friend, is another example of a typical middle-class Indian woman. She is a dedicated housewife who always submits and surrenders. She has surrendered so much that like Jaya who becomes Suhasini after her marriage in *That Long Silence*, she has readily accepted the name 'Geetanjali', the name given to her by her husband after their marriage. Her life moves around 'he', her husband. She is always ready to do all the things her husband wants to do. Saru remembers Nalu accusingly saying to Smita: "Ah! There it is! 'He'! There's always time to do all the things 'he' wants to do, but never any time for doing the things you want to do. You just tag on to him and drift . . . a small boat towed by a large ship . . .". (Deshpande 117). Her talk is always littered by her own 'he'. She never gets tired of speaking about him. She feels proud when she says: "He used to read Tagore in those days . . . And he hates anyone calling me Smita now. He gets very annoyed if anyone does that. He calls me Anju himself". (Deshpande 118). She is happy with her role of a typical wife, a loving mother and a meek and obedient housewife. She wants nothing more in her life. She breathes and lives only for her husband.

She has no liberty even to buy a sari for her sister-in-law on her nephew's thread ceremony. She does not feel sorry for that. She does not feel shy to borrow one hundred rupees from Saru. She says: "Saru, can you lend me some money? . . . Can you give me a hundred? You know I came here for my nephew's thread ceremony. He gave me just enough to buy a small gift for the boy. But I had to buy a sari for my sister-in-law as well. It would have looked very mean if I hadn't . . . Now if I tell him I've bought a sari as a gift, he'll be furious". (Deshpande 118-19). Though deprived of liberty, she is happy with her husband believing that true happiness lies in accepting life as it is. She, thus, proves herself to be a typical middle class woman who is totally dependent on her husband for everything. Her passionate response to her husband's sexual hunger is at the root of their happy marital-relationship. However, she faces a common problem being faced by most Indian women. She shares her problem with Saru: "I never get a chance to read anything these days. There's housework and the children the whole day, and if I try to read at night, he won't let me". (Deshpande 120).

Smita, Nalu and Saru are the symbols of three totally different attitudes and sensibilities of Indian women. Saru stands for a combination of her professional life and her personal life with her different roles in her family. She tries her level best to reconcile between her role as a doctor and that of a wife and a mother because she knows that success and happiness of a marital life depends on understanding, compromise and reconciliation. Smita represents a complete wife, a loving mother, and a complete housewife, while Nalu, a spinster, has been dedicated only to her job and career. Nalu, who never married and who always carried a world of bitterness within her, believes that Smita as a woman has been degraded by marriage and men. She is entirely different both from Saru and Smita. Saru says: "There was a whole world of bitterness within her, ready to spring to the surface at any moment. She complained about her brother and his family with whom she lived, her students and colleagues, the administration of the college . . . politicians, the government, everything . . . It is easy to generalize and say that she is bitter because she never married, never bore a child. But that would be as stupid as calling me fulfilled because I got married and I have borne two children". (Deshpande 121).

Mrinal, Madhav's sister is a typical young girl with romantic ideas and dreams. Madhav once scornfully said: "Poor girl! She's a silly girl . . . She reads stories in magazines and books, and dreams of love and all that nonsense. She thinks it will happen to her too, and that she will escape that way". (Deshpande 123). Mrinal suffers because she is a girl. Neglected and misunderstood, she seeks consolation in romantic stories and fancies. She views herself as a romantic heroine in films and literature. She seeks to break her ties with her parents. She hates her village and a kind of life she has been leading. She is not happy with her life that goes on and on, doing the same things day after day, bringing water, looking after the kids, helping her mother and what not. She is fed up with this dull and mechanical life where there is no change, no pleasure, and no beauty. She desires to set herself free from her parental authority as early as possible by delivering herself up, passive and docile, into the hands of a new master. She is prepared to marry anyone who will take her away from that place. She wants to do so because she is not treated as a free, independent and autonomous individual. She is compelled to stay at home; her comings and goings are watched by her parents. She is not allowed to take charge of her own amusements and pleasures. She, therefore, awaits and looks for the man for fulfillment and escape.

Saru, being a lady doctor, is familiar with all the ugliness and indignities of the woman's life. The woman, she knows, keeps her sorrows and sufferings, complaints and problems to herself. She schools and trains herself to live and endure everything in silence as if she is born to be a mute and silent sufferer. Saru is right when she thinks: "The myriad complaints, the varying symptoms, if put together would provide a world of data for a treatise on the condition of women, backache, headache, leucorrhea, menorrhagea, dysmenorrhea, loss of appetite, burning feet, an itch 'there' . . . all the indignities of a woman's life, borne silently and as long as possible, because 'how do you tell anyone about these things?' Everything kept secret, their very womanhood, a source of deep shame to them; stupid, silly martyrs . . . idiotic heroines. Going on with their tasks, and destroying themselves in the bargain, for nothing but a meaningless modesty". (Deshpande 107). She has a bitter attitude towards these women who endure their diseases in silence. Their unconscious, unmeaning heroism, born out of the myth of a self-sacrificing martyred woman, does not arouse either pity or admiration in her. However, though she is resented by the capacity of endurance and tolerance of these mute sufferers, she continues to advise, suggest and prescribe them with enthusiasm. She believes that it is difficult to change a woman's pathetic condition as long as she is silent and unwilling to change.

According to *Mai Kaki,* Saru's mother was a brave woman, a woman of courage who never complained, and during her illness, she endured her pain and agony with courage. She told Saru: "She never told anyone about what was happening to her. The amount she ate . . . I tell you, a sparrow would have eaten more. Your father never noticed because he never ate with her . . . She was immensely strong. There aren't many women like her now. For the smallest pain, they rush off squealing to doctors, tonics and injections and what not; but not your mother. She lost so much weight, her *cholis* were hanging on her. And her bangles came up to here". (Deshpande 108). Though ill, her sense of hatred for her daughter was so strong and bitter that when she was asked to go to a doctor for treatment, she refused. She was not ready even to see a doctor's face only because her daughter was a doctor. After her death, Saru, who was angry with her dead mother, bitterly said: "I hate her, sapping me of my happiness, of everything. She's always done it to me . . . taken happiness away from me. She does it even now when she's dead". (Deshpande 109).

Padmakar, deprived of his maleness because of his feminine name 'Padma' was one of the few boys with whom Saru was comfortable. His parents compelled him to marry soon after his graduation because his father needed dowry in the form of money, a social evil, to be spent on Padma's sister's marriage. Padma's father-in-law agreed to look after a newly married couple until he completed his postgraduation. On learning this, Padma gave up the idea of doing his MD and began his career as a general practitioner. He was not at all happy with his wife who was orthodox and traditional in her relationship with her husband. To Saru, he says: "My wife! She can't talk about anything but servants and the children, and prices. I earn enough, but she's perpetually trying to economize. She never has her food until I go home and have mine, she cooks just what I like, and she never calls me by my name". (Deshpande 132). She proves to be a typical middle-class Indian wife, the ultimate purpose of whose life is just to obey and please her husband.

Sarita remembers her visit along with her husband to a family where they were invited for tea and where she found the woman who was fearfully silent. The woman, to Saru's surprise, was totally ignored and neglected by her husband. She recollects: "But there is one family . . . one couple, one woman specifically . . . The man sat and talked to us. The woman came in later with trays of food, cups of tea and glasses of water. She came in silently, unobtrusively, like a shadow and went out in the same way, her husband's conversation not interrupted even by a fraction of a second by her presence. He did not introduce her to us, and so strong was the man's disregard of her presence that we ignored her too. We ate our food, sipped the tea and gulped the water as if they had been brought to us by a nameless waiter in a hotel . . . I smiled at her. She did not respond. Her face was unchanged, expressionless, as if she had fallen in with her husband's desires and successfully effaced the person that was her . . . She stood under a light . . . I looked down at her feet and saw that there was no shadow. For some reason the words came to my mind . . . If I cast no shadow, I do not exist". (Deshpande 158-59). She is shocked to see the woman who does not exist at all for her husband.

An Indian woman believes that the beginning of periods leads the girl towards womanhood. Saru is tortured and irritated by various restrictions imposed on her during the periods. For her, it is a strange sensation, something too fantastic, something too shameful and frightful to be revealed to anyone, something that naturally and inevitably happens to all girls. She feels: "It was torture. Not just the three days when I couldn't enter the kitchen or the *puja* room. Not just the sleeping on a straw mat covered with a thin sheet. Not just the feeling of being of a pariah, with my special cup and plate by my side in which I was served from a distance, for my touch was, it seemed, pollution. No, it was something different, much worse. A kind of shame that engulfed me, making me want to rage, to scream against the fact that put me in the same class as my mother". (Deshpande 62). Though, womanhood is one of the greatest experiences for the woman, she doesn't want to be a woman like her mother. While studying anatomy and physiology in the first year of her medicine, she learns: "I was a female. I was born that way that was the way my body had to be, those were the things that had to happen to me". (Deshpande 63). She accepts that she is a female born to go through periods and also to have one of the greatest experiences of a woman's life in the form of motherhood. The very thought of motherhood makes her sworn that she will never fail her children in love and understanding. She has been buoyed up through all the months of pregnancy by the thought of a miracle of motherhood awaiting her. However, she is outraged at the indignity of motherhood, a day-long struggle, pain and shock as a baby's head forces itself out, her posture, her grunts, and her animal-like cries, the prelude to motherhood. However, about the unbearable pain of motherhood, Manohar says: "It's necessary pain, Saru, it's the link, the bridge you have to cross before you reach perfect love". (Deshpande 162). He means to suggest that in order to taste the fruits of perfect love it is necessary for her to bear the pain.

5.2.2 Plight and Predicament of the Indian Woman in 'Roots and Shadows'

The novel, *Roots and Shadows*, portrays a realistic picture of typical Indian women with their unending issues and problems, sorrows and sufferings in a joint family. An Indian woman, a meek and submissive member of a patriarchal society, a puppet following five paces behind the man blindly and mechanically, a lifeless doll dancing on the commands of the man, an spiritless creature suffering on account of male-ego, prejudice, conventions and traditions, is expected to be silent and tolerant, and yet gentle and gracious, caring and loving, kind and considerate right from the ancient days. Though, like a man, she is born free, she is caught in chains in one way or the other and is deprived of freedom. Various restrictions hampering her growth and development have been imposed on her right from her childhood.

Indu, the protagonist of the novel, is born and brought up in an orthodox Brahmin family which denies freedom to its female members. The family is controlled and dominated by Akka, a widow with no child of her own. She is portrayed as a woman who is bound by the restraints of orthodox norms and conventions of Indian patriarchy. Right from the beginning Indu has been trained only to submit and to accept. She has been repeatedly told that the woman has no choice and she is born without wills. She remembers her grandmother who had always been a timid and subdued woman, only a shadow of her husband. She is disgusted and irritated to see the house ugly with the aftermath of an eaten meal, and also to see the strewn plates and the scattered remnants. She feels pity for women who patiently clear up the mess with their bare hands after each meal. She also feels pity for the women like *Kaki* eating from the same dirty plate their husbands had eaten in earlier. She calls them stupid fools not knowing what they really want and do. She interrogates herself: "What do I want? . . . What a large, what a cosmic question that is. I will have to live the whole of my life to know what it is that I want . . . How can I live without knowing what I want? I must know. To live without fear . . . fear of being unloved, misunderstood, displeasing, without the fear of failure". (Deshpande 174). She is surprised to realize that the Indian woman lives without knowing what she wants.

Indu rebels against Akka, her dominating authority, her conventional world with rigid rules, norms and values, and the oppressive atmosphere in the family where women have no choice but to submit, surrender and to accept their lot silently and ungrudgingly. It has been drilled in her mind that, being a female, she has to be obedient and unquestioning, meek and submissive. She thinks that Akka is an obstacle in her way leading her to achieve her goal of attaining freedom and completeness. Right from her childhood, there has been only resentment and dislike in her mind for Akka. She believes that she is too narrow-minded, too bigoted to think of others. It is difficult for her to live happily and freely in such type of suppressed atmosphere. She, therefore, revolts against Akka and marries Jayant, a man of different caste but of her choice, and leaves her ancestral home. She uses 'marriage' as a tool to attain freedom and to become independent and complete in herself brushing aside all the age-old beliefs and superstitions prevalent in Indian society. Though for others, she is capable of anything, she realizes that she, as a human creature, is incomplete, almost nothing without her husband. This is the attitude which is basically responsible for her sorrows and sufferings, her subjugation and exploitation. It is because of this attitude that in the course of her marital life she becomes fluid with no shape, no form, no desire, and no aspiration of her own. However, as it happens with many women, very soon she gets frustrated and disillusioned in her marital life.

Like Deshpande's other anti-patriarchal women protagonists, she, too, strives to attain freedom, recognition and acceptance as an independent member of a society. She, who is a journalist and a writer, has a strong desire to be complete and independent in her writings. She does not dream of winning recognition, acclaim and appreciation as a writer. She believes that rave reviews, worldwide fame and the best seller that stun the world exist only in the fantasies, immature minds and publishers' blurbs. However, she, out of curiosity, asks a question to herself: "But can I withstand other pressures? The desire to be known, to succeed for Jayant's sake . . . will they not impel me to compromise, to write the kinds of things that are acceptable, popular and easily sold? If ever I am in danger of doing so, the memory of that time when I succumbed is there to shame me". (Deshpande 15). Her tragedy is that she cannot enjoy liberty as a journalist and a writer.

She recollects an interview of a soft-spoken, articulate, sincere and dedicated woman who had been given an award and an important office in recognition of her social services, her services in the cause of the welfare and betterment of women, in particular. She is shocked to read a piece, a story about the same woman brought to her by the little old man in a grimy *dhoti* and a black cap. She fails to digest "the story of shameless exploitation of ignorance, poverty and need, a story of ruthlessness and unscrupulousness in the pursuit of fame, power and money". (Deshpande 16). She is wrong in her feeling that no one will believe in the story of these exploited beings. When she goes to her editor with the story, he laughs and contemptuously says: "There's nothing new in this. I knew all this long back . . . Don't tell me, Indu, you really believed all that you wrote! . . . Did you truly think that woman was all this? . . . But we can't print it . . . I never knew you were such an idealist". (Deshpande 16-17). The editor has the age-old abusive and hostile approach to women. She loses her temper at his cynical and contemptuous approach to women in general. She gives an expression to her fury and says to herself: "I could have fought against anger, abuse, and hostility. But I could do nothing against this ridicule. I looked at myself through his eyes and saw myself not as brave, but as foolish and naïve . . . Foul-mouthed, cynical, having no illusions about anyone or anything. And I . . . taking care to present to him the image he wanted". (Deshpande 17).

Though unhappy in her marital life, Indu, like many other typical Indian women, feels that to live without a husband is the greatest calamity in life. The irony of her life is that though she is not completely happy with her husband, she cannot live without him. Her life and her thoughts, always, move around her husband. She thinks of her husband when she dresses herself, she thinks of him when she undresses herself, she thinks of him when she looks in the mirror, she thinks of his wants, his dreams, and his way of life. She forgets her 'self' and her 'identity'. She looks for her 'self' and 'identity' in her husband's. It is the marriage that gives her a gift of submissiveness, subjugation, insult and mutilation. It makes her a typical submissive woman whose identity is nothing but an extension of her husband's. She herself is shocked to see herself change into a wife living her life as per her husband's wishes and ideas. She realizes that she has been consciously or unconsciously trying to shape, mould and change herself according to her husband's needs and desires. She understands that her attachment to Jayant is quite disturbing and her total surrender to him quite frightening. She has dreamt of a happy and complete married life with Jayant, but unfortunately, her calculations go wrong and her dream remains merely a dream.

Knowing about Akka's illness, she returns to her ancestral home where a new role of a guardian of Akka's property is waiting for her, she learns a lot from Vithal, an orphaned student, a pauper picked off the streets, brought home and supported by Kaka, and staying with the family but eating in different homes on different days and always busy with his books and studies. He tells Indu that he has to concentrate on his studies with all the pinpricks in the family as he is an outsider, and that he has no other choice. His statement 'I have no choice' makes Indu think about her life with her husband. She, who has the potentiality to stand out sharp and clear as Indu, an individual, admits: "For had I not, so very often, felt myself just a mouthing, grimacing puppet, dully saying the lines I had to, feeling, actually, nothing? Had I not felt myself flat, one-dimensional, just a blurred figure merging into the background?" (Deshpande 143). She regrets that she has been a mute puppet after her marriage. Her life is filled with deceptions and betrayals. She realizes that her husband expects her to conform to his views and ideas. Deceived and disillusioned, she accepts a conventional role of an Indian wife. She, now, gets a chance to forget a bitter and sordid reality of her marriage on her return to her ancestral home where Akka is lying on her death bed.

Indu contemptuously calls an Indian woman, a martyr, a heroine, just a stupid fool carrying a world of darkness in herself, a pure female animal, a subordinate creature in the world filled with ignorance, prejudice and superstition, or a typical breed only interested in getting married, bearing children, having sons and then grandchildren. She is only known and recognized by her relationship with others. Indu remarks: "These women . . . they are called *Kaku* and *Kaki*, *Atya* and *Vahini*, *Ajji* and *Mami*, as if they have to be recognized by a relationship, because they have no independent identity of their own at all. And, in the process, their own names are forgotten. How does it feel not even to have a name of your own? There are women who are proud of having their names changed by their husbands during their wedding ceremonies". (Deshpande 117). The woman's pattern of life, Indu regrets, is fixed. Decision-making has no role to play in her life. She depends on her male-counterpart almost for everything. Her husband and children, her home and household activities, her cooking and cleaning, her meals, her *pujas* and fasts, her rites and rituals matter most in her life.

She trains herself to adjust and adapt herself with circumstances. She also trains herself to get closely involved with a family having different interests and conflicting feelings. It is surprising that though the female members in a family dislike one another, they do not fail to understand one another. About Sunanda-atya, Indu says: "She was the eternal female . . . cunning, greedy, devious and unscrupulous . . . As a child she had learnt that, being a female, she could neither assert, nor demand or proclaim". (Deshpande 132). Indu has a kind of distaste for the female function, the function of feeding a child, the function that gives her a feeling of motherhood. She is shivered to see Sunanda-atya sitting down with the child on her lap, opening her buttons and pushing a flaccid nipple into his mouth; and the child taking a long shuddering breath and sucking with loud noises. She, in many respects, is different from other women in the family. She has no love for jewellery. Sunanda-atya rightly says: "Yes, Indu never wears anything . . . What does she need such things for? Her education is her real jewellery. It's only poor fools like us who need all that". (Deshpande 141). But there is a shocking dead silence when women in the family hear Indy say: "I never had any jewellery. Maybe that's why I never wore it. Now that I have such a lot of it, perhaps I'll start wearing it". (Deshpande 141). When she says so, it is difficult to make out the faces of women in the dim light, but the air in the room is charged with surprise, dismay, anxiety and fear of losing their share of jewellery.

Indu has heard a lot about Saroja, Naren's mother. She remembers Kaka who said: "I remember her very distinctly, a little thing like you, but very quiet. And when she sang . . . God, what a voice she had!" (Deshpande 50). But unfortunately, she is a typical woman who has no freedom even to learn what she likes and loves. Indu exclaims excitedly and impatiently: "I've heard that and of how she wanted to learn music and how Akka put her foot down. What—learn music from a strange man! Sit and sing in front of strangers! Like those women? Are we that kind of a family? Isn't it enough for you to sing one or two devotional songs, one or two *aarti* songs? What more does a girl from a descent family need to have?" (Deshpande 50). Kaka always felt that it was incorrect not to allow her to learn music, but he was too helpless to do anything but to feel sorry for her. Saroja tolerated everything quietly without complaining. Is it not strange and ironical that in a patriarchal set-up, a woman's desire to learn music is suppressed by a woman? It is the woman who becomes an obstacle in the way of a woman; it is the woman who decides the destiny of a woman. The woman herself is her destiny. And that is why Indu does not blame her husband, who, according to her, has not compelled and pressurised her to live her life the way he wants. She confines herself in the cage willingly.

Indu has a bitter sense of hatred for Akka, a dominating figure in the family, who was against Indu's marriage. She remembers her words: "Such marriages never work, different castes, different languages . . . it's all right for a while. Then they realize . . .". (Deshpande 68). She knows nothing about Akka's marital life. However, she is shocked to hear a tragic and pathetic story of her marital life from Atya. She thinks of the story innumerable times and whenever she does, the story comes back to her in Atya's words: "She was just twelve when she got married. And he was well past thirty . . . Six months after her marriage, she 'grew up' and went to her husband's home. What she had to endure there, no one knows. She never told anyone . . . But I heard that twice she tried to run away . . . a girl of thirteen. Her mother-in-law, I heard, whipped her for that and locked her up for three days, and starved her as well, and then, sent her back to her husband's room. The child, they said, cried and clung to her mother-in-law saying, 'Lock me up again, lock me up'. But there was no escape from a husband then . . . He had a weakness for women . . . And Akka could never give birth to a living child . . . But every time she had a miscarriage, her mother-in-law blamed her for it and made life hell for her. And then, when Akka had been married for more than fifteen or twenty years, he took up with one woman . . . I heard he was crazy about her . . . And then, one day, he had a stroke . . . Akka looked after him . . . He couldn't speak; I remember . . . He was trying to say something. One day Akka found out what it was he was trying to say . . . He wanted her, that woman, his mistress . . . And then Akka said, 'If that's what you want, you can go on wanting. She won't come here. I won't let her . . . Listen to me. It's my turn now. I've listened to you long enough. She came here twice. I threw her out. You'll never see her again". (Deshpande 69-71).

Akka is one of the victims of a child-marriage and a marital-violence. She has been given an inhuman and beastlike treatment both by her husband and her mother-in-law. She has spent almost every night in her marital home crying. However, inspite of injustice done to her in each and every form, she, a typical Indian woman, proves herself a dutiful wife by looking after her bed-ridden husband. Indu, now, feels guilty for having judged her without knowing anything about her. The story of Akka's married life speaks a lot about a tragedy of a married woman, her physical and sexual harassment, her mental torture and suppression, her silently enduring her life, her pain and agony, her sacrifice and exceptional tolerance, her inner strength to accept and face her life as it is, and her capacity to adjust herself to the entire adverse situations.

Vithal's mother is another example of a meek, silent and suffering wife who has been a victim of the sadistic anger of her husband. Indu learns from Old Uncle: "Vithal's father . . . a grim man who rarely spoke and never smiled, there was a streak of cruelty in him that came out in his relations with his meek, silent wife. The boy, as a child, had been a frequent spectator of scenes in which the father had worked out his sadistic anger on the mother for the merest trifles. And then one day, when the man was out on the job, the mother just disappeared. She had not even bothered to cook a meal for the child. When the man returned after a three day job, he found the boy starving. The mother never returned. And neither the boy nor the father ever mentioned her name again. Now the man started on the boy. Not physical cruelty . . . it was as if that instinct had fled with the wife . . . but cruelty of a different kind". (Deshpande 138). Vithal's mother, another typical Indian woman, has tolerated not only physical cruelty but mental torture as well.

Indu is uneasy to learn that Mini's parents are in a hurry to give Mini away in a marriage. She feels sorry for Kaka, Mini's father, who says: "Padmini is past twenty-four now. And there's her horoscope, and the problem of finding a family with a status of ours. And when everything clicks, there's the dowry hurdle. What am I to do? Let the girl stay unmarried? It's all right so long as I'm alive. When I'm gone, can you see her brothers looking after her? May be the boy is a little ugly, may be a little stupid . . . but everything else is fine. The family is good, it's known to us, and they have money. She'll be quite comfortable". (Deshpande 51). Indu has never seen her Kaka so earnest, so helpless, and so worried about his daughter. She is also uneasy to know that Mini, too, is in a hurry to marry any man. To her surprise, she is interested in a marriage and not in a man. In a response to Indu's question, with whom she is getting married, she says: "Oh, what does it matter who it is". (Deshpande 31). Indu learns from Kaka: "He's passed his S.S.C. . . . He doesn't need a job. They have plenty. He can live in comfort like a lord on what they have. And what's the use of these degrees? Can they guarantee a job?" (Deshpande 50). Kaka prefers property to education, which, according to him, does not guarantee jobs. Mini, too, does not bother about education, job, land, property and all these things. She says: "I'm past twenty four. I have to get married. What else is there to think about? . . . What choice do I have? . . . Of course I'm marrying him because there's nothing else I can do.

I'm no good at studies . . . There's only one thing I'm really good at . . . looking after a house". (Deshpande 125).

Mini highlights the plight of an unmarried girl eager to marry when she says: "Any man, Indu. Yes, any man, any man who says 'yes'. You don't know what it has been like, watching Kaka and Hemant . . . running around after eligible men, and then, sending the horoscope and having it come back with the message, 'It doesn't match'. And if the horoscopes matched, there was the meeting to be arranged . . . and all those people coming and staring and asking all kinds of questions. And if we heard they were old-fashioned people, I would dress up in an old-fashioned manner and they would say, 'She's not modern enough'. And if I dressed up well because someone said the boy wanted a smart wife, they would say, 'She's too fashionable for us', or too short, or too tall, or too dark, or something, and Kaka trying to laugh and talk to those people . . . and I, feeling as if I had committed a great crime by being born a girl . . . and if finally, everything was fine, there was the dowry. You know nothing of this, Indu. You're lucky. You escaped all this . . . And now when someone has agreed, can I refuse just because the man isn't . . . Oh, I don't know. And I don't care. He'll look after me. And no one can say to me, 'How old are you? And not married yet! What a pity!' I'm tired, Indu. I don't care what kind of a man he is. Once we are married, and he becomes my husband, none of his flaws will matter". (Deshpande 126). It is unfortunate that most Indian girls are to go through this process as they do not have their own choice of selecting their life partner.

Like Saru, in *The Dark Holds No Terrors*, Indu has a deep sense of hatred for the unclean womanhood. She has never thought of her womanhood until the knowledge has been thrust unexpectedly, brutally and gracelessly on her the day she has grown up. Kaki has told her that she is a woman now and she can have babies herself. She also asks her not to forget that she is unclean for three days now and that she can't touch anyone or anything and she is barred from the *puja* room. Indu helplessly rages against the rules which have made her an outcast and thinks to herself: "I, a woman? My mind had flung off the thought with an amazing swiftness. I was only a child. And then, she had gone on to tell me, baldly, crudely, how I could have a baby. And I had, for the first time, felt an immense hatred for it". (Deshpande 79). She knows that it is the birth of a child that opens the door of motherhood for a married woman like her. Her family members are eager to see her with her own child. She remembers Akka who said: "I suppose you're taking some of the things they take now to prevent having children. When are you going to have one?" (Deshpande 38). Indu is mature enough to know that a typical Indian woman has a strong desire to be a mother of a child, especially a male child.

5.2.3 'That Long Silence': A Portrayal of the Endemic Imbalance in a Marriage

Jaya, like other women protagonists, has been a silent sufferer right from her childhood. The process of silencing Jaya, being a female child, began in her infancy itself. She was not allowed to enjoy songs on Radio Ceylon as listening to these songs was considered a shameful and furtive affair. Her father unsuccessfully tried to make her love Paluskar and Faiyas Khan, classical singers instead of Mohmad Rafi and Lata Mangeshkar. Her grandmother was not pleased with her inquisitiveness. She said: "I feel sorry for your husband, Jaya, whoever he is . . . Look at you—for everything a question, for everything a retort. What husband can be comfortable with that?" (Deshpande 27). She was not allowed to speak out and question. Her curiosity and inquisitiveness was suppressed in Indian patriarchy. She was told the stories of Sita, Sivitri, Gandhari and Draupadi. However, her father did not want her to be like other ordinary women scared of cockroaches, lizards, insects, afraid of darkness and loneliness, nervous about electric gadgets, hopeless at technical matters, and lazy about accounting. He did not want her to be a stereotype of a woman, incompetent and always needing male help and support. He wanted her to be bold, courageous and confident enough to face life. He always wanted her to be different from other women only performing *pujas*, taking interest in household activities, feeling pride even in scrubbing and cleaning the toilet to make it free from stains and smells, and just accepting the destiny of being wives and mothers.

Her suffering in silence continues even after her marriage with Mohan. The tips given to a future wife; 'a husband is like a sheltering tree; and husband's happiness depends on his wife' lays the foundation for her marital life. She accepts Mohan as a sheltering tree. Inspite of being bold and courageous, she becomes a typical Indian wife who follows Mohan's footsteps blindly and obediently. She, like any other typical woman living within Indian patriarchy, suppresses her own likes and dislikes, dreams and aspirations, and lives her life in silence as per the dreams and aspirations of her husband. She herself admits: "I had learnt it at last—no questions, no retorts, only silence". (Deshpande 143). She always takes delight in pleasing her husband as if that is the only duty assigned to her. She is like a sparrow in the story of a foolish, improvident, irresponsible and gullible crow building his house of dung, and a worldly-wise, cautious, responsible, caring, dutiful and shrewd sparrow building hers of wax. She is like a sparrow which keeps the crow waiting for hours, and finally, in the guise of providing sympathy and shelter, kills it. In Indian male-centric society, she feels, it is difficult to appreciate this story in which, the crow, a victim, is a male; and the sparrow, victorious, is a female. However, she believes in a dreadful moral of the story: "Stay at home, look after your babies, keep out of the rest of the world, and you are safe . . . Safety is always unattainable. You're never safe". (Deshpande 17).

Jaya, thus, becomes Suhasini for whom marriage means: "to be at home, to take care of her husband, of her children, of her family . . . Close the doors, stay in and you're safe". (Deshpande 139). For her, marriage is: ". . . a husband and wife care for each other, live with each other until they are dead; parents care for their children, and children in turn look after their parents when they are needed . . . a state of being". (Deshpande 127). She accepts her husband as her profession, career, and a means of livelihood. She believes that she does not have an independent existence apart from her husband. She is content only to be a wife, a mother and a housewife.

For her, there is something positive, something definite about marriage and wifehood. She begins to feel that wifehood is something auspicious whereas widowhood inauspicious. She always remembers her mother looking earnestly into a mirror, applying her *kumkum* with the tip of her ring finger, gently spreading the red powder, making the circle larger and larger, and finally a large, perfect red circle shining in the middle of her forehead; which, according to her, is marriage.

The woman, represented by Suhasini, is a soft, gentle, smiling, placid, sensitive, loving and motherly woman. She is a woman who lovingly looks after her husband, children, family, and home. She becomes her husband's *Ardhangini*. She is a *Pativrata* who faithfully submits herself to her husband and who is physically and emotionally loyal to him. She accepts the role of a devoted wife and a dutiful and responsible mother. Questions, complaints, and retorts have no place in her life. She, gradually, changes into a stereotype of a woman for whom her husband, children and home are of prime importance. She even sacrifices her role of a creative writer in order to play a conventional role of a wife and a mother successfully. She initially follows the footsteps of Sita and Savitri, legendary and mythological female characters, whose energies were directed towards the welfare of their husbands, and not towards liberation of their self. However, she knows that these women followed their husbands willingly whereas she does not do so willingly. She admitts: "And I knew I was not free. I could feel the burden of his wanting, the burden of his clinging". (Deshpande 29). She rotates around her husband and his world. She feels that her identity is in a dilemma and that she is totally disoriented. She is forced to suppress her wants, needs, desires and aspirations. She is passive and submissive even in her marital sex while Mohan is callous, aggressive and dominant. She is taught to tolerate her pain, to bite on it and not to let it escape.

She has been a symbol of love and affection, patience and silence, endurance and tolerance. She is concerned about her children, Rahul and Rati. One of the prime objects of her life is to look after them. However, she is not contented with them.

It is Jaya who has chosen the name Rahul for her son. She recollects: "I had named him after that infant by whose side, it is said, his father lingered, looking at him with love, before leaving home forever to become Buddha. At least, I consoled myself, I had not named him Ananda, after the beloved disciple of Buddha. Yes, I had thought of that name too. 'Ananda'—that would have been ironic indeed; for I had, I realized it then, little joy out of my son. From the moment of his birth, when I had heard his cry, that infinitely heart-rending, breathless cry of the new-born, he had filled me with a sense of foreboding. My love for him had always been touched with pity, tinged by calamitous colours. Rati I really worried about; she seemed in some way to be armed against unhappiness. But Rahul seemed to me totally vulnerable". (Deshpande 77). Though uneasy with her children, she knows that she can experience the taste of motherhood only because of her children.

When Kusum is brought to Mumbai for treatment, she cannot bear her staying away from her children. She goes on saying: "Jaya I must go . . . home . . . to my children . . . I want to see all my children . . . I do not need any treatment, and I am all right . . . I need them". (Deshpande 20-21). She goes home only to die. Nayana, too, is loving and affectionate to her daughters. When her eldest daughter was sick, she tells Jaya, she pawned her anklets with the *Marwari* for money that she needed for her treatment. After having tea and some bread with Jaya, she takes some bread with her and says: "That is for my girls". (Deshpande 28). Her love and concern for her children is one of the virtues of Indian woman, rich or poor. She prefers motherhood to mere wifehood. As a wife she is not a complete individual, but motherhood naturally makes her a complete individual. Simone de Beauvoir writes: "Now, it is precisely the child that according to tradition should assure to woman a real independence in which she is relieved of devoting herself to any other end. If as wife she is not a complete individual, she becomes such as mother: the child is her happiness and her justification. Through the child she is supposed to find self-realization sexually and socially; through childbearing, then, the institution of marriage gets its meaning and attains its purpose". (Beauvoir 501).

The woman's identity is, generally, defined in terms of her relationship with a man as a daughter, a sister, a wife, and a mother. She, in a sense, does not have an identity of her own in a male-dominated society in which rules and conventions are made by the males. Jaya, being a woman, has no place in the family tree prepared by Ramu-kaka. Ramu-kaka gets excited when he looks at the tree. He says: "Look, Jaya, this is our branch. This is our grandfather—your great grandfather—and here's father, and then us—Laxman, Vasu and me. And here are the boys—Shridhar, Jannu, Dinkar and Ravi . . .". (Deshpande 142). Jaya is surprised not to find herself in the family tree. When Jaya interrupts him, he says: "How can you be there? You don't belong to this family! You're married, you're now a part of Mohan's family. You have no place here". (Deshpande 143). Jaya wants to question him, but she does not do so as the female is not allowed to question in Indian Patriarchy. The question she wants to ask is: "If I do not belong to this family, what about the *Kakis* and *Ai*? They married into this family, didn't they? Why are they not here? And what about *Ajji*, who single-handed kept the family together, why isn't she here?" (Deshpande 143).

The woman is, thus, rejected, neglected, and victimized in Indian patriarchal system. She has a subordinate role to play in her parental home as well as her marital home. She is not allowed to enjoy the status and dignity of being a person, being an individual who is equal to the male in each and every respect. She, in a state of subjection, does not behave the way she wants to, but as the man and his masculine world defines her and wants her to behave. She, therefore, tries her level best to satisfy her husband and his sexual needs. She dreams of finding her happiness only through her husband. Jaya, now and then, remembers Vanitamami's words: A husband is like a sheltering tree and the woman is nothing without her husband, without *kumkum* on her forehead. The institution of marriage in India generally subordinates a wife to her husband.

Women, in most cases, allow themselves to be the victims of Indian patriarchy. Jaya's maid-servant, Jeeja, gives her full support and co-operation to her good for nothing husband. She does not oppose him in having another wife in order to have children. She says: "God didn't give us any children—that was his misfortune as well as mine. How could I blame him for marrying again when I couldn't give him any children? How could I blame that woman for marrying him?" (Deshpande 52). Jeeja, after the death of her husband and his mistress, willingly and happily, brings up their son, Rajaram, and even takes the responsibility of his wife, Tara and her three children. Jeeja, who is basically a practical realist and a pure professional, works hard to earn money that she badly needs. She never complains in her life. She never loses her temper. She says: "With whom shall I be angry? My parents didn't intend marrying me to a drunkard. He was not a drunkard then. He had a good job in a mill, and we lived in a decent room in a chawl, not in the slums. He lost all this during a strike. That was not his fault, others misled him, and he believed whatever his friends told him. He started drinking after that . . .". (Deshpande 52). She accepts her tragic lot and moves on with her life with courage.

Jeeja's daughter, Tara, always curses her husband, Rajaram who drinks and beats his wife. Her marital life is not different from that of Jeeja. Jeeja never blames her fate, but Tara moans her fate and cries: "So many drunkards die, but this one won't. He'll torture us all to death instead". (Deshpande 53). However, her mother, Jeeja scolds her and says: "Stop that! Don't forget, he keeps the *kumkum* on your forehead. What is a woman without that?" (Deshpande 53). When Rajaram is admitted in the hospital, Jeeja, followed by Manda, goes to Jaya for help and co-operation. Though poor, she does not want any money from Jaya, she just wants Jaya to talk to the doctor from the hospital so that Rajaram can get a special and timely treatment. She earnestly says: "If you speak to the doctor there, they will look after him better; they will give him special care. Otherwise no one cares, no one is bothered about poor patients, and they won't tell us anything if we ask them. They bark at us as if we're dogs . . . *Tai*, help us . . . If he dies, what will happen to this child . . . and that girl, let her have her *kumkum* on her forehead. What is a woman without that? Her husband may be a drunkard, but as long as he is alive, no one will dare cast an eye on her". (Deshpande 160). Jaya's brother, Ravi, too, wants Jaya to advise his wife and tell her: "Go home like a good girl, Asha. Go back home and obey your husband. And never mind whatever it is he has done, he's your husband, after all, and a husband can do no wrong". (Deshpande 115). Both Jeeja and Ravi highlight the importance of a husband, even though he is wrong, in the life of the woman.

Mohan's mother is a concrete example of a victimized woman in Indian patriarchy. She is mercilessly humiliated and ill-treated by her husband. It is difficult for Jaya to forget an image of the woman "crouching in front of the dying fire, sitting blank and motionless, the huddled bundles of sleeping children on the floor, the utter silence, the loud knock at the door . . . They had all had their food, except her . . . she always waited for him . . . she cooked rice for him again . . . she had his plate ready . . . he sat down, drank a glass of water, poured some into his palm to sprinkle ritually around his plate . . . and then he paused. 'Why is there no fresh chutney today?' he asked, not looking at her. She mumbled something. The next moment he picked up his heavy brass plate and threw it, not at her, but deliberately at the wall . . . he stood up and . . . walked out of the house . . . she put some rice on the fire and began grinding the chutney . . . she was still sitting there in front of the fire, silent, motionless". (Deshpande 35-36). We need to salute her inner strength in the form of silence, patience and tolerance. Mohan can see strength in her mother, silently sitting in front of the fire, whereas Jaya despair.

There is something common between Mohan's mother and his sister, Vimla, something that links the destinies of the two, silence in which they died. Being typical Indian women, who are caught in a trap of Indian patriarchy, silence is the only weapon they use to survive in Indian patriarchy. Their life has been a story of unbearable pain and agony. Jaya remembers Vimla's words: "Strange, isn't it, how different I am from my mother? Five years married now—I performed my fifth *Mangala-Gouri puja* this year—and I have no children. While *Avva* . . . almost all my childhood I remember her as being pregnant. She didn't want that last child, she'd lost four or five babies by then, and she was desperate . . . But then, I was only a child, and her behaviour that day frightened me. It was only a week or two before she died, she was cooking . . . she began hitting herself on the face . . . she went on and on hurting herself . . . she began to cry. I tried to make her lie down, I tried to make her drink water, but she just went on saying, 'I can't, I can't' . . . A week later, she died". (Deshpande 37-38). She cannot tolerate herself being treated merely as a child-bearing machine. She dies as a Suhasini, as a fortunate and blessed woman with her husband still living, and frees herself forever and forever. Vimla, too, dies in the hospital with her silence intact. Their tragic destiny is that 'endurance' and 'silence' are the words written on their foreheads.

Mukta, Jaya's immediate neighbour, tortures herself by fasting. She has more days of fast than days on which she can have her normal and regular meal with a purpose to avoid widowhood. But Arun, her husband falls out of the train and dies. Her fasts fail to save him from death, the ultimate truth of human life. Vanitamami performs numerous *pujas* and observes fasts with the hope of having children, but in vain. A poor, childless Vanitamami adopts a feeble and spiritless Kusum. Both Vanitamami and Kusum, weak women, are born failures, born losers. However, they, somehow, manage to have their own way in their life. Vanitamami, much worried and concerned about Kusum, asks: "Why don't you teach our Kusum some English, Jaya? . . . Her English is very weak. Why don't you ask your husband to get our Kusum's husband a better job? Why don't you take our Kusum to a lady daughter? . . . A poor thing, she has three daughters, at least let the fourth be a son. Why don't you take Kusum to Bombay and show her to a good doctor? She is behaving funnily . . .". (Deshpande 21). She has true love and affection for her daughter. Kusum, a poor, frightened, defeated woman, kills herself by throwing herself into a well in order to set herself free from the unbearable pain and agony of her life. She uses 'suicide' as a means to put an end to her tragic life.

5.2.4 'A Matter of Time': A Horrifying Tale of the Loss and Agony of the Woman

A Matter of Time projects the plight and predicament, pain and loss, oppression and exploitation of four women, Manorama, Kalyani, Sumitra and Arundhati representing four generations of the same family. It is about a middle-class family of Gopal and Sumi with their three daughters, Arundhati, Charulata and Seema. Sumi and her daughters are the victims of Gopal's desertion which disturbs the very peace, happiness and balance of the family. The failed marriage of Gopal and Sumi brings Sumi back to the Big House. Gopal's desertion is a matter of shame and disgust both for Aru, her eldest daughter and Kalyani, her mother, who herself was the cause of dissatisfaction for her mother, Manorama who failed to give a gift of a male heir to the family. Manorama, for whom Kalyani was timid, dull, and unsure of herself, was not at all happy with her. With the mother like Manorama and her own sense of inadequacy, Kalyani was excited by the letters she received from a young man. On knowing about the letters, Manorama thought that Kalyani had done something immoral and obscene. She asked her questions the girl did not understand and answer, and her silence confirmed her guilt for her mother. This was the end of Kalyani's schooling. She was not allowed to go out of the house after that and within a year she was given away in marriage to Shripati. For her mother, she was a symbol of failure as she did not fulfil any of her dreams she had seen for her daughter. She had thought that her daughter would be beautiful and accomplished and would make a happy and brilliant marriage, but this dream remained unfulfilled.

Kalyani becomes a typical Indian woman after her marriage. Sumi is frightened to see the photograph of her parents. She watches: "A classic post-wedding picture, bride and groom formally posed against a dark background, the bride sitting in a chair, the groom by her . . . She is looking not at the camera, but at someone standing by the photographer, the uncertain look of a child seeking approval . . . The man on the other hand is stern, his eyes hooded, arms folded across his chest in the usual 'manly pose' . . . And the way he is standing, he gives the impression of being by himself, wholly unaware of the girl standing by him, his wife". (Deshpande 25-26). This is indeed a photograph of a middle-class husband and wife, the husband standing with sternness and pride, while his wife sitting with uncertain look and the absence of confidence on her face. There has been a frightening, oppressive and mysterious silence between them. Aru is haunted by a number of questions when she finds dead silence between her grandparents. She interrogates herself: "Why doesn't *Baba* ever come down? Why doesn't he have his meals here with the rest of us? Why doesn't he ever speak to Kalyani? She is his wife, isn't she? And why is she so frightened of him?" (Deshpande 39).

Aru learns from Premi that while coming home to Bangalore for the holidays, Kalyani lost her mentally retarded son, Madhav at the V.T. station. Premi says: "*Baba* had gone to check the reservations, leaving *Amma* with the children. When he returned, the boy wasn't there . . . He was never found . . . This happened in the afternoon. At night someone came to Anil's house . . . asking them to go to the station . . . She was still there, sitting on the platform, her luggage and children about her, waiting for *Baba* . . . They didn't see him for nearly two months. He was searching; he went about the city like a madman . . . Anil's grandfather sent word to *Amma's* father. He went to Bombay and brought her back here. *Baba* has not spoken to her since the day it happened". (Deshpande 140). Kalyani's real tragedy begins with the missing of her four-year-old son. In a response to Aru's question asked with a doubt, "Do you think she let him wander away and said nothing?" (Deshpande 141), Premi says: "I don't think so, Aru. How could she? No mother could possibly do such a thing. It was an accident . . . I've seen mothers with retarded children—they're so vulnerable, the mothers are so protective . . . No, it's impossible". (Deshpande 141-42). She believes that a mother's affection for a baby, a baby boy, in particular, inspite of his being mentally retarded, will never allow her to do it deliberately. How can Kalyani, who loves children, especially babies, do so with her own son? Aru does not agree with Premi. For her the question remains: "And if she didn't do it, why didn't she explain? Why didn't she defend herself?" (Deshpande 143).

Aru finds Kalyani's silence inexplicable and mysterious. What she minds is injustice done to her. She does not agree with Premi who says that she must have been scared of her husband. According to her, it is important and necessary for the woman to speak out, to state the truth, to stand up and to defend herself so that she is not misunderstood and misjudged. She wants her grandmother to break her silence and speak of the act of public desertion, of those long hours at the railway station with her daughters, surrounded by the strangers. Kalyani, however, uses 'silence' as a weapon to bear the sordid reality of her marital life. She proves her miraculous strength by surviving intact inspite of what her husband did to her. Sumi, Aru and others are surprised at Kalyani's living her life silently and ungrudgingly. Sumi feels that a fear of widowhood, perhaps, has made her tolerate everything in her life. She wonders: "Is this what has helped Kalyani to endure everything, the fact that she is a wife and not a widow . . . and that she has the right to all the privileges of the husband of a living husband?" (Deshpande 167). She is reminded of a tray of *kumkum*, *paan-supari* and coconut, the symbols of wifehood and also the old woman's words, 'What is a woman without a husband?' She interrogates herself: "Is it enough to have a husband, and never mind the fact that he has not looked at your face for years, never mind the fact that he has not spoken to you for decades?" (Deshpande 167). She feels that Kalyani tolerates everyrthing only because her wifehood allows her to move in the company of women with pride.

On Sumi's return to her parental home after Gopal's walking away from their marriage, Kalyani is worried to find the history repeating in the life of her daughter. The family tries to take her into confidence and to know the reason of Gopal's desertion. However, Sumi, a puzzle difficult to be solved, a mystery, and an enigma, is not ready to open the door of her heart and to disclose the reason. She knows that getting answers to the questions beginning with 'why', will not give a full stop to her plight. She thinks to herself: "The 'why' that all of them are pursuing leaves me cold. I know that they find it impossible to believe that I have not asked him anything. The truth is, I could not have spoken to him that night—no, it was impossible. But even if it had been possible, if I had asked him 'why', would I have got an answer I could have made sense of? . . . And yet, if I meet Gopal I will ask him one question, just one, the question no one has thought of. What is it, Gopal, that makes a man in this age of acquisition and possession walk out on his family and all that he owns? Because . . . it was you who said that we are shaped by the age we live in, by the society we are part of. How then can you, in this age, a part of this society, turn your back on everything in your life? Will you be able to give me an answer to this?" (Deshpande 27). But unfortunately, she, being an Indian woman, keeps these questions to herself. She is destined to live without her husband for the reason nobody knows. The plight of an Indian woman, represented by Sumi and her mother, lies in the fact that she has to accept the decision of her husband. She has no 'say' in her marital life.

Kalyani and Sumi are not the only women who suffer a lot in Indian patriarchal set-up. Almost all women in the novel are the victims of subjugation and exploitation within and outside the institution of a family in one way or the other. Aru, a representative young girl of the fourth generation, finds Manorama as a domineering figure, Kalyani, an enduring figure, and Sumi, a cold and indifferent figure in marriage. With her knowledge of unhappy marriages around her, she steps into her womanhood with a decision not to marry. She is mature enough to be conscious of the curtain beyond which her parents and grandparents lived or did not live their life together as husband and wife. She is, therefore, frightened and irritated at the very thought of marriage. She is uneasy and restless after her father's desertion. Her reaction to her mother's words, 'I don't care' is sharp, bitter and violent. She bursts out: "That's wonderful. You don't care about his having gone, you don't care where he is, you don't care what people think—but I care, yes, I do, I care about *Papa* having left us, I care about not having our own house. I don't want to live like this, as if we're sitting on a railway platform, I want my home back, I want my father back". (Deshpande 21). She is pining for her father, for her own house. Though, she tries her level best, she fails in her attempt to bring her parents together.

Premi, Sumi's sister, now a successful professional, a mother of a seven-year-old son and a wife of a prosperous lawyer, is worried about Sumi's failed marriage. The moment she comes to her parental home, her professional success, her happy family dwindles into nothing and she once again gets into the skin of a frightened child and is reminded of her father's blank stare with a question: 'Why are you here?' Her husband had not believed her when she told him that her father did not speak to her until she was ten. The atmosphere in the house was always surprisingly tense and fearfully silent with her father in his room upstairs, never coming out, never speaking to anybody; and her mother always silent. The first time her father talked to her was when she completed her medical education. Actually, she was summoned to be told that she would be marrying Anil. She could never experience father's love for a daughter. Though happy in her marital life, she, now, is much worried about her sister, Sumi, a deserted wife.

Devaki, a woman entrepreneur, plays a role of a typical Indian wife by moulding herself in the kind of life her husband, Vasudev Murthy, a successful architect from a distinguished family, wants her to live. The blossoming of Devaki after her marriage into a chic young woman is like a modern-day Cindrella story. Seeing an old picture of Sumi, Premi and Devaki, Charu had exclaimed: "I can't believe this is you, Devaki-mavashi". (Deshpande 103). Devaki laughs at herself in the picture, a skinny, awkward girl in glasses, wearing a short, straight dress, scowling, as if conscious of the unpleasing image she was presenting to the camera. She, the dark one in the family of the fair people, has deliberately remade herself and successfully lopped all the awkward corners off herself. And after her marriage, she has gained confidence and fitted herself into the mould of an Indian woman. She, too, is worried about the breakdown of Sumi's marriage and unsuccessfully attempts at reconciliation between Sumi and Gopal.

Goda, a typical Indian woman, always takes delight in making complaints against her husband, Satyanarayan, an easy-tempered man, a good provider and a cheerful companion, laying his jokes at Goda's feet like homage, and even after forty years of marriage, devoted to his wife. She is lucky enough to have a loving husband like him. However, during her weekly visits to the Big House, Goda's complaints about her husband seem to be at the centre of conversation between Kalyani and Goda. She complains about his cheating on his diabetic diet, about his insistence on driving their old car, about his extravagance in buying and so on. Kalyani, as per her habit of sympathizing, responds to her sympathetically with a constant repetition of 'you poor thing'. The moment we compare marital lives of Goda and Kalyani, it seems odd for Kalyani, who has been living with her husband in a strangely oppressive silence, to pity Goda whose husband has been devoted to her.

Manorama, Kalyani's mother, was a beautiful woman interested in rich saries and diamonds. Kalyani proudly said: "You should have seen my mother's saris. She never wore anything but silks. Such silks! And her diamonds—you could see them flashing a long distance away. My father used to say you didn't need a lantern at night if she was with you". (Deshpande 117). For Goda, she was as fair as milk. She was sent to Yamunabai's school at a time when schooling for a girl was something that could come in the way of her marriage prospects. Yamunabai, a daughter of a well-to-do landlord, who had come back to her parental home as a young widow, decided to devote herself to the realization of her vision of setting the girls and women free from the slavery of endless drudgery and childbearing and exposing them to the vastness and beauty of the world around them. It was Yamunabai who made a drastic change in Manorama, a young a girl trapped in the drudgery of looking after her younger siblings. She was turned into a girl who caught the attention of the people and the result was her marriage with Vithalrao. Manorama ruthlessly cut herself off her family immediately after her marriage. She was not happy in her marital life as she failed to give birth to a son. She was not pleased even with Kalyani, who, after her marriage gave birth to three daughters and a mentally retarded son.

The Image of an Emerging New Woman in Deshpande's Novels

CHAPTER 6

6.1 Making of a 'New' Woman in *The Dark Holds No Terrors*

The Dark Holds No Terrors is a story of a man's unquestionable domination on a woman who is treated as a martyr and a paragon of all divine virtues like silence, patience, tolerance and sacrifice. It is about Saru, a modern woman, who strongly resents the attack of Indian patriarchal society on her identity and individuality. She is a symbol of a progressive woman who always tries to exercise her influence on others. She sees her mother as her rival in the game of power. Being a female child, she has been neglected and humiliated by her mother in the name of gender-discrimination. She wants to join medicine in order to be economically independent, but her mother is against it. However, with the support of her father, she goes for her medical education. Being ambitious and revolutionary by nature, she rebels against her parents and marries Manu and leaves her parental home. However, it is unfortunate that she is refused freedom even after her marriage. Her marriage proves to be a failure on account of her sadist husband with his male-ego, his marital violence and sexual assualts imposed on her. For her, marriage becomes a complete surrender of her 'self', a total surrender, a gate that closes all the roads leading to freedom. On hearing the news of her mother's death, she returns to her parental home after fifteen years, and thus gets a chance to save herself from the violent and aggressive sexual attacks of her husband.

She, who is lonely, helpless and frightened, seeks support from her father. Without breaking her silence, without sharing her problem with her father, how can she expect any help from him? Her father is eager to listen to her. He says: "Do you know, Saru, I often feel sorry that we left so many things unsaid, your mother and I . . . Silence had become a habit for us. Now . . . go on, tell me. Tell me everything". (Deshpande 199). She does not find words to open her heart. Finally, she makes up her mind and says: "My husband is a sadist . . . Don't you understand, *Baba*? Don't you know the meaning of the word? . . . He's cruel to me . . . in bed . . . Look, there we were, a normal husband and wife, like any other normal couple, absolutely like any other couple. And one day . . . yes, what happened? A girl came to interview me . . . And as we were talking, he came in . . . I introduced him to her. And while we were having our tea, she asked him . . . 'How does it feel when your wife earns not only the butter but most of the bread as well?' . . . He attacked me like an animal that night . . . I could do nothing against him. I couldn't fight back". (Deshpande 201). She tells him everything about her husband's cruelty in bed at night, his taking revenge upon her by attacking her like a wild animal, her unbearable pain and agony, about everything. She feels relieved after having opened the door of her heart; she gives herself a kind of cathartic treatment by sharing her pain and agony with her father. The question to her husband, 'How does it feel when your wife earns . . . ?' hurts his pride, ego and complex, and brings out a total change in his approach to his wife. She wants her father to help her. She, very frantically, says: "But you've got to help me, you've got to. You did it once. And because you did it I went to Bombay, met him and married him". (Deshpande 204). Her father is worried and concerned about her.

She feels fresh, comfortable and relieved in the company of her father and Madhav. Her stay with them is a kind of relief and escape from her sexually aggressive husband. She begins to take satisfaction in simple household activities such as making tea, washing the tea things, stacking the saucers on the small wooden shelf, hanging the cups on the hooks, changing their places and arranging them on another shelf. She finds herself enjoying the bath, her body responding with pleasure to the warm water, the smell of soap, looking into the mirror and applying her *kumkum*. She stops thinking about herself as a woman, a prey to her husband's sexual desire. Madhav's determination not to spoil his life for his irresponsible brother, Satish, brings out a total change in Saru's approach to her life. He says: "I can't spoil my life because of that boy. It's my life, after all". (Deshpande 208). Saru goes back to her bed, thinking of the words, 'It's my life'. The words torture her mind. She tries to turn her thoughts to other things but in vain. She begins to look at her life with a new and fresh outlook. She says to herself: ". . . it's true. We come into this world alone and go out of it alone. The period in between is short. And all those ties we cherish as eternal and long-lasting are more ephemeral than a dewdrop". (Deshpande 208).

She accepts her loneliness. She realizes that every man is born to be cold, lonely and alone. When she receives a letter informing her that her husband is coming, she is terrified. She does not want even to see him. She decides to leave her parental home and to go away only to avoid her husband. Her father does not want her to run away from the problem. He pleads: "You can't run away this way, Saru . . . Give him a chance, Saru. Stay and meet him. Talk to him. Let him know from you what's wrong. Tell him all that you told me . . . Meet him . . . Don't go without meeting your husband. Talk to him. Tell him what's wrong". (Deshpande 216-17). She feels too tired to face her husband. She holds herself responsible for everything. She blames herself. She thinks: "My brother died because I heedlessly turned my back on him. My mother died alone because I deserted her. My husband is a failure because I destroyed his manhood". (Deshpande 217). She wants her father not to open the door for her husband when he comes. Her father fails to persuade her and walks away helplessly. She does not like her father walking away from her. She thinks: "It's my fault again. If mine had been an arranged marriage, if I had left it to them to arrange my life, would he have left me like this?" (Deshpande 218). She feels that there is nobody to help, understand and forgive her.

She is reminded of Duryodhana's story, the story in which he was waiting for his enemies to come and kill him. She remembers Madhav's words: 'My life is my own'. She experiences a sudden change in her internal behaviour. She realizes that self-trust plays a great role in human life. She, now, believes: "If we can't believe in ourselves, we're sunk". (Deshpande 220). She remembers *Baba's* thought-provoking question: "Are you not sufficient for yourself?" (Deshpande 220). She comes to the realization that she has been her own enemy. If she has been a puppet, it is only because she has made herself one. She herself is responsible for her own plight and predicament. Her temperament itself is her destiny. She decides to change herself. With a renewed knowledge and realization, she emerges as a 'new' woman ready to face her life with courage and confidence. She decides to assert her 'self' and to fight her own battle. She believes that her life is her own and she will shape and mould it the way she likes. With this strength and determination, she decides to go back to Bombay to face her life. She, confidently, says to her old father: "And, oh yes, *Baba*, if Manu comes, tell him to wait. I'll be back as soon as I can". (Deshpande 221).

6.2 *Roots and Shadows*: Projection of Indu's Vision of a Free, Independent and Complete Individual

Roots and Shadows is a projection of Indu's feminine vision and dream of making herself a free and independent individual in a family that denies true freedom to the woman. It is an exploration of her inner urge for self-discovery and self-identity and a portrayal of her emerging as a 'new' woman who defies orthodox conventions and traditions. By nature, Indu is modern, rebellious and revolutionary. She is a member of a joint family dominated by *Akka*, a matriarchal figure representing blind faiths and superstitions deeply rooted in Indian patriarchal system. Nobody in the family has the courage to oppose or to rule out *Akka's* domination and authority. Indu knows: "Since the day *Akka* had come back, a rich childless widow, to her brother's house, she had maintained an absolute control over her brother's children. *Kaka*, even after becoming a grandfather, could be reduced to a red-faced stuttering schoolboy by *Akka's* venomous tongue". (Deshpande 22). For Indu, she has been ruthless, dominating, bigoted and inconsiderate. She enforces rigid rules especially on girls who are expected to be meek and submissive, obedient and unquestioning. Indu is made to feel like a criminal for being bold, inquisitive and curious, and for being non-conformist and passionate about things around her. She, a motherless child, lives in the family because of Anant-kaka, who understands her, Narmada-atya, who always cares for her and Old Uncle, who has always been her support and refuge, a true friend and confident ally. Inspite of the love and support that she receives from them, she cannot enjoy freedom in the family.

Tired of the suffocating atmosphere in the family, just out of a bitter hatred for *Akka*, she marries Jayant a man of her choice and leaves her parental home to enter into a new world. She, thus, by marrying a man of different caste, rebels against *Akka* and her conventional world. She loves her husband, but for her, her love for him is no more than surrendering her body and soul to him. She, like any other typical woman, feels that she can attain completeness only through her husband. As a wife, she is left with no other choice but to follow her husband meekly and obediently. She finds herself totally merging into her husband. Her husband suppresses her feminine voice and vision, and turns her into a silent creature with no choice, no urge, and no aspiration of her own. She lives according to her husband's wills and desires. Her marriage begins to suppress her femininity and her natural human demands. She is not happy with him who takes her for granted and expects her only to submit and surrender. Inspite of her rebellious and interrogative nature, she, unconsciously, conforms to the image of an ideal Indian wife by shedding her 'I' and losing her identity in her husband's.

Her husband takes decisions on her behalf. Though, she offers to resign from her job as a journalist, he, without understanding the reason behind her offer to resign, advises her to continue with her job. He just listens to her and says: "That's life! . . . Don't forget, we have a long way to go". (Deshpande 17). She, hating herself, hating her job, feeling trapped, finding herself endlessly chained to the long dusty road before her, takes his advice, and quietly and obediently goes back to work. Her feminine instinct has been curbed and suppressed. She realizes that her existence is not for herself, but for her husband. She feels unsafe and insecure with her husband. She silently moves on with her marital life which encloses and imprisons her true 'self' and 'identity'. She moves on with her marital life because she wants to avoid the conflict with her husband and to prove to her parental family that hers has been a happy and successful marriage. Her husband becomes the root cause of her anxiety and distress. With a call from *Akka*, she gets a chance to get away from her husband and her marital life.

During her stay at her ancestral home, away from her husband, she gets a chance to think about her strained marital relationship, and about the unfulfilment of her dreams and aspirations. She also learns about the tragedy of *Akka's* marital life, the debate and conflict in the family for money and property, and about the family members living together inspite of their diverse interests. She fails to understand Old Uncle who says that people need to follow certain rules in life and that the measures of freedom can be found within these rules. People should find happiness in simple things in life. They should not live only for their own selves. Happiness and success are not measured in terms of earning and spending. She does not agree with him. He feels amazed and sorry for her when she says: "Isn't that the ultimate truth? That's what really matters . . . one's own self". (Deshpande 105). She is confused at his question: "Tell me, Indu, what do you want?" (Deshpande 105). The question strikes her like a blow in her middle because she is aware that she does not know what she wants in her life. She finds herself on the verge of a complete bankruptcy. Old Uncle's question, 'Are you happy in your marital life?' makes her heavy and rigid. She also does not know whether she is happy or not. Instead of directly answering the question, she just says Jayant is a right person for her, but her marriage has made her dependent. He tells her that to make the partner depend on the other is an unavoidable and inevitable part of a marital life, and that marriage, the success of which depends upon love and attachment, is the only thing that matters in life. Indu is caught between Naren's philosophy of detachment and Old Uncle's philosophy of attachment. Old Uncle tries his level best to explain to her the true meaning of a marital life. She learns that to find happiness in little things, to find freedom within the obligations of duty and responsibility, and not to feel shameful in depending on others is the only solution to any problem in a marital life.

Indu, *Akka's* successor and a guardian of the house, is expected to be as bold and decisive as *Akka*. She realizes that it is very difficult to please each and every member of her ancestral family interested only in his or her share of property. She is worried about Naren and Old Uncle. But she can do nothing for them. She receives a letter from Jayant. He writes: "I don't understand you, Indu. What's the problem? Surely you don't have to get involved with the problems of every Tom, Dick and Harry in the family. What have they ever done for you? Not one of them bothered to see whether you were alive or dead these last ten years. Shake the dust of that place off your feet, my dear, and come home soon. We can make our plans when we are together". (Deshpande 142). She, contemptuously, laughs at the idea of their making the plans together, when she says: "Plans . . . shall we buy an ambassador, or a flat? Shall we go in for a house, or a trip abroad? Shall we buy a carpet or a new painting for the drawing room?" (Deshpande 142). She experiences Hamlet-like internal conflict. She is too confused to make decisions and to arrive at concrete conclusions. She fails to be strong and confident enough to give justice to the role of a guardian of the house.

Her mind goes back to her childhood and she remembers: ". . . how I had once, as a child, in an idle hour, played with an ant that seemed doggedly bent on getting to some place. And, I, equally determined that it should not go there, had pushed it back again and again, And that silly ant, not understanding, getting more and more wildly confused, had turned round again and again, trying to get back to its original road. And gleefully, triumphantly, I had pushed it back thinking . . . You have to do what I want". (Deshpande 144). Indu considers herself silly and confused like the ant which is compelled by her to do what she wants. She sees no difference between the ant and herself as she, too, is trained to do what her husband wants. However, she is surprised to realize that the ant does not give up her struggle to get back to its original road. She appreciates determination of the ant. The ant is determined to move on with her life inspite of obstacles. She wants to be as determined as the ant. She is filled with an exalted sense of confidence within herself. She realizes that it is the determination that plays a great role in human life. She gathers strength, courage and confidence to move on with her life expecting possibilities both for growth and grace. She ultimately realizes that she has been chasing shadows, leaving her roots behind.

She, therefore, decides to return to her husband with courage, confidence and determination and not to submit to anyone's dictates, not to be suppressed by her husband in the matters of her career. She is determined to confront her problems with courage and to do what she feels right. She decides to hide her relation with Naren and to live an honest life with her husband. She decides to come out of her emotional struggle and to lead a meaningful life with her husband. She is bold and confident when she says: "Nevertheless I knew I would not tell Jayant about Naren and me. But there were other things I had to tell him, that I was resigning from my job, that I would at last do the kind of writing I had always dreamt of doing, that I would not, could not enrich myself with *Akka's* money, and that I would, on the other hand, pay for Mini's wedding". (Deshpande 187). She hopes that her husband would understand her. She has conquered her fear and is ready to assert herself by making her own decisions. Equipped with courage and confidence, she returns home to face the challenge of her marital life, and to restart her marital life built on the foundation of truth and honesty. She, finally, emerges as a new and independent individual.

6.3 Jaya's Emerging as a 'New' Woman in *That Long Silence*

Jaya, like any other typical Indian woman, caught in the trap of Indian patriarchy, has been a mute sufferer right from her childhood. She finds her likes, dreams, desires and aspirations suppressed; and her female self and identity effaced. After her marriage with Mohan, she lives in the shade of a sheltering tree in the form of her husband. She is happy with her husband and two children. However, she experiences unbearable mental pain, agony, loneliness, uneasiness, consternation, anxiety, dismay and confusion after Mohan's leaving her. Mohan leaves her after accusing her of not caring about him and their children, of isolating herself from him and his concerns, and of despising him for his failure. He shouts in anger: "But it did not matter to you, nothing mattered to you, only your needs, you could see nothing else . . . But I know that I've never mattered to you, not really. You married me only because Dinkar told you to . . . How can I expect you to have any feelings for me?" (Deshpande 118). Jaya is terribly shocked and bewildered by these charges. She is full of a sense of angry confusion, guilt and resentment. Owing to her typical submissive nature, she cannot defend herself against these charges.

Her silence has been her enemy. She silently cries in agony: "What was he charging me with? And, oh God, why couldn't I speak? Why couldn't I say something? I felt foolishly inadequate, having nothing to offer to him in exchange for all these charges he was pouring on to me. It was only when he said, 'I've never come in your way, I've let you do what you want . . .' that there was a sudden painful quiver in me and suddenly overcame my aphonia . . . 'My writing' . . . I gave it up because of you . . . I've done everything you wanted me to . . . I've sacrificed my life for you and the children". (Deshpande 119-20). Mohan did not accept the charge that his wife gave up writing because of him. Instead, he said: "Your writing? . . . When I've been so . . . so upset, I've been careful; I've tried not to disturb you when you were writing. From the very beginning, I've allowed you to write, I've encouraged you, I was proud of you . . . You know it was I who spoke to the editor of the Sunday paper about that weekly column. I don't want to take any credit I don't deserve, but it did make a difference—my speaking to the editor about you". (Deshpande 119). Mohan and Jaya, husband and wife, parents of two children, quarrel like anything.

Jaya kills Suhasini in her when she hears Mohan accusing her: "I've always put you and the children first, I've been patient with all your whims, I've grudged you nothing. But the truth is that you despise me because I've failed. As long as I had my job and position, it was all right; as long as I could give you all the comforts, it was all right. But now, because I'm likely to lose it all . . . Do you think I haven't seen how changed you are since we came here, since I told you about my situation?" (Deshpande 121-22). Jaya cannot bear this ugly accusation. She tries to control her anger, her hysterical laughter; but she fails. Laughter bursts out of her. When she recovers herself, she finds herself alone in the room. She feels herself gasping, almost drowning in the darkness. She compares herself with Kusum. She thinks: ". . . am I going crazy like Kusum? . . . But I know I'm not, I know I'm sane". (Deshpande 125-26). She is haunted by the ghost of Kusum who was ready to welcome her to the world of unwanted and deserted wives. She admits that like Kusum she has been rejected by her husband. However, she cannot follow 'poor Kusum' who was bold enough to take the biggest decision of all, the only decision that mattered in life, the decision to kill herself by throwing herself into the well. Jaya and others think that Kusum opted for madness and death, but they are wrong. The fact is that Kusum did not opt for anything; rather, she was pushed into it by circumstances.

After the clash between Jaya and Mohan, Jaya feels that her marriage is almost over. Mohan does not return for days. She receives no news from him. She eagerly waits for his return. She goes to her Churchgate apartment with the hope to see him there, but she is disappointed. She is mentally disturbed. Her mental stress is so intense that she falls sick. She is taken care of and brought back to health by Mukta, her daughter, Nilima, and a servant girl, Manda. She thinks and thinks to herself. She thinks of her childhood, of her life before and after marriage, of her children, of everything. Now she is afraid of being alone without her husband. Being a typical Indian woman, her wants are simple. She wants: "Just to live. To know that at the end of the day my family and I are under a roof, safe, enclosed, in a secure world. If it's dark outside, what does it matter? I can close the door and windows, switch on the lights and the darkness will recede. But now I knew that I could never shut out the darkness; the darkness had invaded me. The knowledge of what had happened to us was terrifying. Even if Mohan came back, even if this trouble blew over, could we go back to being what we were? Something had been lost, only an illusion may be, but its loss had left such a rent in our lives that it seemed impossible for us to mend it so that nothing showed. And yet I knew no life but this one . . . if Mohan returns . . . if only Rahul and Riti come back, we can begin living afresh . . .". (Deshpande 181-82). Her mind becomes a battlefield of fear, doubts and confused thoughts.

In the morning, she goes to the balcony and stands there staring at the road, looking into nothingness. For one crazy moment, she dreamily sees: "Mohan and the children were coming towards me, running steadily, all three abreast. When they came closer, I saw they were a father and two daughters, running effortlessly and in unison, all three with healthy trim bodies, relaxed faces. Then they came even closer and I saw that one of the girls was running reluctantly; she stopped, panting, a hand to her side, her face agonized—the father said something angry while the other girl waited, a look of resignation on her face. Then the laggard resumed running and I watched them until they moved round the corner, out of sight". (Deshpande 182). Again she thinks of Kusum standing at the window, "flailing wildly in agony, crying out—I want to die; I want to die, with her face terrorized, her eyes blank, her nose running". (Deshpande 183). She is also frightened and shocked to recollect Nilima saying: "You know, auntie, what I'm going to do one of these days? . . . I'm going up on the terrace and WHOOSH . . . they'll find me down there on the pavement". (Deshpande 183). She is talking of killing herself. But her mother, Mukta knows her well. She says to Jaya: "She often does. That's just talk. I know she'll never do it. She is curious about life; she'll always want to know what happens next . . . She's tough . . . And I know Nila needs a family". (Deshpande 183). She means to suggest that it is difficult for the woman to live without a family.

Jaya thinks of the words, 'she is tough, she needs a family'. She realizes that both toughness and a family play a great role in the woman's life. Unfortunately, she does not have both after her husband's leaving her alone. She considers herself a patient suffering from the disease of loneliness. She has a strange feeling that nothing is left in her life. She is wondered by Mukta's peace of mind, her courage, her toughness and readiness to face her life with the shadow of her dead husband behind her and the monstrous cloud of *Mai* floating over her daily life. Though, it is difficult for her to relate to the world without her husband, she decides to follow the footsteps of tough and bold Mukta. The thought that the woman needs to be tough and bold, and the picture of a girl, a child, wearing a dress with pockets for the first time, thrusting her hands in them, feeling heady with the excitement of finding unexpected resources within herself, from the magic peepshow, all of a sudden, give Jaya a new idea, a new thought and strength to start life afresh. She decides to begin with the child with her hands in her pocket.

Jaya remembers Sanskrit words from the *Bhagwadgita*, the words she saw in *Appa's* diary, the final words of Krishna's long sermon to Arjuna: *Yathecchasi tatha kuru*, the words that mean, 'Do as you desire'. She interprets these words in her own way. For her, the words mean: "I have given you knowledge. Now you make the choice. The choice is yours. Do as you desire". (Deshpande 192). She, finally, realizes that she has to make choice on her own; she has to decide on her own. She considers herself responsible for her destiny. She is, now, determined to live her life with courage and confidence. She is confident when she says: "I'm not afraid any more. The panic has gone. I'm Mohan's wife, I had thought, and cut off the bits of me that had refused to be Mohan's wife. Now I know that kind of fragmentation is not possible. The child, hands in pockets, has been with me through the years. She is with me still . . . Two bullocks yoked together—that was how I saw the two of us the day we came here, Mohan and I. Now I reject that image. It's wrong. If I think of us in that way, I condemn myself to a lifetime of disbelief in ourselves". (Deshpande 191). She is ready to start a life anew with Mohan when he returns. She decides to speak out and to listen, to erase the long silence between them. She, armed with new outlook, vigour and enthusiasm, decides to face her marriage. She, thus, emerges as a 'new' woman ready to assert her self and individuality.

6.4 Sumi and Aru: Strong and Determined Indian Women

A Matter of Time is a portrayal of Sumi, the deserted wife, who is brought to the shelter of the Big House, the parental home, with her three daughters, Aru, Charu and Seema, by her father, Shripati. Sumi, a woman of courage, confidence, determination, dignity, responsibility, self-sufficiency and self-fulfillment looks after her daughters even in the absence of her husband. Gopal walks out of marriage, a trap, by leaving Sumi, his wife for the reasons not clearly known to both. Sumi is watching a movie. When Gopal comes in, she is enjoying a melodious song sung by the clown; *Jeena yahan, marna yahan, iske siwa jana kahan*. She fearfully feels that something unexpected, something unpleasant is going to happen in her life. He says that he wants to talk to her. She silently listens to what he has to say to her. There is no communication as such between them. He looks at her for a reaction, but she just gazes at him, saying nothing as if there is nothing to be said between them. She just looks at him in surprise and is spellbound. Her silence itself is her reaction to what he says. What he says is not revealed by the novelist herself. He goes out as quietly as he had come in. She watches the movie until the end. She, then, goes to bed with the song still going on in her mind. She tries to interpret the song over and over again. She gets tired and falls asleep. She gets up at three in the morning only to see herself alone in the bed.

After Gopal's desertion, though, Sumi appears to be calm and composed, her grief, anger and humiliation are so deep and intense that she becomes uneasy and restless. She is silent and impatient. Her silence becomes a cry of despair. She feels lonely and emotionally disturbed. She tries to comfort herself when she says: "It takes time to get used to sharing your life with another person, now I have to get used to being alone". (Deshpande 23). She is not afraid of loneliness any more. She decides to accept and adjust herself with her tragic lot. She is worried about her daughters. She is haunted by a variety of questions related to her daughters. She asks herself: "Am I the enemy? Do my daughters blame me for what Gopal has done? Do they think it is my fault? Why can't I talk to them, tell them what I feel, how it was? Why can't I open my heart to them?" (Deshpande 23). But with the thought that her life needs to move on with her daughters and for her daughters, she accepts her husband's desertion as her fate. She decides to manage her family in her adversity on her own without her husband. Though struck with grief and humiliation, she tries her level best to keep herself calm, controlled and composed especially for the sake of her daughters. She and her daughters are united in a kind of friendship and companionship of wordless and rhythmic work with the thought that they need to confront their life as a joint journey and a cooperative venture.

Sumi's mind is crystal clear. There are no signs of anger, irritation or annoyance in her. Her routine, getting out of bed, washing, making tea, going into her daughters' room, everything remains unchanged and undisturbed. She answers her daughters' questions with infinite and unbelievable silence and patience; she listens to their repeated exclamations with peaceful and composed state of mind. Her daughters are astonished to find their mother's routine, as usual. Aru, her eldest daughter, realizes that she, with her sisters, is trapped into an activity by the greatest fear, the fear of losing face. For them, their father's leaving the family is not just a tragedy but shame and disgrace as well. It is a matter of shame and disgrace even for her mother, Kalyani, who, on confirmation of Gopal's desertion, cries out: "No, my God, not again". (Deshpande 12). She begins to cry in pain. Sumi, too, joins her and gives way to the dam she has built. Aru is unable to understand the nature of her surroundings, people around her and their pain and distress. In helplessness and distress, she questions herself: "My God, what's happening to us and what am I doing, lying here on the floor like a refugee?" (Deshpande 12). However, in the course of time, Sumi and her daughters begin to adjust themselves in the Big House which now becomes a place of refuge for them. They are not on the verge of crisis now, but they mould themselves in the household routine in which grief and fear have little place. Realizing that now she has to carry out the responsibility both of mother and father of the girls, Sumi develops a new habit, the habit "of touching them, holding their hands, smoothing their hair, as if this physical contact is a manifestation of some intense emotion in her". (Deshpande 33). When Aru finds her mother in the kitchen, she feels that a heavy weight of distress and humiliation has been lifted off her, and that she will be all right now. But there is a kind of purposeless extravagance about her movements which is certainly different from her normal vivacity and quickness.

Though, Gopal's desertion is the cause of great worry and concern for her family members, this unexpected crisis in her life gives her a chance to prove her inner strength and potentiality. She strongly accepts the role of a deserted wife. She does not encourage any discussion over her failed marriage and prefers to be silent. Self-trust, self-confidence and self-respect are the important traits of her personality. Her self-respecting nature does not allow her to accept any monetary help from her close relatives. She does not expect any pity or sympathy from any of her relatives. She is determined to accept the challenge of her life thinking that real happiness lies in accepting challenges. Sumi's decision to learn to ride the scooter indicates that she is confident enough to live her life all by herself. We learn: "She begins all by herself . . . Aru is there to help her the next day. But it is not long before she dispenses with all help and rides it herself, going in circles round the pond, slowly, ready to put her foot down the moment she feels unsure of her balance . . . The next day, Sumi suddenly gathers speed and in a burst of confidence, goes out of the gate . . . Aru is anxious too; she wanders to the gate and waits there until Sumi returns and runs back in after her. Sumi stops and holds both her arms above her head in a triumphant gesture". (Deshpande 33-34). Her experience of learning to ride the scooter proves that she is, to the surprise of her family members, exceptionally confident, unbelievably determined and fully prepared to live her life with her daughters on her own.

Aru, being the eldest, tries her level best to give her full support to her mother. She tries to be a responsible member of a family. She leaves Charu free for her studies in her important second year of the college. She is made strong by adverse circumstances. When Aru insists on going with her mother to the dentist, Sumi thinks that she wants to be the man of a family, she wants to take her father's place, she wants to fill the blank Gopal has left in their lives. She tries to steer her mother and her sisters through the stormy passage of change that has taken place in their lives. Kalyani is unwilling to accept any help in the household activities either from Sumi or from her daughters. In a response to Kalyani, who says: "Aru should be studying, Sumi, she should be having fun, she shouldn't be involved with this—this mustard seed of domestic life". (Deshpande 36), Sumi readily responds: "And at your age, you shouldn't be burdened with us, either. God knows none of us wants it, but there it is, we're stuck in this situation. So let's make the best of it . . . *Amma*, if we're going to stay here, and who knows how long it's going to be, you'll have to learn to take everyone's help. If you can't, it's going to be hard on all of us". (Deshpande 37).

She is worried about her daughters, who, on the surface, seem to live a normal course of their lives, but Sumi notices some change in them. They have withdrawn into themselves. Aru's reserve has changed into secretiveness. Charu has become a single-minded book worm. Seema keeps aloof both from her mother and her sisters. Uneasily, she thinks: "I don't want my daughters to live with a hand clasped over their mouths, like Premi and I had to". (Deshpande 59). She wants her daughters not to be silent sufferers. It is difficult for her daughters, especially for Aru, to forget what her father has done to them. She does not want even her mother to forget it.

She wants her mother to consult the lawyer and do something against him. Sumi does not agree with her. She just laughs and says: "Gopal has outsmarted the law. He's given us all that he had. And he has nothing now, not even a proper job . . . So what can the law make him do? . . . Do you want to punish him, Aru? I don't. I'm not interested. I just want to get on with my life . . . Let him go, Aru, just let him go. This is not good for you". (Deshpande 61). Sumi and Aru, have different approaches to Gopal. Aru wants him to realize what he has done, Sumi doesn't. Aru has a deep sense of bitterness for her father, who, she feels, is responsible for their sense of loss and displacement, for their shame and disgrace. During her visit to her father, she speaks to him of her mother, of unexpected change in her, her indifference to her husband, of Charu and her desperation and of her own feeling of having been deserted. She calls him a callous father, a cruel husband and an unfeeling man. She expresses her anger and hatred in a question that she asks him: "Why did you get married at all, why did you have children?" (Deshpande 62).

Sumi begins to feel that she and her daughters are intruders, interlopers in her parental home. She, with pride, says to her father: "I have no right to be here. I feel a parasite . . . You don't know how easy it is to become a parasite . . . There's Ramesh ready to give me money, and Devi and Premi, of course. And now you're asking me if I need any money . . . I'm looking for a job, *Baba*, I have some money right now . . . And don't worry, if I need any money I will ask you. But living here free, I think I can make what we have lost quite a while". (Deshpande 71-72). What she says to her father underlines her self-respect, which does not allow her to accept any financial support either from her father or from her relatives, and to live in her parental home as a parasite; her determination to look after herself and her three daughters on her own. She knows that her father too has always encouraged her to be strong and independent. In a stern voice, he says: "Parasite? What do you mean? . . . Don't talk nonsense. This is your home. You belong here . . . And don't speak of parasites. I would never encourage you to be one; I always wanted you to be independent". (Deshpande 71-72).

She does not accept any help from Ramesh who earnestly says: "But it's your money, didn't you hear me, Sumi? It's yours. My father intended *Guru* to have it . . . That flat in Bombay is as much Guru's as it was my mother's, don't you see? And *Guru* got nothing out of it . . . This isn't charity we're offering you. We are not giving you even half the value of the flat, we can't do that. It's only a token". (Deshpande 123). Sumi knows that he has been trying to help her. In a response to him, she says: "Don't think I'm being high minded, Ramesh. It isn't easy for me to turn my back on money. I want it, my God, I want it so badly! I want so much to feel secure; I want to know that my girls won't lack for anything. It's so stupid of me, Ramesh, I never imagined such a thing happening, I never prepared myself for this". (Deshpande 124). She too begins to feel that money plays an important role in the life of a deserted wife.

Sumi begins to search for a rented house thinking that it is better for her and her daughters to leave her parental house. She thinks: "I must move out of the house. I must look for a house for my daughters and myself. I can't go on living here". (Deshpande 76). Though, she tries, she fails in her attempt to search for the rented house. During her search for the house, she happens to meet her husband for the first time since the day he left home. They do not feel comfortable when they speak to each other. A burden of unsaid things lies between them. They just stare at each other in silence as if they have nothing to say to each other. She realizes: "We can never be together again. All these days I have thinking of him as if he has been suspended in space, in nothingness, since he left us. But he has gone on living; his life has moved on, it will go on without me. So has mine. Our lives have diverged; they now move separately, two different streams". (Deshpande 85). They are living without each other; their lives are moving on without each other. They are like two different streams going in opposite directions. She realizes that nothing can save their marriage. They are now two poles apart. With this realization, she starts a new phase of her life with her daughters.

Devaki, her sister, has been hit hard by the breakdown of Sumi's marriage. Her efforts to talk to Gopal, to know the reason of his desertion have failed. It is Devaki who has a strong desire to bring Sumi and her husband together, who tries her level best to bring them together. She arranges a party, which is no more than an attempt at reconciliation, to which she invites both Sumi and Gopal so that they can get a chance to meet each other. It is Devaki, not Sumi, who is anxiously waiting for Gopal. When he comes, he sees Sumi who smiles at him without any reserve, confusion and embarrassment, and introduces him to a young man she is talking to. Gopal is amazed and awed to see her talking even to strangers with ease and comfort. Devaki wants them to speak to each other, to spend their time together in the party. Sumi does not seem to be prepared for this. She says: "Devi, I knew you were a romantic girl, I can still remember those awful mushy romances you used to read, but surely now that you're a businesswoman, you've changed? Did you expect Gopal and me to fall into each other's arms in your living room?" (Deshpande 107). Sumi is clever enough to know what Devaki is hoping for.

Devaki is confused and surprised to realize that Sumi is not interested even to talk about her failed marriage with Gopal. She is too sensitive to control her tears. Sumi removes Devaki's glasses and gently wipes her tears with her own sari. She says: "I've never been able to cry easily, you know that. And what do I say, Devi? That my husband has left me and I don't know why and maybe he doesn't really know, either? and that I am angry and humiliated and confused . . .". (Deshpande 107). She does not know what to say, why to say and how to say. When Gopal watches her, a strange thought strikes him: "She is attractive, she can get married, and maybe I should divorce her, set her free". (Deshpande 108). So thinking, he leaves the party silently, deciding again, to leave his wife to live her life with her daughters. On her way back, Sumi sees Gopal walking slowly and steadily by the side of the road, with his head down, absorbed in his thoughts, unaware of the car that stops near him. Murthy wants to give him a lift but Gopal does not accept it. He just gestures as if to say: "I'm all right, you go on". (Deshpande 109), and without a word even with Sumi, who is in the car, he begins to walk again. Sumi too says nothing and silently accepts his walking away, walking away from the car, walking away from her and from her life. There is a strangely passive acceptance of separation, of desertion thrust upon her by her unfavourable fortune.

Sumi learns a lesson from a spider. She constantly looks at the spider's web, glittering in the morning rays of the sun, and finds the spider tirelessly working on its web, its shelter, scuttling to the centre and then back, over and over again. With a smile on her face, she thinks that the spider is busy with the business of its life. She learns that it is necessary for her to be busy in the business of her life. She realizes that to pine for her husband, who has left her with her daughters, cannot be the purpose, the business of her life. The only business of her life, now, is to weave a new web for herself and her daughters. She decides to forget everything about her failed marital life. She prepares herself for her future life, for the job which she is soon to start on. She decides to keep herself busy with her job. She realizes the truth that things change with time, circumstances too change, and that nothing in life is constant, and it is better to change with changing time and circumstances. She, therefore, decides to change and to move on till she takes the last breath in her life.

She accepts the challenge of writing a play for the inter-school play competition. She writes the play, *The Gardener's Son*, the play based on the story that she heard from Godamavashi, the story of the king, his only daughter and the gardener's son. She finds herself filled with excitement and exhilaration while working with the girls and rehearsing them. She almost forgets herself, playing her role as a teacher. She wants to forget everything about her marital life. However, she is worried about Aru who has a sense of bitter hatred for her father. She wants to take revenge upon her father. She says: "I only want him to realize he can't get away scot-free. He shouldn't be able to do this and just walk away". (Deshpande 137-38). She meets Surekha, a lawyer in order to go to the court against her father, but Surekha advises her not to do so.

Sumi does not like Aru's consulting the lawyer. She asks her not to have the burden of other people's actions on herself. Sumi knows that she is a revolutionary young girl in the true sense of the term. She is a rebel who rebels against her own father. She wants to know the reason behind the strange nature of her father.

Aru is critical even to the hopeless relationship between her grandparents. She fails to understand the reason behind Kalyani's accepting injustice, torture and humiliation silently. She says to Charu: "When I was a child, I used to think that as you grow older, you become wiser, more sensible, that you can cope with things better because you know so much more. But look at all of them . . . what a muddle, God in heaven, what a muddle! What's the point going on if that's all we can do, go on muddling forever? It seems pointless. I'm not sure I want to go on". (Deshpande 143). The flame of anger burns brightly and steadily in her when she thinks of her grandfather and of her father. She seems to be in utter despair. She confesses to Charu: "I can't go on . . . If we can do nothing but to go on muddling this way forever, I don't want to go on at all". (Deshpande 183). In her mood of despair, she begins to consider every mother a victim, and every father a betrayer. She loses her belief in the institution of marriage itself. She says with seriousness and determination: "I'm never going to get married". (Deshpande 76). The tone in which she says so makes it clear that she means what she says. Sumi does not want Aru to be possessed by such type of negative thoughts. She does not want her to live her life with a kind of negative generalization on the nature of man-woman relationship.

For Aru, Gopal's desertion does not merely imply an empty space in the family, but a complete disintegration of the family. She feels: "There is no family left. We are five separate individuals, all of us going our different ways, five units that don't add up to a whole". (Deshpande 184). She has a sense of having lost her very foundation and support in the world. She believes that the things are wrong and that they cannot be right again. But Sumi knows that Aru will not be in despair for a long time. She will certainly come out of it; she will go on with her life. She will make sense of what is happening around her; her consciousness will move outside herself and reach out to the others as well. Right now, she is confused, she is fumbling, not knowing what she wants, not knowing what she has to do. Sumi, who has full trust in Yamunabai's *mantra*, the article of her faith, '*Nimittamatram bhava savyasachi*', meaning 'we must never forget that we are only instruments', and Lord Krishna's advice to Arjuna on the battlefield: "Be thou only the instrument, Arjuna" (Deshpande 188), is sure that her daughters will stand on their own feet. She knows that Aru is bold and courageous enough not to be affected by these adverse circumstances and that she is capable enough to take her life as it comes to her lot.

Seema, Sumi's youngest daughter, wants to see her father. She is taken to him by her mother. She leaves her alone with Gopal. As per Shankar's request, she goes inside and waits in his house, drinks a glass of coffee offered to her by Manju, Shankar's wife. She is uneasy as her mother-in-law talks to Sumi. She just moves about with a sense of repression. She neither sits down nor speaks to Sumi. She leaves the role of the hostess to her mother-in-law. Sumi is irritated by the old woman's question and advice. She asks abruptly and unexpectedly: "When are you going back to your husband? You should be with him. Look at his state! It's all right to stay with your parents for a while, but that's not your home. When my daughters come home, I don't let them stay long. Go back to your husband, he's a good man. If you've done wrong, he'll forgive you. And if he has—women shouldn't have any pride". (Deshpande 161). The old woman's advice and question surprises and upsets her. She fails to understand as to why the woman is held responsible for the strained relationship between husband and wife. She actually detests the generation represented by the old woman holding the woman responsible for the marital crisis. Shankar, too, wants Sumi to do something for Gopal. To him she says: "I can't do anything for Gopal. He's going his way and I have to go mine". (Deshpande 161). When she sees Seema and Gopal descending the stairs, unaware of each other, Sumi's anger turns from the old woman to Gopal. She thinks to herself: "He had no right to do this to me, to let the world into our relationship". (Deshpande 162). She does not like Gopal allowing others to poke their nose in their relationship. She also does not like him to do injustice to her daughters.

Sumi always tries to keep her feelings about Gopal's desertion to herself. She knows that she can cope with the reality of her life by keeping her feelings to herself. Her image that she presents to the world is that of grace and courage, of confidence and determination, the image to be admired rather than to be pitied. Inspite of her condition, she is determined to go on living on her own with the support of her stoic pride. During her final visit to Gopal, she, with a sparkling face and an exceptional vivacity, says to him: "I'm getting a job, Gopal, I think I'm going to get it . . . It's in Devgiri . . . And Seema can be with me, she can join the school, we can be together, I want the job so much". (Deshpande 223). Her inner strength does not allow her to lose her courage and confidence. She wants to do so many things in her life. She wants to start her life afresh especially for herself and her youngest daughter, Seema. She decides to accept a job in the residential school and to leave the Big House. She decides not to take Aru and Charu with her. With a renewed enthusiasm and impulsiveness, she says to Aru: Now we'll be on our own . . . Be happy for me, Aru. This is the first thing in my life I think that I've got for myself. I was sure I wouldn't get it . . . But one of the members of the Board saw my play . . . And do you know, Aru, I'm already thinking of another one. It feels so good, you can't imagine! I've been so lazy all my life. And suddenly I want to do so many things . . . There's *Amma* and *Baba*. I feel good to think that you'll be with them . . . You'll be all right, won't you? . . . You'll come to me often, I'm getting my own place, just a room and a kitchen, but we can be together". (Deshpande 230-31). On hearing her mother speaking so excitedly and enthusiastically, Aru bursts into tears. Sumi holds her daughter close and tries to soothe and comfort her.

Sumi and Shripati meet a tragic death in an accident. The family in the Big House is shattered to pieces by their unexpected demise. Aru does not believe her ears when she receives the news. She is speechless. She looks at Kalyani and Goda who are crying out in a terrible voice. She rushes at Kalyani who slumps to the floor unconsciously. Kneeling by Kalyani's huddled body, she says: "*Amma*, I'm here, I'm your daughter, *Amma*, I'm your son, I'm here with you, *Amma*, I'm here . . .". (Deshpande 233). She is strong and competent enough to take charge of everything. She handles and controls the situation with full concentration of a rope-walker, holding the weight of her grief in her two hands, not as if it is a burden, but to balance herself. She reads the play, *The Gardener's Son*, the day after Sumi's death. She feels guilty when she reads it. She thinks to herself: "It's only for children, she said to me, but it's not, I know it's so much more. Sumi is saying something here which I must know. But I can't get it, not now, it's impossible. I can't think of anything but Sumi who is dead. Her figure keeps coming between me and her words; it won't let anything come through. I wish I'd read it earlier, I wish I'd spoken to her about it. I thought she didn't care about what *Papa* did, I thought she was uncaring, indifferent, I said angry words to her, but I know now that was not true. It's too late now, I can never speak to her, it's too late". (Deshpande 240).

She understands her mother only after her death. As she does not cry like her sister, Charu, her grief and guilt remain suppressed in her. She just stoically endures the pain-spiked guilt that lies heavy and sharp within her. Her father, who cannot share his grief with anyone, too, is helpless and does nothing to assuage her pain and grief. Aru tries her level best to keep her promise made to her grandmother by keeping herself always by her side as her support and guardian. Gopal is to leave the Big House, now Kalyani's house. Charu goes with Premi-mavashi. Aru, Seema and Kalyani are now prepared to live in the house. When Gopal turns to Aru, she breaks down. It is the first time she has given way to her grief since her mother's death. She cries bitterly taking the name of her mother again and again. Gopal, who is invaded by a piercing pain, tries to console her. Aru controls herself and says to her father: "Yes, *Papa*, you go. We'll be all right, we'll be quite all right, don't worry about us". (Deshpande 246). Aru is ready to prove herself a 'new' woman prepared to live her life with Seema and Kalyani.

Glossary

Anamat:	A daughter brought up by parents to be given away in marriage.
Abhangas:	Hymns, a type of verse.
Aarti:	A form of worship of god waving small lighted oil lamps in a circular motion.
Ardhangini:	Wife.
Agni:	A sacrificial fire, lighting the pyre in Hindus.
Ajji:	Grandmother.
Avva, Amma, Ai, Ma:	Mother.
Atya:	Father's sister.
Appa, Baba, Papa:	Father.
Behnji:	Sister, also used as a term of address.
Bhau-bij:	A day during Diwali festival when brothers are honoured by their sisters.
Bharatnatyam:	A dance form.
Champak:	A flower tree.
Cholis:	Bodices, Breast covers.
Chawl:	A long and narrow building.
Devi:	Goddess.

Ekpatni:	A husband true to his wife.
Ganapati:	The elephant-headed god.
Ganapati Bappa Morya:	A joyous chant hailing Ganapati.
Guru:	Teacher.
Ghumar:	A dance form.
Gharba:	A dance form.
Hartalika:	A day of fasting for women a day before Ganapati festival.
Haldi:	Turmeric used in Hindu religious ceremonies an auspicious mark on the forehead of a married woman.
Haldi-Kumkum:	A celebration by married Hindu women.
Hindu Mahasabha:	A militant political organization.
Hindi Chini bhai bhai:	A slogan praising Indians and Chinese as brothers.
Kumkum:	A red powder used in Hindu religious ceremonies. Also an auspicious symbol of wifehood on the forehead of a married woman.
Kaka and Kaki:	Uncle and Aunt.
Kshatriyahood:	Behavioural pattern peculiar to the class of warriers.
Kuchupidi:	A dance form.
Kathakal:	A dance form.
Lavani:	A dance form.
Mama and Mami:	Father-in-law and Mother-in-law, Maternal uncle and aunt.
Mudras:	Gestures, a term used in Indian dance, a particular Yogic state.
Mantra:	An incantation, a principle, a formula of prayer.
Marwari:	A moneylender or a pawnbroker.

Mangala-Gouri puja: A ritualistic worship by married Hindu women for the first five years of their marriage.

Namastes: Greetings with respect.

Paan-supari: A betel-leaf and a betel nut offered to guests on auspicious occasions.

Pativrata: A true and faithful wife.

Puja: A ritualistic worship of the gods.

Pindas: Oblation of the departed dears, a ball of rice offered to the dead.

Raksha-bandhan: A festive day celebrating a bond of affection between brothers and sisters.

Rajas: Kings.

Ram Nam Satya Hai: A choral chant accompanying the dead on their last journey.

Runmukta: Freed from debt.

Suhasini: A married woman with her husband alive.

Shira: A sweet dish made of semolina.

Sa-hriday: Emotionally united.

Swa-janam: Members of one's own family.

Tulsi: A basil plant worshipped by Hindu women.

Tulsi-puja: A worship of a basil plant by Hindu women.

Tanjore: A painting form.

Vahini: An elder brother's wife.

Bibliography

Ahuja, Ram. *Indian Social System*. Rawat Publications, Jaipur and New Delhi, 2002.

Amur, G.S. 'Literature Alive'. An Interview.

Beauvoir, Simone de. *The Second Sex*. H.M. Parshley. (Trans. and ed.), Penguin Books, New Delhi, 1972.

Bhatnagar, Parvati. "Search of Identity: A Study of Shashi Deshpande's *The Dark Holds No Terrors*". *Quest*. Vol. 15. No. 1, June, 2001.

Brien, J.O. *Violence in Divorced Families in Theorizing Patriarchy*. Berley Black Well, Oxford, 1990.

Das, Veena. "Reflections on the Social Construction of Adulthood". Sudhir Kakkar (ed.), *Identity and Adulthood*. OUP, New Delhi, 1992.

Deshpande, Shashi. *The Dark Holds No Terrors*. Penguin Books Ltd., New Delhi, 1980.

Deshpande, Shashi. *Roots and Shadows*. Orient Longman Ltd., New Delhi, 1983.

Deshpande, Shashi. *That Long Silence*. Penguin Books Ltd., New Delhi, 1988.

Deshpande, Shashi. *A Matter of Time*. Penguin Books Ltd., New Delhi, 1996.

Deshpande, Shashi. "Why I am a Feminist". *Ibid*. 83, 2002.

Deshpande, Shashi. An Interview. *The Times of India*.

Gangadharan, Geetha. 'The Fiction of Shashi Deshpande'. An Interview.

Gangadharan, Geetha. 'Indian Communicator': An Interview. 20th November, 1994.

Gokak, V.K. *The Concept of Indianness with Reference to Indian Writing in English*. Ramesh Mohan. (ed.), Orient Longman, Madras, 1978.

Gupta, Ramesh Kumar. "Image of Woman in Shashi Deshpande's Novel, *Roots and Shadows*: A Critical Study." *Poetcrit*, Vol. 15, No. 1. January, 2004.

Harding, Sandra. Quoted from Friedan, Betty. 'Feminine Mystique'. Dell Publishing, New York, 1984.

Iyenger, K.R.S. *Indian Writing in English*. Sterling Publishers, New Delhi, 1993.

Jain, Jasbir. *Gendered Realities, Human Spaces: The Writing of Shashi Deshpande*. Rawat Publications, New Delhi, 2003.

Kakkar, Sudhir. *Intimate Relations: Exploring Indian Sexuality*. Penguin Books Ltd., New Delhi, 1989.

MacIver, R.M. and Charles H. Page. *Society: An Introductory Analysis*. Macmillian India Ltd., New Delhi, 2001.

Palkar, Sarala. "Breaking Silence: Shashi Deshpande's *That Long Silence*". *Feminism and Recent Fiction in English*. Sushila Singh (ed.). Prestige Books Ltd., New Delhi, 1991.

Riti, M.D. Wasafiri. An Interview, 1993.

Sandhu, Sarabjit K. *The Image of Woman in the Novels of Shashi Deshpande*. Prestige Books Ltd., New Delhi, 1991.

Sheshadri, Veena. *That Long Silence*. Literature Alive, 1988.

Shri Swami Vishveshwarnandaji, H.H. Keynote Address at the Conference at Haridwar on 18th December, 2008.

Vishwanatha, Vanamala. An Interview. 'Literature Alive'. December, 1987.